D0579116

Education and Values

370.11
Ed831u

EDUCATION AND VALUES

DOUGLAS SLOAN, Editor

Teachers College, Columbia University

Teachers College, Columbia University
New York and London   1980

Library
I.U.P.
Indiana, Pa.
370.11   Ed 831u
c. 1

Copyright © 1979 and 1980 by Teachers College,
Columbia University. All rights reserved.
Published by Teachers College Press,
1234 Amsterdam Avenue, New York, NY 10027.

Library of Congress Cataloging in Publication Data
Main entry under title:
Education and values.
    Includes bibliographical references.
    1. Education—Philosophy—Addresses, essays,
lectures. 2. Values—Addresses, essays, lectures.
I. Bertocci, Peter Anthony. II. Sloan, Douglas.
LB41.E3343   370.11   79-19832
ISBN 0-8077-2574-9

8 7 6 5 4 3 2 1   80 81 82 83 84 85 86 87
Manufactured in the U.S.A.

Contents

Preface

Several years ago Professor Charles Muscatine of Berkeley wrote: "Either the university of the future will take hold of the connections between knowledge and human values, or it will sink quietly and indistinguishably into the noncommittal moral stupor of the rest of the knowledge industry."[1] Now, nearly a decade later, and despite much recent interest among educators in moral education, values clarification, and citizenship training, it is not at all clear that the university — and with it, the rest of American education — has even begun to grasp that essential connection, to which Professor Muscatine pointed, between "knowledge and human values." Raising the question of education and values elicits more often than not discussion of such topics as attitudes, character, concerns — all crucial, but conceived almost always as somehow fundamentally separate from knowledge, from knowing, and from the knower — as at bottom basically alien to the very substance of education.

The intent of *Education and Values* is to contribute to the efforts of those who are seeking to pick up that connection. It will not satisfy those who gladly welcome any concern with values as a call simply to reassert the important but secondary virtues of frugality, industry, obedience, and duty, but who reject those moral efforts and perspectives that threaten to cut through all the conventional pieties and normal assumptions whereby we prop up our "okay world" — whether that be the world of tradition or of modern rational technology. Nor, it is the editor's hope, does the volume make many concessions to those myriads of mild cynics who would relegate values to the domain of the superfluous amenities with which we reward ourselves after having seen to the necessities: First, a living, then art and morality; first, survival for our financially beleaguered colleges and universities, then a philosophy of higher education;

---

1 Charles Muscatine, "The Future of University Education as an Idea," in *The Choice before the Humanities,* ed. Arnold S. Nash (Durham, N.C.: Regional Education Laboratory for the Carolinas and Virginia, [1970]), p. 18.

1

first, social change, then cultural purpose, or, as one of Bertolt Brecht's oft-quoted characters put it more bluntly, "First Grub, then values." Such a view is as jejune and banal as it is modish, dealing as it does on one level with mere truisms, and on another with falsehoods, since it is a rationalization for misconstruing the true nature of the issues altogether. The problem lies much deeper than either the sentimentalist or the cynic is willing to admit. The overarching issue is one of perception and understanding: What is the nature of the human being and of the world in which we live? It is not a question of values or no values, of morality or no morality, but of which values, which morality. What values are nourished by the world we know and the way we know it? Conversely, what do the larger values of whose potential for realization we do, indeed, have presentiments, however dimly, what do they suggest, what judgments do they bear, regarding the limitations in our present knowledge and modes of education?

Fortunately, there exist those today who are attempting to reestablish the connection between knowledge and human values. A perusal of their work suggests some starting points and guideposts for any beginning effort to rethink the relation between education and values.

Fundamental to all is a recovery of the ancient notion that any genuine new knowledge is inextricably rooted in wonder. An education at whatever level that does not nourish the capacity for wonder is not merely deficient, it is a blight, and is no doubt of the sort that led Blake to say, "There is no use in education. I hold it to be wrong. It is a great sin." E. F. Schumacher has described those who seek knowledge about everything and understand nothing.[2] It is wonder—not mere curiosity, one of the lower virtues common also to cats, but wonder, a sense of enchantment, of respect for the mysteries, of love for the other—that is essential to the difference between a knowing that is simply the garnering of information and techniques and knowing that seeks insight and understanding. It is wonder as the source of knowledge that reveals how intimate is the relation between knowledge of the other and knowledge of the self, between inwardness and outwardness. An education that fails to attend to self-knowledge and inner development can never attain to genuine knowledge of the world. For all its triumphs it can in the long run only lay waste.

Wonder is the starting point, but in our times, especially, wonder is not enough. The connection between knowledge and human values is also to be seen in the peculiar nature of human problems. There are some prob-

2 E.F. Schumacher, *A Guide for the Perplexed* (New York: Harper & Row, 1977), pp. 1-14, passim.

lems, Joseph Weizenbaum has written, that are amenable to being solved logically and for which techniques and mechanisms for arriving at final solutions can be derived. There are others, he writes, that "cannot be 'solved' (by man *or* by machine) in the sense that 'answers' can be found that forever dispose of them and all their consequences." Weizenbaum gives some examples of such human problems: "How to serve truth and yet be a university professor; Maintaining good relations with one's children; The world pollution problem; How to reduce tension in one's neighborhood; etc."[3] Like these, and we could all add further examples of our own, are the peculiarly human problems, the most important problems of education. Others have made similar distinctions between those problems for which there can be in principle complete solutions and those that remain always because they are the manifestation of what it means to be human. Schumacher speaks of convergent and divergent problems; Jacques Ellul of dualistic and dialectical thinking.[4] What all are pointing to is that the central human problems are those that are "solved" only by maintaining the tension between polarities — between freedom and discipline, between the individual and society, between the conscious and the unconscious, between rationality and instinct, and so forth. They are problems not to be wished away in a spurious harmony that denies conflict, nor to be solved by forcing all to conform to one or other of the opposing sides.

Emerson once set forth the first and prime criterion by which he would judge the adequacy of every educational method and educational system. "Let me say before all other considerations," he wrote in one of his early essays on education, "that I think it the main guard to a correct judgment, I may say the bulwark of all that is sacred in man — not to accept degrading views."[5] For a start, that which is sacred in man surely involves the peculiarity of the essential human problems — value charged, value conflicting, value realizing, value destroying. There is much in our education and in our sanctioned, orthodox views of the world — the various determinisms, environmentalisms, behaviorisms, scientisms — that when taken as total or final knowledge fail Emerson's first test: They

3 Joseph Weizenbaum, "Limits in the Use of Computer Technology, Need for a Man-Centered Science," in *Toward a Man-Centered Medical Science*, ed. Karl E. Schaefer et al. (Mt. Kisco, N.Y.: Futura Publishing Company, 1977), pp. 83–97.

4 E.F. Schumacher, "The Greatest Resource — Education," in his *Small Is Beautiful* (New York: Harper & Row, 1973), pp. 89–90; Schumacher, *A Guide for the Perplexed*, pp. 120–36; and Jacques Ellul, *The Betrayal of the West* (New York: The Seabury Press, 1978), pp. 164–69.

5 Ralph Waldo Emerson, "Education," in *Early Lectures of Ralph Waldo Emerson*, vol. III, ed. Robert E. Spiller and Wallace E. Williams (Cambridge: Harvard University Press, 1972), p. 291.

degrade the human being, they seek to simplify the human problems, and, thus, they reduce the human potential to something other and lower than itself. And degrading man they visit their degradation upon the earth, upon the beasts and creatures, and now threaten to do so upon all of life. The peculiarly human problems, along with their potential for human development, cannot even be recognized, let alone engaged, without constant attention to the connection between knowledge and values.

However, if this connection is to be established it demands a far more adequate conception of reason than has become dominant in our times. Jacques Ellul has identified the central problem of Western civilization, whose great achievements Ellul is second to none in appreciating, as "the betrayal of reason by rationalism."[6] In our scientistic, technologizing ways of thinking we have nearly succeeded in eliminating all that partakes of insight, intuition, wonder, feeling, dreams, and culture, and, thereby, have reduced reason to only one of its lesser dimensions: a quantifying, engineering, controlling logic. We have in Ellul's terms rejected a dialectic for a dualistic approach that divides the world into irreconcilable opposites — such as the rational versus the irrational — and bids us choose one over the other, rather than realizing that the true task is to maintain the tension of polarities. Do we not realize, Ellul asks, "that dreaming is no less important, basic, and decisive for man than reason, or rather, that reason ceases to exist if there is no dreaming, no lightheaded imagination, no myth and poetry?"[7] The truncation of reason in its full sense has resulted in the curious and extreme irony that we are saddled with a rationality that in its monomaniacal drive to control everything, to eradicate all traces of uncertainty, is deeply implicated in all those things that now threaten final chaos.

Peter Abbs, editor of *Tract*, the lively British journal of cultural criticism, has argued that an overemphasis on a reductive, technologizing rationalism also promotes a false opposition between knowledge and true culture. "At crucial stages," Abbs writes,

the life of culture requires the critical energy of the alert mind. At the present moment, a divorce between knowledge and culture is taking place. There is a danger that the powers of the mass media and the powers of the educational system, working in isolation from each other and appealing to completely different levels of the psyche, will together

6 Ellul, *The Betrayal of the West*, p. 164.
7 Ibid., p. 154.

conspire to create a man who is, at once, technically knowledgeable and culturally infantile. Functional civilization may squat heavily in the center of such a man's brain, but Caliban-like impulses, inchoate and dangerously confused, will beat through his undeveloped heart. The emergence of such a man, outwardly knowledgeable, inwardly blind: preoccupied with techniques and not with teleologies: responsive to the dictates of scientific progress, but not to the imperatives of human culture, should serve to unsettle us all.[8]

Lest there be any mistake, this is not a call for a return to the spontaneous, to the instinctive, to the irrational—that is *schwärmerei* and by now we should all know where it leads. What is being pointed to is the urgent need for a recovery of reason in its fullest sense. Indeed, it is the reductive and technologizing educators who, by creating an intellectual, moral, and spiritual vacuum, pave the way for the black-magic educators who are only too willing to step in and fill the emptiness.

The connection between knowledge and values, it would seem, can be reestablished only by means of a thorough transformation of our present conceptions of knowledge and of knowing. Recently, in addressing himself to the tragedy of the People's Temple in Guyana, Professor John E. Smith of Yale University pointed out that the need for an adequate rationality is not one that can be solved by teaching more courses in logic, epistemology, and the philosophy of science as these are now conceived. "The fact is," writes Professor Smith, "that the dominant *philosophical* outlook of those who have been teaching these subjects in recent decades has helped to create the problem. The 'rational' and 'meaningful' have been so narrowly defined that religious, ethical, and metaphysical beliefs have been excluded from the domain of reason and cast on the junk heap of the meaningless and the emotional, where no critical evaluation is possible. An entirely new approach is called for."[9] Such a new approach, if it is really new, will mean reestablishing imagination, insight, intuition, and human values where they belong, at the heart of reason. The implications of doing so are radical and risky, for new ways of seeing can very well bring the perception of new worlds far different from the one to which we have grown accustomed.

Because perception and perspective are involved, a first and absolutely necessary step in exploring the question of education and values is to pay heed to a variety of different views and concerns that can shed light on

8 Peter Abbs, "Mass Culture and Mimesis," *Tract*, no. 22 (n.d.): 10.
9 John E. Smith, Letter to the Editor, *New York Times*, December 4, 1978.

6

the way. "What we need," the personalist philosopher Ralph Tyler Flewelling once wrote, "is depth, and we shall never get the depth, which is perspective and insight, until we include in our vision the whole scheme of relations, physical, temporal, biological, social, mental, and spiritual."[10] It is wholeness that must be sought. To this end we have invited as contributors to this book outstanding representatives of a number of different views, scientists, philosophers, theologians, historians. Their outlooks are not all fully compatible with one another—in some instances they are in outright conflict—and most should prove controversial. Each, however, is seeking an education capable of comprehending and promoting the truly human.

A version of this volume first appeared as a special issue of *Teachers College Record* (February 1979). Without the devoted and expert work of the *Record* staff—Frances B. Simon and Nanette L. Ferguson—this volume would not have been possible. The editor takes pleasure in expressing his deep appreciation to them.   DS

10   Ralph Tyler Flewelling, *Creative Personality* (New York: The Macmillan Company, 1926), p. 60, quoted in Ralph Tyler Flewelling, *The Forest of Yggdrasill* (Los Angeles: University of Southern California Press, 1962), pp. xlvii.

On Insight and its Significance, for Science, Education, and Values

DAVID BOHM
Birkbeck College, University of London

INTRODUCTION

The major part of our systematic thinking consists generally of an attempt to solve problems. Such an attempt arises when something has happened that cannot properly be dealt with by means of the knowledge and thought that are ready to hand. One may begin by searching one's memory to see if an answer can be found there. If not, one may ask someone else if he knows the answer or else one may engage in a search of the relevant literature. If this does not work, one may try through reasoning to "figure out" an answer, by drawing conclusions logically from what is already known. And if none of this works, one's mind is still in a state of readiness, waiting for an answer, perhaps suggested by an intuitive intimation of knowledge that is "unconscious," or by a happy chance combination of ideas that have been buried in the background of one's mind.

Although this whole process is evidently both necessary and useful, indeed indispensable, for any sort of practical activity, there is an important respect in which it is inadequate for meeting the challenge of life as a whole. For however far it goes, it cannot get beyond the field of all that happens to be known at a given moment, along with what can be developed from this field by principles and methods that are already known, as well as with what may be implied and intimated in a looser and more general way. From time to time, however, challenges arise that require a creative and original response, going beyond the entire field of the known. One who is incapable of meeting this challenge will be like a person who is tethered to a fence post by a rope. He will think he is free to go

7

as far as may be necessary in any given situation, but when he tries, he eventually feels the jerk of the rope and can go no further.

What is it that is required to be free of the limitations of the field of the known? In this article, I shall propose that what is needed is a certain *insight*, which is (as the word indicates) inward perception. As outward perception (i.e., through the senses) may bring us into contact with new kinds of actual facts that have never been known before, so inward perception (i.e., through the mind as a whole) may bring us into contact with new forms and areas of reason that have never been known before.

In this article, we shall begin by considering how insight takes place within the discipline of scientific research with which I am the most familiar. We shall then discuss the relationship of insight to reason, and from there go on to more general areas, first to that of education, and then to the whole question of values, which is so important for the overall order of our lives. In all of this we shall see the ultimate inadequacy of the attempt to proceed solely from the necessarily limited field of the known, and we shall indicate the sort of insight that is needed to go beyond such limitation.

INSIGHT IN SCIENTIFIC RESEARCH

One of the clearest ways to see what insight means is to look at those scientific theories that aim to provide *universal* laws that would be of *fundamental* significance for the *totality* of matter, *independently* of the conditions of time and space. As far as we know, the notion that theories of this kind could be proposed and discussed freely began with the ancient Greeks. (Before that, such theories had generally been incorporated into systems of religious beliefs, so that there were strong psychological and social pressures that interfered with this sort of freedom.) And indeed, as is well known, Greek philosophers proposed and discussed with great passion a wide range of fundamental, universal theories, including, for example, the notion that all is fire, all is water, all is air in various degrees of condensation, and so forth.

In these discussions, there emerged a certain basic notion of *universal order*, which turned out to be important for later developments because it was carried along by the Scholastics to the beginnings of the modern era. This is that between earth and the heavens there is an order of increasing perfection (going on up through the seven crystal spheres). The perfection of celestial matter was supposed to express itself through motion in the most perfect and beautiful of orbits, which was considered to be that of a circle. By contrast, the imperfection of earthly matter expressed itself in the complicated disorderly and ugly motions that so frequently take place in this lowest of spheres.

The Greeks engaged in fairly extensive astronomical observations, which led them to the discovery that the planets do not actually move in circular orbits. This did not, however, bring about the abandonment of their notion of a universal order of increasing degrees of perfection from earth to the heavens. Rather, the observed fact was *accommodated* by the further proposal that actual orbits consisted of a set of epicycles (i.e., circles superimposed on circles). In this way, they were able to fit the facts while in essence retaining their general notions of order.

The idea of epicycles turned out to be quite useful, both for navigational and for astrological calculations. Nevertheless, it is clear that in a deeper sense it served as a means of evading a challenge to the prevailing basic notions of order, since almost anything that might be found in astronomical observations could be made to fit by introducing a sufficiently complicated set of epicycles. Such evasion of challenges is indeed one of the principal impediments to insight (as we shall bring out in more detail throughout this article).

Now, for the ancient Greeks, *reason* was generally taken as the highest value. As has been seen, they did, of course, engage in a certain amount of observation. But for the most part, they tended to take such evidence of the senses as at best a kind of supplement to reason, which latter was regarded as the sole vehicle of truth. (This is perhaps in part why astronomical observations did not lead them to abandon their rationally expressed principle of universal order of degrees of perfection.) Toward the end of the Middle Ages, however, there arose a revolutionary new approach, first indicated by Roger Bacon, who suggested that observation and experience (extended later to experiment) have to be given a value at least as high as that of reason. This was, of course, the germ of the modern *scientific approach*, in which what is actually observed and is perceived may be taken as a fundamental challenge to ideas that have thus far appeared to be reasonable.

As this new approach began to take hold, observations and experience accumulated that implied that celestial matter is not actually fundamentally different in quality from earthly matter. Thus, Copernicus indicated that one could fit the facts in a simpler way by supposing that the sun, and not the earth, was at the center of the planetary system. Kepler showed that the actual orbits were ellipses for which the notion of the perfection of the circle had no significance. Later observations with the telescope showed that the moon had highly irregular mountains, as "imperfect" as any to be found in the earth. Also, other planets had satellites, so that the earth was not unique, not even in this regard. In short, it was implied that all matter is basically the same in nature, independent of its place relative to the earth.

By the time of Newton, such knowledge coming from observation and experience was available to the scientific community and was present as a sort of background that was perhaps hardly noticed. People were, however, generally not aware that this knowledge implied a question that constituted a fundamental challenge to the prevailing ideas about the nature of matter. It was Newton who sensed this question, and faced the challenge. How it happened is that he saw the apple falling, and asked himself, "Why doesn't the moon fall?" His answer was that the moon *is* falling (but that, because of its motion in a curved orbit, it is continually being accelerated in such a way that it never reaches the surface of the earth). Since all matter is basically of the same nature, it follows that each body attracts all others through a universal force of the same kind as the gravitation experienced on the surface of the earth.

The next stage in Newton's work arose out of the need to make some *hypothesis* as to how the gravitational force falls off with the distance. What probably happened was that he took up the already known idea that light intensity falls off as the square of the distance from the source, and extended this by analogy to the intensity of the gravitational force. By a happy coincidence, this turned out to work (i.e., to give numerically correct predictions for the orbit of the moon, and for the planets more generally). But if this hypothesis had not worked, he could have tried another, and another, until he found one that was suitable. This entire procedure of searching for a suitable hypothesis would evidently have consisted of operations within the overall field of the known, as delineated earlier in this article.

Newton's original discovery of universal gravitation was, however, not a hypothesis. Rather, it was (for Newton at that time) an inward perception, or insight. As has already been pointed out, what was generally available when Newton did his work was the fairly well confirmed idea in the background of scientific thought that celestial matter is not basically different from earthly matter. What Newton saw, in a flash, is that *if* this is so, then universal gravitation must follow from the fact of earthly gravitation.

The above may seem fairly obvious *now*, but in the context of his times, Newton's ability to have such perceptions was an indication of a certain quality of genius that is not at all common. This quality involves in an essential way an intensity of interest in questioning what is commonly accepted that amounts to genuine passion. When this sort of passion is absent, the mind is working in a state of low energy in which it cannot go beyond certain habitual frames of thought, in which it feels comfortable, safe, secure, respectable. It therefore cannot properly face the challenge that requires questioning basic notions, of which it is at best only dimly conscious.

Thus, in Newton's time, though it was commonly known by scientists that celestial and earthly matter are basically similar, the general mode of thought was to put this into one compartment, which was not allowed to disturb another compartment. In this other compartment was the idea that there is really no problem, and that, in fact, the moon does not fall because, of course, its celestial nature makes it stay in the heavens where it belongs.

Such rigid compartmentalization is, like carrying adaptation of existing ideas too far, another way of evading fundamental challenges. It was the intense energy and passion in Newton's inquiry that dissolved these compartments and opened the way for his new discovery. What is being proposed here is that the *germ of insight* is this energy, which in effect perceives the subtle and yet powerful forces in the mind—emotional, social, and still others that are beyond description—that hold it in rigid compartmentalization of functions and ideas.

This perception is essentially of a nature that cannot be put into words. But when it happens, *reason* is then free to move in appropriate ways, to lead to new notions. Thus, once Newton was free of the prevailing, largely unconscious compartmentalization of earthly and heavenly matter, it was just good reasoning to say that if all matter is the same, the moon must be falling. Many scientists of his time were as good at such reasoning as Newton was, but few had that quality of passion which makes possible an act of creative and fresh insight.

The theoretical ideas flowing out of Newton's many insights (of which the notion of universal gravitation was only one) continued to dominate physics until early in the twentieth century. Einstein brought about the first set of fundamental challenges to these ideas. Even when he was only fifteen years old, he was already asking himself the question: "What would happen if an observer were moving at the speed of light, and he tried to look at himself in a mirror?" It is clear that the light would never leave his face, so that he would see nothing.

The deeper meaning of this question can only be appreciated when we consider a certain Newtonian conception prevailing at that time, which was that any velocity, however great, can in principle be reached, and indeed overtaken, by a material object if it is given enough acceleration.

For example, it is now common experience that an airplane can catch up with and overtake the speed of sound. It was implied in Einstein's question, however, that there was an essential difference between the speed of light and any other speed (such as that of sound). For if we were to reach the speed of light, some of the basic relationships common to all matter would cease to make sense.

One can bring this out even more sharply by noting that all matter is assumed to consist of atoms, held together by electromagnetic forces, to make up stable arrangements that constitute large-scale bodies as we know them. If a material body were to go faster than light, the electromagnetic forces would be "left behind" as shock waves are left behind in the air when an airplane exceeds the speed of sound. And as a result, there would no longer be forces between the atoms. They would drift apart, and such a material object would simply disintegrate. Since an observer *is* such an object, there can be no observer who exceeds (or even reaches) the speed of light.

So Einstein's question "What would happen to an observer reaching the speed of light" has a simple answer. This is that *no material body can ever reach the speed of light*. Rather, the latter is like a horizon that recedes indefinitely no matter how one tries to reach it. This was already the essentially new notion underlying the special theory of relativity. In the next ten years or so, Einstein worked out hypotheses that put this notion into a definite mathematical form that was indeed confirmed by experiment and observation. However, it is clear that the germ of all this was in the original insight he had at the age of fifteen.

Those who knew Einstein will agree that his work was permeated by great passion. It was the perception growing out of such passion that could dissolve mental barriers. In the case of special relativity, one of these barriers was the idea that because they had worked so well for several centuries, all of Newton's basic concepts were absolute truths that it would be pointless to question. Such an idea evidently constitutes yet another impediment to insight.

Few scientists had the energy of mind needed to question ideas with such great prestige, and, yet, Einstein did not mean to disparage Newton in doing so. Rather he said that if he saw further than Newton, it was because he stood on Newton's shoulders. Newton himself revealed a similar humility when he said that he felt like one walking on the shores of a vast ocean of truth, who had picked up a few pebbles that seemed particularly interesting. The essential point here is perhaps that the ordinary state of mind tends to be one of *hubris*, in which each person is inclined to think that his basic notions are some kind of final truth. This may well be one of the greatest barriers of all to insight. Only when such hubris is absent can the mind flow freely in new directions that allow reason to develop in original ways.

INSIGHT AND REASON

To sum up what has been said so far, insight is an *act*, permeated by intense passion, that makes possible great clarity in the sense that it perceives and dissolves subtle but strong emotional, social, linguistic, and intellectual pressures tending to hold the mind in rigid grooves and fixed compartments, in which fundamental challenges are avoided. From this germ can unfold a further perception that is not contained in the entire previously existent field of the known, within the structure of which such grooves and compartments had hitherto been an inseparable constitutent for all those who had been working in the field. This perception includes new orders and forms of *reason* that are expressed in the medium of thought and language.

Let us now go on to discuss further what the essential nature of this unfoldment is.

First, it is often useful to go to the roots of words, which may show a deeper and more universal meaning that has been lost in the routine usage of the word that has developed out of tradition and habit. The word reason is based on the Latin *ratio*, which in turn comes from *ratus*, the past participle of *reri*, meaning "to think." This has been further traced back, though somewhat speculatively, to Latin, Greek, and Indo-European roots meaning "to fit in a harmonious way." With all these proposed meanings in mind, let us consider the word "ratio." Of course, one may have a numerical ratio or proportion expressed as

$$\frac{A}{B} = \frac{C}{D}$$

And it was quite common in ancient times to relate harmony, order, and beauty to such ratios (e.g., in music and in art). But ratio actually has a much more general qualitative meaning, which can be put as: A is related to B as C is related to D, which can in turn be more succinctly expressed as $A:B::C:D$.

It takes only a little reflection to see that such ratio permeates the whole of our thinking. Consider, for example, a sequence of similar objects, or points — A_1, A_2, A_3, A_4, and so forth, that are ordered along a line, or else appear in time as an order of succession. The essence of the quality of sequentiality is that each element is related to the next one as the next one is to the one that follows, and so on. Thus we may write $A_1:A_2::A_2:A_3::A_3:A_4$, and so forth.

But now, we can carry this notion of ratios much further. Thus, consider a different sequence, represented by B_1, B_2, B_3, B_4, and so forth. It is evident that these two sequences are basically similar, in that $A_n:A_{n-1}::B_n:B_{n-1}$ (where n stands for any number). Indeed, all sequences are similar in this way, and the quality of sequentiality is expressed in its purest form by the sequence of the numbers (the integers), so that every sequence can faithfully and accurately be denoted by a set of numbers. Thus we have come to an example of universal ratio; that is, that ratio which expresses the essence of any and every sequence.

The notion of sequence contains implicitly and in principle unlimited hierarchy of further development. Thus, consider any straight line, regarded as made up of a sequence of small equal segments, A_1, A_2, ... A_n. Then, because it is straight, each segment is to the next as the next is to the one that follows. Or $A_1:A_2::A_2:A_3::A_3:A_4$, and so forth. Let us denote this whole relationship or ratio by R_1. Now consider another line, perpendicular to the first one, with segments, B_1, B_2, ... B_n, whose corresponding relationships are denoted by S_1. But it is clear that now any pair of perpendicular lines is related in the same way. Thus, if R_2 and S_2 are the respective ratios defining a second pair of perpendicular lines, it follows that $R_1:S_1::R_2:S_2$. And so we obtain a *ratio of ratios*, or a relationship of relationships. Such a notion is capable of indefinite development and unfoldment to give rise to a vast and ever-growing harmonious and orderly totality of relationship in the form of arithmetic, algebra, and various other kinds of mathematics.

This totality of ratio is not restricted to thought and language. Thus, the ratio of sequences that is expressed above can be directly perceived by the senses, for example, in a row of objects, such as trees or houses. So ratio is a content that may pass freely from reason to the senses and back again. Indeed, ratio is to be perceived also in the emotions. Thus we may sense that a certain emotional response is, or is not, in proportion to the actual occasion that provoked it. It is thus clear that ratio in its totality (i.e., reason) may be universal, not merely in the area of thought and language, but, more generally, in that it permeates every phase of experience.

As an example in the field of science, let us consider once again Newton's discovery of universal gravitation. The ancient Greek notion of the cosmos implied that the fundamental ratio was that between different degrees of perfection. Newton, however, perceived that the fundamental ratio was in the sequence of positions covered by a material body in successive moments of its motion, and in the strengths of the forces suffered by this body as it underwent these movements. This was stated as a *law of motion*. Such a law is an expression of ratio, which is considered to be both *universal* and *necessary*, in the sense that anything other than this form of ratio is not thought to be actually possible.

However, such necessity has always been found in fact to be limited, and not absolute. As indicated earlier, Einstein (and later still others) showed that some of Newton's ideas were only approximations, and that new laws were needed, containing those of Newton as simplifications, as special and limiting cases. Thus, whereas Newton had, for example, considered space and time to be separate, each independent of the other, Einstein introduced the notion of a fundamental ratio or relationship between space and time. (This is indeed what is meant by the term "theory of relativity.")

What is indicated by this kind of development (which has in fact occurred in all the sciences) is that there is no fixed and final form to the totality of ratio, but that it is capable of continual unfoldment. And as we have seen, the germ of this unfoldment is the act of insight. This is an overall perception that penetrates inwardly very deep, not only in the sense that it is not restricted or confined to certain fields, but also in that it permeates the very roots of consciousness and mental activity in general. This perception then branches out into various particular media, which include the senses, the emotions, and thought (i.e., the intellect). It may thus be said that reason is perception of new orders of relationship in the medium of thought. But, as we have pointed out, though its conditions are determined by the medium of thought, its implications go through the other areas of experience.

As the expression of reason in thought and language is repeated, it tends to become relatively fixed in terms of what may be called "formal logic." It is this that constitutes the main core of our ordinary thinking. Such thinking is, as we have said earlier, both necessary and useful in practical life. However, it has to be noted that it also tends to combine with fixed emotional and social responses to produce rigid grooves and closed compartments, with an attendant hubris that attributes final truth to whatever may be the prevailing general notions. And thus the formal logical approach, developed into habit and routine, has generally become a major barrier to further insight.

INSIGHT AND EDUCATION

To go on with seeing some of the implications of what has thus far been developed, it will be useful first to ask what is essential to education. We shall suggest here that this is to be found by considering the deeper significance of the verb "to teach." The root of this word is in a group of Greek and Latin verbs meaning "to show." This implies that true education consists in *showing* the student something that he can then see for himself, or explore and discover for himself. Such an approach is, of course, not compatible with one in which the main object is to convey a certain content to the student, give him a certain set of facts and principles to learn, skills to accumulate, and so forth.

A striking example of education in the sense of showing is afforded by considering the well-known case of Helen Keller, who became blind and deaf at an early age and was thus unable, also, to develop the use of language. When her teacher Anne Sullivan first met the child, she perceived a "wild animal" who could not communicate or engage in any significant relationship with other people. However, she had a strong feeling of love for the child, and this gave her the energy and passion needed to face the apparently insurmountable difficulties of teaching someone with whom she had so little contact.

After some discouraging attempts, Anne Sullivan discovered a promising approach. She began to bring the child into touch contact with various objects, and to scratch the name of each object on the palm of her hand. As Helen Keller herself later commented, she regarded all this as a game. Through this kind of game there was established in her mind a connection between a considerable variety of objects and the patterns of scratches on the palm of her hand that were to be associated with them. Then, as she says, one morning she was put in contact with water in a glass. This was puzzling, because it was not clear whether what was meant was the solid glass or its nonsolid contents. Later, in the afternoon, she was exposed to water from the pump (which was, of course, not solid at all). When the same name was scratched on her palm, she had a sudden flash of perception whose meaning was "everything has a name." This was the germ of a very far-reaching transformation of her whole life. For she began to learn words rapidly, and in a day or two could begin to exchange sentences with her teacher. From here on, she ceased to be a wild animal and developed rapidly into an affectionate child, with a lively intelligent mind, who was eager to learn and to communicate, and who was thus capable of close relationship with other people. This is indeed an example of a point that we have already made, i.e., that reason is present in every phase of experience.

It is worthwhile to go a bit more carefully into the nature of Helen Keller's perception. If we let N_1 stand for the name of a certain general class of objects O_1, N_2 for the class O_2, and so forth, what she saw was the universal ratio $N_1:O_1::N_2:O_2::N_3:O_3$, and so forth, that is, the relationship of name to the class of objects of which it is the name as universal. Moreover, if we let N stand for the word "name," we can express a yet deeper perception implied in her statement as

$$N: (N_1:O_1::N_2:O_2::N_3:O_3, \text{ etc.}): \ :N_1:O_1::N_2:O_2, \text{ and so forth.}$$

That is to say the word "name" is to the general relationship involved in naming as the name of any class of objects is to the objects in that class. But, of course, she did not know the word name at that time. It is thus evident that she must have had a nonverbal perception of the naming relationship, along with the implication that this too must have a name. So, what she saw was the germ of a vast hierarchy of universal ratio, which did indeed begin to unfold immediately and to develop very rapidly from that moment on.

A little further reflection will show that this perception could not have come from a state of low mental energy. Rather, there must have been great passion, which was capable of dissolving all the older modes of thinking built up from very early in her life. So we are justified in calling what happened an insight, in the sense in which we have been using the word. The teacher, Anne Sullivan, must likewise have had an insight to have discovered (also mainly nonverbally) the key significance for linguistic communication of the fact that each general class of objects or relationships has a name.

What happened with Helen Keller shows clearly that reason is not restricted to being a technico-practical instrument, useful mainly to order our daily activities, to organize society, and to increase the productivity of industry. Rather, it has also a much deeper and more inward significance in the sense that totalities of ratio (such as that perceived by Helen Keller in the instance cited above) permeate the whole of what we are, so thoroughly indeed that we would be hardly human without them. And here we are especially emphasizing that what plays this part is not so much the ordinary process of reasoning through formal logic, but, much more, that perceptive reason which emerges from the great energy and passion involved in insight.

With all this in mind, let us now go on to consider education as it is generally carried out throughout the world. It requires hardly a glance to see that, with perhaps a few notable exceptions, little or no attention is given to insight in this field. Rather, what is generally regarded as most important is to have the student accumulate certain kinds of knowledge and skill that, it is hoped, will enable him to adapt to the society in which he will grow up and will perhaps be useful for that society. Few teachers are likely to have passion and insight of the kind shown by Anne Sullivan, and few pupils would be able to respond as Helen Keller did. Yet, one can see that such insight is crucial if mankind is ever to get out of mental grooves and compartments that hold it prisoner and force it to go on repeating patterns of thought and behavior that lead to fragmentation into conflicting races, nations, classes, groups, and to the endless continuation of practices that have brought about our present series of world-wide crises (overpopulation, pollution, destruction of nature and so forth.

How can this challenge be met in education today? One might propose that serious attention be given to the teaching of insight in schools. But evidently, this would require that the teacher *show* the student what insight is, and (as happened with Anne Sullivan) to do this is possible only when the teacher is already capable of such insight. Who is going to teach the teacher? Evidently, he has to discover for himself what insight is — and how he can have it.

A good point at which we can start in doing this is to ask what the main factors tending to *prevent* insight are. A little reflection shows that one of these factors is that insight is generally given little value, not only in our schools, but in society as a whole. Rather, as has already been indicated, there is a very strong tendency to give the highest value not to having the student discover for himself what the teacher is showing, but rather to having the student conform to what the teacher asks of him; and this, in turn, arises because in society in general, such conformity is given a very high value while insight is either regarded as of little importance or, at best, something that might occasionally be useful if applied to the existing body of knowledge and generally accepted practices. But this attitude is in itself enough to prevent insight. For example, if Helen Keller had regarded language as nothing more than a useful adjunct to her previous more or less solitary life, this would have negated the basic significance of her insight, and, even more, would have got in the way of the dissolution of mental grooves and compartments that is the very essence of insight.

We see then that the question of values is crucial in this context. We will never give energy and passionate attention to something that has for us little or no value. Insight can come about only if insight is itself seen as having a very high value, beyond that of accumulating useful knowledge and indeed beyond that of adapting to the existing values in society. But here, of course, we have to be very careful, since a revolt or rebellion, arising out of a mere reaction against such values, has no more significance than that of the conformist attitude of accepting them. Rather, as shown in the many examples given in this paper, insight requires a quality of energy that can dissolve any fixed or habitually adopted set of grooves or compartments, and to do this is, of course, not compatible with jumping from one set of values to an opposing set.

INSIGHT AND VALUE

It is clear from what has been said so far that we now have to go more deeply into the question of values. As a first step, let us consider the derivation of the word from the Latin root *valere* meaning "to be strong and vigorous" (the words "valiant" and "valor" have the same root). At this rate, to be of value is to have a certain virtue, that is, the power to do some specific thing. It is the value of a thing or an idea that makes it desirable or useful to us and that can give rise to an urgent demand for us to have it or to realize it. As indicated earlier, we have little care for an interest in something that we regard as having no great value. People can love only whatever is *dear* to them (i.e., of very high value), and only what is felt to be of high value can give rise to the energy of passion.

Clearly, then, our values permeate the whole of our existence and are a major factor in determining what sort of human beings we are and how we will behave. It is particularly important in this connection to notice what actually happens when we make *value judgments*. In effect, these are conclusions concerning what is and what is not of value, and such conclusions are, of course, imprinted in memory as *presuppositions*. We then act immediately from this kind of presupposition, generally with little or no conscious awareness that this is what is actually happening.

Presuppositions are indeed common in every phase of life, and are not restricted to being the results of value judgments. For example, if we are walking on a level path, the conclusion that it *is* level becomes a largely unconscious presupposition, determining how the various functions of the whole body are "set" so as to respond to what is assumed to be a "level path." But if one suddenly encounters an unseen pothole, the body is not properly disposed to meet it, so that one trips. Similarly, conclusions concerning values can be fixed, often very early in life, and these become presuppositions from which we unconsciously "evaluate" each new situation. Quite often, these fixed values turn out to be inappropriate, and our response to new situations is then disorganized and confused (i.e., our "wrong" values can be said to "trip us up"). Unfortunately, it is much harder to be aware of such inappropriate values than it is to be aware of holes in the road. Indeed, we tend to avoid such awareness by blaming our confused response on something else that can be seen, rather than on presuppositions concerning values, of which we have little or no consciousness.

By the time a person has grown up he has absorbed from parents, friends, school, and society in general an enormous range of such presuppositions about values. And when he sees evidence of something wrong with these values, he tends to adopt instead an opposing set of value judgments, leading to contrary presuppositions, implying the need to struggle against the first set. But, of course, these are not basically different in nature from those that he wants to give up. Both are inadequate in that they are too fixed and static and cannot respond properly to the ever new and changing reality in which each person finds himself from moment to moment.

It takes only a glance to see how pervasive such systems of presuppositions concerning values actually are. For example, it is (and has always been) common to value material security and comfort very highly. Along with this goes a tendency to give very high value to the need to be thought well of by others and to conform to what they expect of one's behavior and general responses. And, indeed, such values do have their place, at least up to a point. The trouble is that we tend to give disproportionately high value to these requirements, in the sense that we often act as if we believe that they should always prevail, no matter what happens. In short, these values have generally become largely unconscious presuppositions from which we are inclined to react almost automatically and mechanically.

Seeing that these kinds of material and social values have widely led to confusion, chaos, and even to disaster, many have concluded in favor of an opposing set of values, which always puts principles first, gives supreme importance to spiritual factors, and rates one's own personal convictions as generally having priority over the consensus of society. But, of course, these values are as fixed, as mechanical and unintelligent, as are those to which they are opposed. This has indeed long been well known, as indicated by the common notion that carrying the "good" to extremes will lead ultimately to the same end as will the "evil" that one is opposing.

How can we then determine an appropriate set of values? This is perhaps a bit like Einstein's question: "What would happen if we reached the speed of light?" Einstein's answer was that matter could never actually reach the speed of light. Our answer here is that there is no way once and for all to determine an appropriate set of values. Any fixed conclusions concerning values leads to a corresponding presupposition from which confused action will in general eventually flow. What is needed is an *intelligent perception*, from moment to moment, of what the right values are for the actual situation at that moment. That is to say, we have to be sufficiently free of attachment to past conclusions so that we are able to see each thing, each idea, each emotional response, each action, each relationship, at its proper value, without any persistent tendency toward bias and distortion (recalling also that the value of something is its strength as virtue, i.e., what it is actually good for, both in itself and in relationship to everything else). If we can do this, then our action may be orderly, harmonious, and generally appropriate. But, as has been indicated above, if our values are so fixed that they cannot change fundamentally, this will be impossible.

We cannot, however, allow the matter to rest at this point. For if we stop here, there will be a genuine danger of just trying to let our values "float freely," and the likely eventual result would be a complete breakdown of private morality and public order. The reason for this is basically that nothing that has been said or done thus far has been sufficient to bring about a significant change in our general conditioning to an overall set of conclusions and presuppositions concerning values. These will therefore continue to act habitually and automatically, and since they are often incompatibly different for different individuals and different groups, as well as within each individual, there is bound to be a general conflict of basic values, leading eventually to violence and destruction. Indeed, the widespread tendency to try to fix values common to all is in essence an attempt to avoid such conflict, which is, however, as we have seen, almost certain to fail because fixed values cannot intelligently meet new situations that are always arising.

Here it is important to emphasize that conclusions and presuppositions about values are not just intellectual activities. Rather, what we value is what we desire, what we regard as necessary, what we feel we need urgently, what we *will* to do, and so forth, and, as has already been indicated, from the presuppositions underlying all these responses there generally arises immediate activity, without an opportunity to reflect, to weigh, or to ponder on the appropriateness of what is happening. (E.g., consider prejudice, which is in essence a prejudgment of low value for particular groups of human beings.) Such unintelligent reactions are indeed the basic root of our *motives*, which mechanically arouse desire and incite the will toward certain ends that are felt to be of very high value. And what is particularly confusing is that we are usually not even aware that this is happening, but are inclined to believe that we have "voluntarily chosen" to do what our conditioned values have actually compelled us to do. Because of such strong reactions, intelligent perception of what is actually valuable in a given situation is seriously impeded and becomes very difficult.

What then is to be done? A helpful clue can be obtained by noting that the presuppositions about values act in a way that is basically similar to that of the emotional, social, linguistic, and intellectual pressures, tending to hold the mind in rigid grooves and compartments, which, as we have seen, prevent new discoveries in science and in other fields. Indeed, as a little reflection shows, these pressures are themselves the outcome of fixed values that have ceased to be appropriate (e.g., the extremely high value generally given to other people's opinion of one's work, etc.). It seems reasonable, then, to consider the proposal that to clear up our general confusion about values we need here the same quality of insight that has been able (for example, in scientific research and in Helen Keller's discovery of language) to dissolve rigid grooving and compartmentalization of the mind. This will allow reason to flow freely in new ways, so that it can give rise continually to fresh perceptions concerning value.

To bring such insight to bear on our whole system of values, which tend to dominate us both individually and socially, is no easy task. Indeed, it requires an energy, a passion, a seriousness, beyond even that needed to make creative and original discoveries in science, in art, or in other such fields. One may readily feel daunted by the prospect of so difficult an undertaking. Yet it is clear that unless mankind begins to engage in this work, very little that anyone does can have any real meaning, at least not in the long run. Perhaps, then, some who perceive the very high value of insight, particularly into what is tending to interfere with clarity in all our values will feel a sufficient sense of urgency to begin to inquire in a creative and original way into those subtle pressures that trap us in our fixed systems of values.

Excluded Knowledge: A Critique of the Modern Western Mind Set

HUSTON SMITH
Syracuse University

The learning of the imagination can remain an excluded knowledge only so long as the premises of material science remain unquestioned and their exclusions undetected.
—Kathleen Raine

The editor of this volume has done something unusual. He has invited me to present my thoughts precisely because they "are not shared by most educators today," which is to say not shared by most readers of this journal. I have been eager to get on with some other work, but I find this concern to get at fundamental issues compelling. I shall write in a personal vein because I think that an indication of how I came to the atypical views that have impressed themselves on me will help throw into relief what those views are. And if (beginning with my title) I sound brash and argumentative, I hope the reader will understand that this is to get huge issues into sharp focus in small compass.

I begin with the journey that brought me to where I now am.

I. PRELIMINARIES

My first book chanced to be on education.[1] It was well received. Robert Ulich, perhaps the grand old man of educational philosophy at that time,

---

1 Huston Smith, *The Purposes of Higher Education* (New York: Harper & Brothers, 1955). "Chanced" is the exact word here, for the book almost did not get written. Had I not run into a professor of speech who said he had been meaning to tell me that he was using a committee report I had written in his choral reading class, that report would have remained buried in my files until discarded. As it was, the idea of a committee report being intoned as art was so bizarre that I unearthed the document and reread it. It was the report of a committee that had been appointed to define the aims of liberal education at the university where I was then teaching (Washington University, St. Louis), and finding that it did read passably, I dispatched it to a publisher. The reply was back in a week. The contents had to be expanded tenfold, but a contract was enclosed.

rated it above the famed 1945 "Redbook," Harvard University's *General Education in a Free Society.*

Thanks to this early and, as the preceding footnote indicates, almost fortuitous venture into educational theory, the professionals in that field seem for twenty years to have considered me one of them — at least I have felt included. When teaching encountered the new medium of television, the American Council on Education asked me to consider the implications.[2] The American Broadcasting Company included me in its 1962 "Meet the Professor" series. I was invited to deliver the 1964 Annual Lecture to The John Dewey Society,[3] and in that same year to assess the state of the humanities for the fiftieth anniversary issue of *Liberal Education.*[4] When T-groups and "encounter" came along, the National Training Laboratories, an arm of the National Education Association, invited me to Bethel, Maine, to consider the role of group dynamics in the learning process;[5] and when political rumbles broke out on college campuses in the late 1960s Phi Beta Kappa asked me for an analysis of the traumas Vietnam and other factors were occasioning higher education.[6] I have lost count of the educational conferences I have participated in, but find that at least two produced printed fallout.[7]

I have included these autobiographical paragraphs to make the point that in education theory I have not been an outsider. For the bulk of my career I have been emphatically "in." Why, then, am I now out? — "out," I want to stress, only in that my views have grown atypical, not that my feelings are estranged. The *shape* of my ideas may have taken a curious turn, but my interest in ideas themselves has never been livelier. I remain a teacher,[8] and I have never doubted that given the vocational slots of the modern world, the university is my home.

2 Huston Smith, "Teaching to a Camera," *The Educational Record*, January 1956.

3 Expanded, it was published as Huston Smith, *Condemned to Meaning* (New York: Harper & Row, 1965).

4 Huston Smith, "The Humanities and Man's New Condition," *Liberal Education* 50, no. 2 (May 1964).

5 Huston Smith, "Two Kinds of Teaching," in Thomas Buxton and Keith Prichard, *Excellence in University Teaching* (Columbia, S.C.: University of South Carolina Press, 1975). Preprinted in *The Key Reporter* 38, no. 4 (Summer 1973); and reprinted in *The Journal of Humanistic Psychology* 15, no. 4 (Fall 1975).

6 Huston Smith, "Like It Is: The University Today," *The Key Reporter* 34, no. 2 (Winter 1968-1969). Reprinted in *The Wall Street Journal*, March 20, 1969.

7 Huston Smith, "Values: Academic and Human," in *The Larger Learning*, ed. Marjorie Carpenter (Dubuque, Iowa: William C. Brown, 1969); and Huston Smith, "Education beyond the Facts" (Charleston, West Virginia, Morris Harvey College, 1962).

8 I almost wrote "born teacher," for when my father built his children a workshop I lost no time in converting it into a school room. Tools were shelved, benches brought in, and my younger brother and the servant's children — we were in China — impressed for pupils. And I? I assumed the podium as if authorized by the Mandate of Heaven if not the Tao itself. The sensation has never left me. Imprinting is too weak. It is enough to make one consider reincarnation.

3 70. 11 Ed 83/u
C. 1

As for the content of my thoughts, which (as has been indicated) now run rather counter to the prevailing academic mind set, they are spelled out in the book that brought the invitation to write this essay. Titled *Forgotten Truth: The Primordial Tradition*, it was published by Harper & Row in 1976; the Colophon paperback appeared a year later. I shall be itemizing the book's key claims and arguing their validity, but before doing so let me enter a final propaedeutic. I want to note how the opposition between truth as I now see it and the prevailing contemporary mind set broke upon my awareness.

It came into view through the conjunction of two elements that, once I got them sorted out, bounced off each other like antagonists. Even so, they had no choice but to keep on interacting—honing my perceptions of each; getting their outlines into clearer and clearer focus—because both were locked *in me*. Call the components East and West or past and present, the facts are that I was born and raised in China and sometime later found myself teaching at M.I.T. A more unlikely conjunction of opposites would be difficult to imagine. China (the China of my boyhood at least) represented tradition and the past, whereas M.I.T. stood for "the future in microcosm," as we liked to say. China was religious (folk religion, mostly, but religion all the same), whereas M.I.T. was secular—its chapel has no windows, as if the architect were saying, "No hope for transcendence here unless you blot out the Institute completely." And China was humanistic whereas M.I.T. was scientific.

Pulled in these opposite directions, my fifteen years in Cambridge were tumultuous. They were also exhilarating, absorbing, and above all instructive. As they progressed I discovered, first, an organic connection between the three terms on each side of the divide: optimally defined, it seemed to me, "traditional," "religious," and "humanistic" have more in common than I had realized, as do "modern," "secular," and "scientific." But then came the surprise. I found that if I stayed with the problem instead of capitulating to accepted ways of construing things—giving in to Bacon's "idols of the theater"—there was no way I could avoid the conclusion that truth sides more with the first of these two sets of triumvirates than with the second.

Before I say why that conclusion seemed forced on me, let me introduce the two antagonists—the two contenders for truth—more properly. For simplicity's sake I shall refer to the first triumvirate as Tradition and the second as Modernity. The gist of their differences is that modernity, spawned essentially by modern science, stresses quantity[9] (in order to get

9 Cf. René Guénon, *The Reign of Quantity* (Baltimore, Md.: Penguin Books, 1972), and this statement by Gerald Holton: "The difficulty has perhaps been not that this new way [of separating primary quantifiable properties from secondary qualitative ones] was too hard, but that it turned out

at power and control) whereas tradition stresses quality (and the participation that is control's alternative). That's the nub of the matter, but the assertion is compact, so I shall amplify it.

The point is this. Before the rise of modern science in the seventeenth century, the entire world, humanly speaking,[10] was wrapped in an outlook that had embraced it from its start, the outlook that in the subtitle to *Forgotten Truth* I designate "The Primordial Tradition." I must describe that outlook of course, but let me back into doing so. As it was science that unhorsed Tradition, if we understand what science is we shall be on our way toward understanding the soul of the perspective it dislodged.

II. THE NATURE OF SCIENCE

I agree with those who say that science is not one thing, but to conclude that its multiple facets are joined by no more than "family resemblances" gives up the hunt too quickly.[11] There is a discernible *thrust* to these facets, which this diagram from my book is designed to identify.

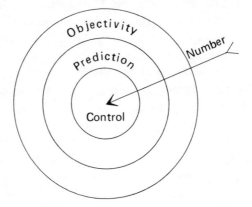

to be all too easy. Once the scientists of the seventeenth century had found the key to this particular gate, the road that opened beyond led more speedily and deeply into remote and fascinating territory, further and further from the original ground of understanding the world" (*Thematic Origins of Scientific Thought* [Cambridge: Harvard University Press, 1973], p. 440).

10   "Entire" overstates the case slightly, but not much. Mary Douglas tells us in *Natural Symbols* that every type of society, from the most secular to the most religious, can be found in the tribal world, but my point concerns proportions.

11   A quick review of the significations that led up to the current meaning of our word *science* can help orient us for what follows. *Scientia* in the classical world meant reasoned disclosure of something for the sake of the disclosure itself. Up to the seventeenth century such disclosure consisted largely of classifications of things that were qualitatively different, but after Galileo it became the search for nature's quantitative laws. The German *Wissenschaft*, however, continues to carry broader denotations than our English *science* and includes all scholarly disciplines; it is in this German sense, for example, that Marxism claims to be scientific. It is my contention that our English

No knowledge deserves to be called scientific unless it is objective in the sense of laying claim to intersubjective agreement. Many things meet this initial requirement, however, without being scientific in any rigorous sense — court testimony, for example. We move closer to science proper when we come to truths that enable us to predict[12] — what cannot be falsified is not scientific — and closer still when we reach truths that facilitate control. Each move we make toward the center finds our knowing increasingly locked into mathematics, number being (as is often remarked) the language of science. Numbers lend themselves to the objectivity and precision science seeks because, unlike words, they are unambiguous — more on this later.

The achievements of this thrust toward truth — I am thinking of the noetic achievements of pure science quite as much as the pragmatic achievements of technology — have been so dazzling that they have blinded us to the fact that they are products of an exceedingly restricted kind of knowing. Look what falls outside its ken:

1. Intrinsic and Normative Values

"Values. A terrible business. You can at best stammer when you talk about them," Wittgenstein remarked, illustrating his point by the form of his very utterance. Science can deal with instrumental values but not intrinsic ones. It can tell us that nonsmoking is conducive to health, but whether health is intrinsically better than somatic gratification it cannot adjudicate. Again, it can determine what people do like (descriptive values) but not what they should like (normative values). Market research and opinion polls are sciences but there can be no science of the *summum bonum*.

2. Purposes

To attribute an intentional character to what happens in nature is anthropomorphic, and anthropomorphic explanations are the opposite of

---

word has come to refer basically to what goes on in the natural or empirical sciences and their mathematical underpinnings. In saying that "physics is a science," no one feels it necessary to warn his hearer that he means that it is a natural science, whereas "sociology is a science" will provoke dispute if the qualifying adjective "social," functioning here as a diminutive, is not added.

12   B.F. Skinner stands as a parody of the lengths to which science's concern for predictability can drive a man. When it was suggested to him sometime back that it would be a mistake for psychology to take a position on determinism that the Heisenberg Principle had shown to be unsupportable in physics, Skinner replied that the "muddle of Physics" was physics' worry, not psychology's. From the fact that electrons are unpredictable, he seemed to be saying, it doesn't follow that human beings are. See T.W. Mann, ed., *Behaviorism and Phenomenology* (Chicago: University of Chicago Press, 1964), pp. 139-40.

scientific ones. For science to get down to work seriously, Aristotle's final causes had to be banished and the field left free for explanation in terms of efficient causes only. "The cornerstone of scientific method is . . . the *systematic* denial that 'true' knowledge can be got at by interpreting phenomena in terms of final causes—that is to say, of 'purpose.' "[13]

3. Global and Existential Meanings

Science itself is meaningful throughout, but there are two kinds of meaning it cannot get at. One of these is global meanings—what is the meaning of it *all?* It is as if the scientist were inside a large plastic balloon; he can shine his torch anywhere on the balloon's interior but cannot climb outside the balloon to view it as a whole, see where it is situated, or determine why it was fabricated. The other kind of meaning science cannot handle is existential: It is powerless to force the human mind to find its discoveries involving. Let the discovery be as impressive as you please; the knower always has the option to shrug his shoulders and walk away. Having no handle on meanings of these two specific kinds, science "fails in the face of all ultimate questions" (Jaspers) and leaves "the problems of life . . . completely untouched" (Wittgenstein).

4. Quality

This is basic to the lot, for it is their qualitative dimensions that give values, meanings, and purposes their pride of place in life. Yet it is precisely this qualitative dimension that eludes the quantitative measuring grid that science must try, at least, to impose on events if they are to become precise data. Certain qualities (such as tones or colors) are connected with quantifiable substrates (lightwaves of varying lengths), but quality itself is unmeasurable. Being a *subjective* experience, it cannot be laid out on a public chopping block; being a *simple* experience, it cannot be dissected even introspectively. In consequence, it is "refractory to measurement"—not just provisionally, but in principle.

> We cannot say that in experience one light has twice the brightness of another. The terms in which we measure experience of a sound are not terms of experience. They are terms of the stimulus, the physical sound, or of the nervous or other bodily action concomitant with the experience. . . . The search . . . for a scale of equivalence between energy and mental experience arrives at none.[14]

13 Jacques Monod, *Chance and Necessity* (New York: Random House, 1972), p. 21.
14 Sir Charles Sherrington, *Man on His Nature* (Cambridge, U.K.: Cambridge University Press, 1963), p. 251.

Qualities are either perceived for what they are or they are not so perceived, and nothing can convey their nature to anyone who cannot perceive it directly. The most that one can do is to compare things that have
a quality with things that do not, and even then the comparison is meaningful only to persons who know from experience what the quality in
question is. Science's inability to deal with the qualitatively unmeasurable
leaves it dealing with what Lewis Mumford calls a "disqualified universe."

This account of what science cannot deal with is certain to encounter
resistance. Not, as far as I have been able to discover, because it is untrue. All that would be required to show that it is untrue would be a
counter-example — a single instance in which science has produced precise and provable knowledge concerning a normative value, a final cause,
an existential or global meaning, or an intrinsic quality. Considering the
importance of these four domains for human life — for three hundred
years mankind has all but held its breath waiting for science to close in on
them — the fact that it has made no inroads whatever would seem to be a
clear sign that science is not fashioned to deal with them. The reason we
resist science's limitations is not factual but psychological — we don't *want*
to face up to them. For science is what the modern world believes in. It
having authored our world, to lose faith in it, as to some extent we must if
we admit that its competence is limited, is to lose faith in our kind of
world. Such loss of faith would be comparable to the crisis that would
have visited the Middle Ages had it suddenly discovered that God was
only semicompetent — that he was not God but just another god. The fall
of a God is no small matter.

The moves to avoid admitting the limitations of science take two turns.
It is argued either that science is not as I have depicted it; or that it is, but
its character will change.

1. *First objection*: Science is not as I depict it. It is more flexible, more
human, and more humane than I make it appear.

a. First version. Scientists are as human as the rest of us.
Their idealism, warmth, and natural piety — a quotation from Einstein
on his mystical feeling for the universe can be expected — is as well developed as the next man's.

Answer: I have said nothing to the contrary. I am talking neither
about the persons who discover scientific truths nor about the ends to
which their truths are directed — ends that obviously can be either helpful
or destructive. I am talking about the character of scientific truth itself.

b. Second version: I make it sound as if there were a single
scientific method that delivers discoveries almost on command, whereas
in fact that method — insofar as there is *a* method in the singular — is as

"human" as any other. It is human both in the noble sense of pivoting on distinctively human capacities for inspiration and imagination, and in the less noble, "all too human" sense of being subject to pitfalls. Science is fallible. False starts, blind alleys, in-house vendettas, and outright mistakes are conspicuous parts of its record. (Citations from Michael Polanyi, Thomas Kuhn, Abraham Maslow, and James Watson's *The Double Helix*.)

Answer: If the preceding confusion lay in failure to separate scientific truth on the one hand from the persons who discover it and the ends to which it is put on the other, the confusion here lies in conflating such truth with the processes by which it is reached—the psychology and sociology of scientific discovery. The routes by which scientists *arrive* at their discoveries may be as inspired, diverse, and fallible as one pleases—I personally think Feyerabend's *Against Method* goes too far, but I agree that the scientific method can never be completely formalized. But again, that is not what I am talking about. My eye is not on how science is acquired: It is on the truth its acquisition-process *arrives at*. Or more precisely, it is on the defining features of such truth—the kind of truth science tries to get at.

     c. Third version: I make objectivity the minimum requirement of scientific knowledge just when we are coming to see that there is no such thing.

Answer: Here the confusion is between two meanings of objectivity. Science need not be objective in the sense of claiming to mirror the way things are in themselves—the so-called camera theory of knowledge. One can even go so far as to say that in its frontier reaches science says very little about what nature itself is *like*; mostly it tells us how it responds to the experiments we direct toward it, with the result that these experiments must themselves figure in our conclusions as to what has been disclosed. Knowing of this kind is indeed subjective in the sense of conforming to a knowing subject. But this kind of subjectivity does not touch the objectivity science demands as its admission ticket, which (to repeat) is consensual agreement. Man may be as implicated in his knowing as you please; science asks only that he be implicated generically rather than idiosyncratically—that he be implicated as physicist, say, rather than as Jones or Smith.

     2. So much for the first objection, that science is not as I have depicted it. The *second objection* accepts my account as applicable for today's science but not necessarily for tomorrow's.

Answer: Obviously science will change in many respects; the question is: Will its changes be of the sort that enable it to deal with the values, purposes, meanings, and qualities it has thus far neglected? (The change from classical to relativity physics was momentous, but it changed nothing in physics' stance toward the four lacunae I keep citing.) If science *is* to deal with these lacunae, it will have to relax the demands for objectivity, prediction, control, and number that have excluded it from qualitative domains while producing its power in quantitative ones. We are free, of course, to turn science in this new direction, a direction that is actually old in that it points back to the pre-seventeenth-century, partly alchemical notion of what science should be. What we must realize is that every step taken toward humanizing science in the sense of moving it into the four fields it has thus far ignored will be a step away from its effectiveness in the sense of its power-to-control. For it is precisely from the narrowness of its approach that the power of modern science derives. An effective and restricted science or one that is ample but does not enable us to control the course of events much more than do art, religion, or psychotherapy — we can of course define the word as we wish. What is not possible is to have it both ways.

As the articles in this book focus on values that include religion, this section on science should perhaps be rounded off by noting that the stress I place on the differences between science and religion runs counter to the prevailing trend, which is to accent their similarities, a trend that has led theologians to appreciate Teilhard de Chardin, Michael Polanyi, and Thomas Kuhn (for all their merits) perhaps extravagantly. I think this bedfellows approach holds dangers. We see, I think, what prompts the approach: If it can be shown that science resembles religion, perhaps the credibility of the first will rub off onto the second. The kicker, however, is this: The similarities that are being made so much of in the current science/religion discussions concern person (the scientist who does science), method (how science is *done*), or application (the uses to which science is put), none of which, taken individually or even collectively, rival in importance a fourth issue, namely the kind of knowledge science *seeks*. Science has advanced to the unrivalled respect it now enjoys by virtue of the kind of knowledge it has discovered and the control to which such knowledge lends itself. It is with reference to *this kind of knowledge*, therefore, that it deserves to be defined and by our society will be defined — alternative proposals by theologians or philosophers are not going to change this. The result is that any credibility rub-off from science onto religion that may derive from associating the two will be outweighed by the pull to conform religious truth to scientific: The more religion is linked with top-dog science, the greater will be the expectation that its truth conform to the top-dog's successful mold. The process is subtle, but very strong. It is at work in the academic study of religion where objectivity has already become an almost undisputed norm.

III. THE TRADITIONAL, AND IN EFFECT
PRIMORDIAL, OUTLOOK

I hope that the preceding section has not cast scientists in the role of white-coated bad guys. I do not know if science has brought more harm or good even to date, much less what the long-term balance will show. Pointing fingers nowhere save at ourselves—at us, we denizens of the modern world in general, and even here there is no finger-pointing really; we would have had to have been prescient demigods for what has happened not to have happened—I am occupied with a single phenomenon, quite a simple one really. When attention turns toward something it turns away from something else. The triumphs of modern science—all in the material world, remember—have swung our attention toward the world's material aspects. The consequence—could anything be more natural?—has been progressive inattention to certain of the world's other properties. Stop attending to something and first we forget its importance; from there it is only a matter of time till one begins to wonder if it exists at all.[15] But let me invoke another voice to make my point more graphically.

In his posthumous *A Guide for the Perplexed*, a book that appeared a year after *Forgotten Truth* and parallels it to the point that it can be read as the same book for a different audience, E. F. (*Small Is Beautiful*) Schumacher tells of being lost while sight-seeing in Leningrad. He was consulting his pocket map when an interpreter stepped up and offered to help. When he pointed on the map to where they were standing, Schumacher was puzzled. "But these large churches around us, they aren't on the map," he protested. "We don't show churches on our maps," he was informed. "But that's not so," Schumacher persisted. "That church over there—it's on the map." "Oh, that," the guide responded. "That's no longer a church. It's a museum."

Comparably, Schumacher goes on to say, with the philosophical map his Oxford education provided *him*: Most of the things that most of mankind has considered most important throughout its history didn't show on it.

---

15 An example at hand: The item I wrote just before starting this present essay was a review of Bollingen's two-volume posthumous compilation of the writings of A.K. Coomaraswamy, so I looked up John Kenneth Gailbraith's review of the set in *The New York Times Book Review*. It was delightful, of course, but he dismissed the second volume of the set, which contains Coomaraswamy's metaphysical writings, with a single sentence: "It worries me in stating as true what can only be imagined" (March 12, 1978).

Or if they did, they showed as museum pieces—things people used to believe about the world but believe no longer.

The anecdote provides an ideal entré to the traditional world view in suggesting that modernity omits something—as the title of my own book puts the matter, it has forgotten something. This something, which constitutes the ontological divide that separates tradition and modernity, is higher realms of being—domains of existence that begin precisely where science stops. "Higher" functions metaphorically here, of course—the additional realms are not spatially removed. But if we discount this literal, spatial sense of higher, they are superior in every (other) way. They are more important. They exert more power. They are less ephemeral. They are more integrated. They are more sentient and therefore more beneficient. And they enjoy more felicity, a felicity that in the highest octaves phases into beatitude. Ontologists fuse these various facets of worth by saying that the higher regions have more being. They are more real.

If the reader finds such notions incredible, his response is completely understandable; the truth I have come to think they represent would not be forgotten, again as in *Forgotten Truth*, if they pressed the "of course" button within us. Theodore Roszak voices the typical incredulity of today's intellectual toward the primordial vision when, in reviewing the Schumacher book just alluded to, he writes: "It does no good at all to quote [Aristotle, Dante, and Thomas Aquinas], to celebrate their insight, to adulate their wisdom. Of course they are wise and fine and noble, but they stand on the other side of the abyss" (Los Angeles *Times*, 11 September 1977). But capacity to believe (or disbelieve) has never been a reliable index of whether the belief in question is true; innumerable social, historical, and psychological factors affect what people are able to believe. I do not argue that the primordial vision continues today to seem self-evident or even (to our practical, workaday sensibilities) plausible. What has escaped me, if it is around, is anything modernity has discovered that shows it to be mistaken. In searching for negative evidence I naturally turned first to science, only to find that when its discoveries are freed of interpretations the facts themselves do not require, they slip into the folds of Tradition without a ripple. Only when negativism intrudes and the successes of science are wittingly (as in positivism) or unwittingly (as in modernity generally) used to erode confidence in realities other than those science can handle—when, in a phrase, science phases into scientism—does opposition appear. Tradition (a word I try never to pronounce with contempt) incorporates science, whereas scientism excludes tradition by fiat. The fact that tradition has the more generous, inclusive purview stands for me as at least an initial count in its favor.

Were I to say in detail what the higher reaches of reality are, there would be no room to suggest before I close some possibilities they hold for education. So, accenting their primordial, near-universal character, I shall say briefly that in addition to practical life, which is grounded in (1) the material or *terrestrial* plane, every known culture has allowed a place for religion, which, to accomodate important differences in spiritual personality types, proceeds on three levels: folk religion, theism, and mysticism. Folk religion is involved with what Plato calls (2) the *intermediate* plane (*to metaxy*), theism with (3) the *celestial* plane (Wilhelm Schmidt's "High God," a supreme divinity manifesting personal attributes, classical theism), and mysticism with (4) the *Infinite*—God in his ineffable mode: the Tao that cannot be spoken, nirvana, sunyata, the Godhead. "The Great Truth about the world," as Schumacher says, "is that it is a hierarchic structure of four great 'Levels of Being.' "[16]

To amplify only slightly:

1. The matrices of the terrestrial plane are space, time, and matter. Science seems to be developing nearly ideal procedures for understanding it. We are so into the scientific way of seeing things that we tend to think of this physical stratum as foundational; we assume that it could exist without the others, but not vice versa. In point of fact, however, from our human point of view, matter (primary qualities, "vacuous actuality") is far from our starting point—it is with experience, not matter, that we begin. Phenomenology has come forward to make this point painstakingly and, as counterpoise to the reductionism that results when we forget it, is an important movement.

2. Human life is so obviously psyche *and* soma, body *and* mind, that the terrestrial and intermediate planes are usually best considered together. Nevertheless, the intermediate plane does contain ingredients that exceed its manifestly human one that phenomenology attends to. These additional ingredients have the looks of a hodgepodge, a grab bag—they constitute the world of tarot cards, tea-leaves, and premonitions, as someone has characterized it. The animate denizens of this world are gods, ghosts, and demons; the "little people" of various description; the "controls" of spiritualists, mediums, and amanuensi; departed souls in limbo, purgatory, and the Tibetan bardos—in a phrase, discarnates generally. Some of these are so suspect that I am embarrassed even to list them, but one man's mush is another man's meaning, so in view of the difficulty of producing reliable criteria for sorting out what has at least some factual basis, it is best at this point to be egalitarian. So much non-

16   E.F. Schumacher, *A Guide for the Perplexed* (New York: Harper & Row, 1977), p. 8.

sense goes on in the name of this intermediate or psychic plane that it takes a bit of courage to say, as Margaret Mead and Gregory Bateson recently have, that *something* does go on. The courage can be less if we depersonalize the contents of the intermediate plane, for as we have now come to assume that the universe that wraps us round by and large is impersonal, it is easier for us to countenance forces or entities that fit this description. Regarded as impersonal, the contents of the intermediate plane turn up as psi phenomena of parapsychology, "coincidences" (as in Arthur Koestler's *The Roots of Coincidence*), Jungian archetypes, and astral influences — again, much winnowing is needed to separate the wheat from the chaff. Dreams seem to have some sort of privileged access to this plane, and Theodore Roszak's *Unfinished Animal* is lush witness that interest in it is not confined to traditional cultures or unsophisticated minds in ours. A leading analytic philosopher recently observed that whereas Freudianism has a marvellous theory but no facts, parapsychology has facts but no theory. The second half of his statement holds pretty much for the intermediate plane generally: Enigmatic energies of some kind seem to be at work, but as we have noted, it is the very mischief to verify them or identify what they are. And let me repeat that it is usually best to think of the terrestrial and intermediate planes together, for on the one hand the terrestrial cries out for infusion from the intermediate to account for the difference between life and nonlife, while the intermediate for its part resembles the terrestrial in being a maelstrom of forces that threaten as much as they sustain us.

3. Impersonally, the celestial plane consists in Western idiom of the Platonic archetypes as integrated in the Idea of the Good. Personally, as we have said, it is the God of classical theism.

4. The Infinite is everything, integrated to the unimaginable point of excluding separations. It can be intuited, but words can depict it only paradoxically, for univocal assertions (being definite) necessarily exclude something, which the Infinite (by definition) cannot.

It bears repeating that the higher planes are not more abstract. Quite the contrary: Each ascending plane, in addition to being incredibly vaster, is more concrete, more real, than the ones below. Only on superior levels are the contents of lower levels revisioned to make the way they first appeared seem, like dreams on awakening, relatively unreal. This last phrase, "relatively unreal," should be glossed to read, "not totally unreal, but requiring revision from the way they appear on planes that are more restricted."

The disappearance of the higher planes of reality from our contemporary philosophical maps — or, to speak more carefully, the decline in our

confidence in such planes — is, as I say, the change that separates modernity from tradition most decisively.[17] In common parlance, our outlook
has become more this-worldly, "this world" being the one that connects
with our senses. And it is clear from what I have said that I think the
change has impoverished our sense of what the world includes and what it
means to be fully human — in giving "ultimate authority to the world view
of a slightly sleepy businessman right after lunch," to invoke G. K. Chesterton's wry formulation, we have lost our grip on the innate immensity of
our true nature.[18] It stands to reason that a new ethos has emerged to fit
this reduced onto-anthropology, and before I turn to saying a thing or
two about education I need to dub in that ethos. My sketch holds, I think,
for our culture as a whole, but again especially for today's university.

IV. THE ETHOS OF THE MODERN WEST

The most pertinent way to characterize the modern ethos briefly is to say
that it is a blend of naturalism and control. The two terms are related, for
it is our wish to control that has brought our naturalism. By way of a new
epistemology, we can add, so we actually have three things going: our will
to power, its attendant epistemology, and the metaphysics this epistemology brings in its train.

1. Promethean Motivation

Can anyone doubt that science has enlarged man's power incalculably,[19]
or that this is the primary reason we are so invested in it? Life by its very
nature is beset with problems, and problems cry out to be solved. Since
science, via technology, is the most effective problem solver we have developed, it is natural that in trying to solve the problems that beset us we
have come to look increasingly in science's direction.

This much seems clear. What we are only beginning to see is that prometheanism breeds a distinctive epistemology.

---

17 "If anything characterizes 'modernity,' it is a loss of faith in transcendence, in a reality that
encompasses but surpasses our quotidian affairs," we read in "Review of *Facing Up to Modernity* by
Peter Berger," *The Chronicle of Higher Education,* January 9, 1978, p. 18.

18 "We are the only people who think themselves risen from savages; everyone else believes they
descended from gods," Marshall Sahlins tells us in *Culture and Practical Reason* (Chicago: University of Chicago Press, 1976). And from Saul Bellow's 1976 Nobel Prize address: "We do not think well
of ourselves; we do not think amply about what we are. . . . It is the jet plane in which we commonplace human beings have crossed the Atlantic in four hours that embodies such values as we can
claim."

19 It has also rendered us as a species more vulnerable, but that has only recently come to light.

2. Promethean Epistemology

Let me introduce Ernest Gellner here, for as a philosopher-sociologist who brings his sociological equipment to bear on analyzing philosophy, his conclusions are more than personal opinions; they claim, at least, to report on the condition of philosophy in general. In his *Legitimation of Belief* he tells us that underlying the seeming variety, chaos even, of twentieth-century philosophy, an "emerging concensus" can be discerned. Having for some time accepted that epistemology is philosophy's current central task, philosophers are now coming to agree, broadly speaking, that to be recognized as legitimate, beliefs must pass certain tests. "There is the empiricist insistence that faiths . . . must stand ready to be judged by . . . something reasonably close to the ordinary notion of 'experience'. Second, there is the 'mechanistic' insistence on impersonal . . . explanations."[20]

Without dropping a word, Gellner proceeds to acknowledge that it is our prometheanism that has established this twofold requirement:

> We have of course no guarantee that the world must be such as to be amenable to such explanations; we can only show that *we* are constrained to think so. It was Kant's merit to see that this compulsion is in us, not in things. It was Weber's to see that it is historically a specific kind of mind, not human mind as such, which is subject to this compulsion. What it amounts to is in the end simple: if there is to be effective knowledge or explanation *at all*, it must have this form, for any other kind of "explanation" . . . is *ipso facto* powerless.

> We have become habituated to and dependent on effective knowledge, and hence have bound ourselves to this kind of genuine explanation. . . . "Reductionism," the view that everything in the world is really something else, and that something else is coldly impersonal, is simply the ineluctable corollary of effective explanation.[21]

Gellner admits that this epistemology our prometheanism has forced upon us carries "morally disturbing" consequences:

> It was also Kant's merit to see the inescapable price of this Faustian purchase of real [sic] knowledge. [In delivering] cognitive effectiveness [it] exacts its inherent moral, "dehumanizing" price. . . . The price of

20   Ernest Gellner, *Legitimation of Belief* (Cambridge, U.K.: Cambridge University Press, 1975), p. 206.
21   Ibid., pp. 206-07.

real knowledge is that our identities, freedom, norms, are no longer underwritten by our vision and comprehension of things.[22] On the contrary we are doomed to suffer from a tension between cognition and identity.[23]

Even so, Gellner concludes, we must accept this tension, for the only alternative to "effective knowledge" is "meretricious styles of thought" aimed at "restoration of the moral order within a cosy world in which identities and moral norms were linked in a closed circle of definitions."

3. Naturalistic Metaphysics

Given the way promethean reason imposes itself on the objects it works with, the world it presents to us can be viewed as the product of a vast display of ventriloquism in which the so-called external world is a dummy; if this comparison, which I take from Philip Sherrard, leans too far in the direction of science-as-construct, it at least gets us past the simplistic model of the archeologist who *dis*covers through straightforward acts of *un*covering. Empiricism and mechanism being ill suited to deal with transcendence and the unseen, the epistemology of prometheanism necessarily conjures for us a naturalistic world. Hannah Arendt stressed this toward the close of her life. "What has come to an end," she wrote, "is the . . . distinction between the sensual and the supersensual, together with the notion, at least as old as Parmenides, that whatever is not given to the senses . . . is more real, more truthful, more meaningful than what appears; that it is not just beyond sense perception but *above* the world of the senses."[24] Emphasizing that "what is 'dead' is not only the localization of . . . 'eternal truths' but the [temporal/eternal, sensual/supersensual] distinction itself," Dr. Arendt continues with some sentences that are serious enough, perhaps even momentous enough, to be quoted in full:

Meanwhile, in increasingly strident voices, the few defenders of metaphysics have warned us of the danger of nihilism inherent in this development; and although they themselves seldom invoke it, they have an important argument in their favor: it is indeed true that once the suprasensual realm is discarded, its opposite, the world of appearances as understood for so many centuries, is also annihilated. The sensual, as still understood by the positivists, cannot survive the death of the super-

22   Ibid. Sartre's "absurd" is a corollary of the positivism that denies any essential meaning that is not empirically verifiable.

23   Ibid., p. 207.

24   Hannah Arendt, "Thinking and Moral Considerations," *Social Research* 38 (Autumn 1971): 420.

sensual. No one knew this better than Nietzsche who, with his poetic and metaphoric description of the assassination of God in *Zarathustra*, has caused so much confusion in these matters. In a significant passage in *The Twilight of Idols*, he clarifies what the word *God* meant in Zarathustra. It was merely a symbol for the suprasensual realm as understood by metaphysics; he now uses instead of *God* the word *true world* and says: "We have abolished the true world. What has remained? The apparent one perhaps? Oh no! With the true world we have also abolished the apparent one."[25]

V. IMPORT FOR EDUCATION

Education has so much to learn. It needs to learn, needs to see, what is happening to it, and what it should do in the face of this happening.

What is happening to it is that it is being pressed increasingly into the service of the kind of knowing that facilitates control. Inasmuch as our will-to-control has cut our consciousness to fit its needs — tailored our awareness to fit its imperatives — our educational attempts naturally conform to this tailoring. I shall not attempt to document this assertion systematically — only to note a few straws in the wind.

Philosophy

The place where philosophy intersects science is of course logic, and the growth of logical concern in twentieth-century philosophy has been dramatic. It is going too far to suggest, as someone recently has, that philosophy departments have in effect now become departments of applied logic, but the trend to "do philosophy" via the formal arguments of symbolic logic is unmistakable. Even in the philosophy of language, Chomsky's mildly metaphysical (Cartesian) interests are being overtaken by Donald Davidson's effort's to apply symbolic logic to natural languages. The other side of the coin is, of course, the "melancholy, long, withdrawing roar" of philosophy's retreat from metaphysics;[26] where world views cannot be avoided entirely, the species that is usually admitted is a brand of mechanism, materialism, or empiricism — a recent *New York Times* report refers to "the materialism that is overwhelmingly predominant in current analytic philosophy."[27] Yet neither Quine nor Kripke — the senior

25   Ibid.

26   On the premise that Westerners are now being forced to turn to Asian gurus, psychologists, and statesmen in other academic disciplines for the comprehensive vision philosophy used to help them toward, a five-day conference is being planned for June 1979, Berkeley, California, under the title "Philosophy, Where Are You?"

27   Taylor Branch, "New Frontiers in American Philosophy," *The New York Times Magazine*, August 14, 1978.

and junior "Mr. Logics" of our time — think that empiricism or materialism are themselves empirically grounded.[28] They have been instated — I
am speaking for myself now — because they are the premises that support
most forthrightly the kind of knowledge that facilitates control.[29]

Economics

"Contemporary economics thinks of itself as a science, heavily quantitative, using mathematics and statistics as its vocabulary. Paul Samuelson
and Wassily Leontief are its giants."[30] In *Small Is Beautiful*, E. F. Schumacher contends that its quantitative orientation has become so excessive, so totally devoid of qualitative understanding, that even the quality
of "orders of magnitude" ceases to be appreciated.

Political Science

"The profound option of mainstream social scientists for the empiricist
conception of knowledge and science makes it inevitable that they should
accept the verification model of political science," Charles Taylor, Professor of Social and Political Theory at Oxford University, tells us. "The
basic premise [of this approach is] that social reality is made up of brute
data alone," data that is objective in requiring no interpretation and being in principle recordable by machines. The consequence, Professor
Taylor concludes, is that a "whole level of study of our civilization . . . is
ruled out. Rather [it] is made invisible."[31]

History

A member of the external examining committee that was appointed a
year or two back to review the graduate history program at my university
happened to belong to the new breed of quantitative historians. At one
point in the committee's deliberations he was reported to have said, "If

28 Quine sees ontological positions — what is finally real — as relative precisely because they cannot be objectively grounded, and Kripke has written as follows: "Materialism, I think, must hold that
a physical description of the world is a *complete* description of it, that any mental facts are 'on-
tologically dependent' on physical facts in the straightforward sense of following from them by necessity. No identity theorist [materialist] seems to me to have made a convincing argument against the
intuitive view that this is not the case" (closing section of his paper "Naming and Necessity").

29 For the reason why persons who are seeking "effective knowledge" (Gellner's phrase) are required to charge persons who work from alternative metaphysical premises with "begging the question," see my discussion of D.C. Dennett's work in *Forgotten Truth: The Primordial Tradition* (New
York: Harper & Row, 1976), pp. 135ff.

30 Adam Smith, *New York Times Book Review*, September 18, 1977, p. 10.

31 Charles Taylor, "Interpretation and the Sciences of Man," in *Understanding and Social Inquiry*, ed. Fred Dallmayr and Thomas McCarthy (South Bend, Ind.: University of Notre Dame,
1977), p. 124.

you can't count it, you might as well be playing football." Granted that his statement was extreme, it says something about our times that a responsible academic could have said it all.

Anthropology

"English-speaking anthropology over the last half century has been and continues to be passionately scientistic in its hopes and claims, and methods. One consequence—and it shares this trait with other sciences—is a built-in positivism and an aversion to history, both general and its own."[32]

Psychology

Insofar as there is a model of man in academic psychology, it seems still to be basically Freudian, and "classical psychoanalytic theory is based quite explicitly on a specific, highly materialist view of man's nature."[33]

The Social Sciences generally

Charles Taylor generalizes the point we quoted him as making about political science as follows:

> The progress of natural science has lent great credibility to this [verificationist] epistemology, since it can be plausibly reconstructed on this model. . . . And, of course, the temptation has been overwhelming to reconstruct the sciences of man on the same model; or rather to launch them in lines of inquiry that fit this paradigm, since they are constantly said to be in their "infancy." Psychology, where an earlier vogue of behaviorism is being replaced by a boom of computer-based models, is far from the only case.[34]

May Brodbeck notes that there are

> two factors within the social disciplines. One of them exuberantly embraces the scientific idea; the other [introducing the distinction between *verstehen* and explanation], exalts its own intuitive understanding as being superior in logic and in principle to scientific explanation,[35]

but Thomas Lawson of Western Michigan University says that recent scholarly critiques of the nonscientific faction have "been so powerful and

32   Robert Ackerman, "J.G. Frazer Revisited," *The American Scholar*, Spring 1978, p. 232.
33   Irving Yalom, *The Theory and Practice of Group Psychotherapy* (New York: Basic Books, 1975), p. 85.
34   Taylor, "Interpretation and the Sciences of Man," pp. 105-06.
35   May Brodbeck, ed., *Readings in the Philosophy of the Social Sciences* (New York: Macmillan, 1968), p. 2 of the "General Introduction."

penetrating that [it is] bankrupt."[36] This seems to justify the following overview in the September 1978 issue of *The Atlantic*:

> The social sciences are, or aspire to be, sciences; they have a scientific methodology. . . . The majority of social sciences have adopted a form of radical empiricism. According to this doctrine, the only sentences that are scientifically acceptable are those that are directly verifiable by experiment. . . .
>
> This methodology was borrowed from the teachings of the logical positivists. . . . Logical positivism was given up long ago by most scientists and philosophers, including many of the positivists themselves. Yet this positivistic doctrine . . . has taken firm root in the social sciences. It has done so because it provides a simple (if oversimple) distinction between fact and value which allows social scientists to make the (sometimes bogus) claim of scientific objectivity.[37]

The Arts

I shall let the poet Kathleen Raine describe the situation here.

> Poets of the imagination write of the soul, of intellectual beauty, of the living spirit of the world. What does such work communicate to readers who do not believe in the soul, in the spirit of life, or in anything that can be (unless the physically desirable), called "the beautiful"? For in René Guénon's "reign of quantity" such terms of quality become . . . "meaningless," because there is nothing for which they stand. . . .
>
> What can be saved from a culture whose premises are of a spiritual order in an iron age peopled by Plato's "men of clay" (the human primate of the scientist) is the quantifiable; the mechanics of construction, in whatever art. And the engineering element in the making of a poem is negligible in comparison with that of the most impressive and typical work of the reign of quantity, the space-ship. What meaning is there, in materialist terms, to the word "poet"; or the essence — the "poetry" — and the quality — the "poetic" — of works of art?[38]

Geography

I save for last a field that shows some signs of a turning tide. Following

36 Thomas Lawson, unpublished paper, 1974.
37 Alston Chase, "Skipping through College: Reflections on the Decline of Liberal Arts Education," *The Atlantic*, September 1978, p. 38.
38 Kathleen Raine, "Premises and Poetry," *Sophia Perennis* 3, no. 2 (Autumn 1977): 58-60.

World War II, geography's classic concern with place lost ground to a
more abstract, geometric concern for space; a recent issue of the *Canadian Geographer* refers to "a generation of geographical treatment of the
man-environment relationship as a measurable, objective, and mechanistic entity which may be examined through concepts and methods derived
from the natural sciences." It goes on, however, to place the "high tide of
[this] scientific geography in the last decade," the 1970s having shown
signs of "a fundamental dissatisfaction with positivist philosophies of
social science and the perceived implications of such study for our social
and geographical world."[39] The geographers at my own university tell me
the empiricist school must still be reckoned the dominant one, but in this
field there seem to be signs of a "rise of soul against intellect," as Yeats
would put the matter.[40]

I have mentioned only a handful of disciplines, and even in these have
done little more than report some straws in the winds that have blown my
way since I started to think about this essay. If they add up to no more
than a straw man, there may be no problem. But if they are accurate in
suggesting that the academic mind is leaning excessively toward the scientific model, what is to be done?

If it is true, as I have argued:

— first, that the exceptional power-to-control that modern science has
   made possible has made us reach out insistently, perhaps even desperately if we feel we are on a treadmill, for ever-increasing control;
— second, that this outreach has forged a new epistemology wherein
   knowledge that facilitates control and the devices for getting at such
   knowledge are honored to the neglect of their alternatives;
— and third, that this utilitarian epistemology has constricted our view
   of the way things are, including what it means to be fully human;

if, as I say, these contentions are essentially accurate, it behooves us to decide if we want to change our direction, and if so, what a better direction
might be.

39 *Canadian Geographer* 22, no. 1 (Spring 1978): 66–67.

40 As this article goes to press, something has come to my attention that suggests that
philosophy, which in a sense is epistemology's custodian, may itself be starting to recover from the
unautonomous way it has related to science thus far in this century. In a book that Hilary Putnam,
Chairman of the Philosophy Department at Harvard, is writing he argues: (1) that it is time for
philosophy to lay aside the debunking posture that has characterized it for the last fifty years; (2) that
the materialism that virtually *is* its current metaphysics and the empiricism that is its epistemology
are both inadequate; (3) that its biggest present job is to develop a model of rationality more adequate than the three present contenders — inductive logic, relativism, and innate ideas *a la* Chomsky;
and (4) this new model should be one that establishes philosophy as a cognitive domain situated between science on the one hand and art on the other.

On the first question, it is obvious from the tenor of my entire essay that I think we can do better than continue down our present path. The main reason I would prefer an alternative is that I think that with respect to things that matter most our present course is taking us away from truth more than toward it, but there is a supporting reason. There are reports that life in the cave we have entered does not feel very good. As I do not trust my own intuitions here — they could easily be self-serving — I shall let a colleague, who as a sociologist studies societies directly, make the point.

It is by now a Sunday-supplement commonplace that the social, economic and technological modernization of the world is accompanied by a spiritual malaise that has come to be called alienation. At its most fundamental level, the diagnosis of alienation is based on the view that modernization forces upon us a world that, although baptized as real by science, is denuded of all humanly recognizable qualities; beauty and ugliness, love and hate, passion and fulfillment, salvation and damnation. It is not, of course, being claimed that such matters are not part of the existential realities of human life. It is rather that the scientific world view makes it illegitimate to speak of them as being "objectively" part of the world, forcing us instead to define such evaluation and such emotional experiences as "merely subjective" projections of people's inner lives.

The world, once an "enchanted garden," to use Max Weber's memorable phrase, has now become disenchanted, deprived of purpose and direction, bereft — in these senses — of life itself. All that which is allegedly basic to the specifically human status in nature comes to be forced back upon the precincts of the "subjective" which, in turn, is pushed by the modern scientific view ever more into the province of dreams and illusions.[41]

If we have trimmed our epistemological sails too close to the scientific desiderata of objectivity, prediction, number, and control (see diagram p. 422), and it is this that has constricted our world view and brought alienation, it seems only sensible to consider alternative guidelines — perhaps even opposite ones to get the matter in sharp relief. The alternatives to objectivity, prediction, control, and number are subjectivity, surprise, surrender, and words. With the exception of the last of these four terms, it sounds odd even to suggest that education might turn toward them.

41   Manfred Stanley, "Beyond Progress: Three Post-Political Futures," in *Images of the Future*, ed. Robert Bundy (Buffalo: Prometheus Books, 1976), pp. 115-16.

This shows how deeply committed we are to the scientific quartet; the question is, are we too deeply implicated with it even to imagine what an education that swung toward the neglected alternatives would look like?

Subjective education would recognize that it is as important to understand oneself as one's world or its part. It would distinguish between objective and subjective (existential) truths, the latter being defined as truths we acknowledge not only with our minds but with our lives as well — we live as if we really do believe that they are true. And it would argue that "truth" deserves the prefix "subjective" as much as the prefix "objective."

Education for *surprise* would begin with, and keep always in full view, its indisputable premise: In comparison with what we do not know, what we do know is nothing. Balancing our present assumption that education's role is to transmit what we know, education for surprise would not reject that premise but would add that it is equally important to remember how much we do not know. Learning theory? Who knows, really, how we learn? Medicine? I go to visit my neighbor Robert Becker at New York's Upstate Medical Center because of interesting things I have heard about his research and he greets me with, "We know *nothing!*" "Welcome to the club," I reply, having studied the skeptical tradition in Western philosophy rather thoroughly. "That's not what I mean," he says. "It may be true generally, but it's especially true in medicine. Here I am, a director of medical research with thirty years behind me, and when I cut my face shaving I haven't any idea what makes it heal." Generalizing Becker's point, education for surprise would remind students that the more we know, the more we see how much we do not know: The larger the island of knowledge, the longer the shoreline of wonder. Noting that neither language nor science is rule-directed in the sense of proceeding by the application of rules we can discern and explicitly state, it would pay special attention to case studies where the long shot carried the day. It might even try to hone students' sensibilities to surprise by asking questions like, "Did anything surprise you yesterday?" On the flyleaves of the training manuals for such education we might paste this statement, titled "The Strangest Age," from *Newsweek*, 25 July 1977:

> Perhaps ours is the strangest age. It is an age without a sense of the strangeness of things . . . .

> The human race has grown up and lost its capacity for wonder. This is not because people understand their everyday world better than people

did in earlier ages. Today people understand less and less of the social and scientific systems on which they depend more and more. Alas, growing up usually means growing immune to astonishment. As G. K. Chesterton wrote, very young children do not need fairy tales because "mere life is interesting enough. A child of 7 is excited by being told that Tommy opened the door and saw a dragon. But a child of 3 is excited by being told that Tommy opened the door." The 3-year-old is the realist. No one really knows how Tommy does it.[42]

Education for *surrender* sounds strangest of all, not only because of the military associations of that word but because it runs counter to the penchant that has created our modern world. Recognizing that it would be working against some of our strongest social instincts, such education would remind us that life proceeds by breathing out *and* in, giving *and* receiving, doing and being, left hemisphere and right, yang and yin; moreover, too much imbalance between the poles can make life capsize. It would show that only in the realm of things — the realm I have called the terrestrial plane — are freedom and the control to which it can be put attractive even as ideals; the last thing a man in love wants to hear from his beloved is that he is free, while to enter a friendship or marriage with intent to control is to sully it from the start. In life's higher reaches, freedom and the will-to-power are symptoms of detachment in its pathological sense of inability to cathect. To be unable to give oneself — to a person, a cause, the call of conscience, God, *something* — is to lack a capacity that is integral to being fully human. It is to be incapable of commitment. Kurt Wolff says that "the seminal meaning of 'surrender' is 'cognitive love,' " and notes certain other meanings that "follow from it: total involvement, suspension of received notions, pertinence of everything, identification, and risk of being hurt."[43] Heidegger's continuing influence on our campuses in the face of his tortuous language and unpopular premises derives in part, at least, from the sense that there is something inherently right in the *Gelassenheit* toward which his philosophy points. Someone has translated *Gelassenheit* as "reverent, choiceless letting-be of what is in order that it may reveal itself in the essence of its being."

Reading, writing, and arithmetic: Education is always involved with *words*, but in opposing them to numbers I am focusing on a specific fea-

42 "The Strangest Age," *Newsweek*, July 25, 1977.
43 Kurt Wolff, "Surrender, and Autonomy and Community," *Humanitas* 1, no. 2 (Fall 1965): 177. See also his "Surrender as a Response to Our Crisis," *Journal of Humanistic Psychology* 2 (1962): 16-30; and *Surrender and Catch* (Holland: D. Reidel, 1976).

ture. Words are symbols, whereas numbers are only signs.[44] Because signs
are univocal, they can lock together in logics that compel assent, but this
cannot be said of symbols, which are multivalent in principle. Their in-
built ambiguity makes logicians flee them for univocal signs,[45] but
humanists prize their equivalence. A biologist has stated their case succinctly:

> Ambiguity seems to be an essential, indispensable element for the
> transfer of information from one place to another by words, where
> matters of real importance are concerned. It is often necessary, for
> meaning to come through, that there be an almost vague sense of
> strangeness and askewness. Speechless animals and cells cannot do this.
> . . . Only the human mind is designed to work in this way, pro-
> grammed to drift away in the presence of locked-on information, stray-
> ing from each point in a hunt for a better, different point.[46]

Language is biological in that we are programmed to learn it, Dr.
Thomas concludes, but it is peculiar in being a "programming for ambiguity." An education-for-words that is alert to their symbolic virtues
would teach that the need to be clear must not be allowed to sterilize language — rid it of the humus of adumbration and allusion that makes it
fertile and capable of reaching into every crevice of the human soul. The
point is crucial for dilating our sense of world. We cannot go back to very
old civilizations where words virtually doubled for things by borrowing
their full substance, but there is no reason why we cannot come again to
see that at its best symbolism is the "science" of the relationship between
alternate levels of reality (al-Ghazali).

The foregoing has deduced the outlines of an alternative education by
reversing the criteria of scientific knowing. I might have gotten to much
the same place if I had asked what education would look like if it at-
tended more to the things science is not skillful with: intrinsic and normative values, purposes, existential and inclusive meanings, and
qualities. But I have said enough for today, save for a quick coda.

I hope what I have written has not contributed to the literature of indictment. I have tried, or hope I have tried, merely to ask myself where

44   Numerology is a special case that need not concern us here. In $2 + 2 = 4$ numbers function
as signs, but in "God is one," one is a symbol.

45   Paul Ricoeur points out the irony in the phrase "symbolic logic" which, as the name for our
ultimate, formal, abstract exactitude, exactly inverts the symbolism's usual meaning (*The Symbolism of Evil*, trans. Emerson Buchanan [Boston: Beacon Press, 1969], p. 17).

46   Lewis Thomas, *Lives of a Cell* (Toronto: Bantam Books, 1974), p. 111.

we are and where it might be good to go. The second half of this question, "Where might it be good to go," does not, I think, implicate me in the homilist's complaint of living in bad times, but it does bring my argument full circle in a way I had not anticipated. Going is a mode of doing, and doing includes an element of control. But will-to-control, having caused our narrowed epistemology and ontology, is what we need to correct — this has been my argument.

The paradox — recommendations issuing from one side of a mouth that preaches *wu wei* (nonwillfulness, noninsistence) with its other side — could be embarrassing were it not in fact a virtue. For it shows that at least we have not been wrestling with a straw man. If motivations (intentions) do breed their respective epistemologies and worlds and it has been our historical destiny to push the problem-solving triumvirate to dangerous extremes, the question remains: What *is* the right balance between participation and control? I do not know the answer. If I were a university president forced to divide short funds between knowledge that furthers participation and knowledge that furthers control, I would agonize. Everything I have written is premised on the intuition that we are top-heavy on control, but those who disagree are powerful and worthy of the utmost respect and even fear. So much so that I shall ask Gregory Bateson to address to them my final rejoinder. His statement appears in an interview with Daniel Goleman in *Psychology Today*.

Goleman: What's to be done?

Bateson: Funny question, "What's to be done?" Suppose I said that nothing's to be done. Way back in 1947, I was asked to address a group of physicists at Princeton. They had all worked on the atom bomb, and then were terribly remorseful about what might be done with it. Robert Oppenheimer had organized a seminar for these nuclear physicists to examine the social sciences to see if there were any remedies. After my talk, I was Oppenheimer's house-guest. The next morning was a horrible, rainy winter day. The children had lost their rubbers and Mrs. Oppenheimer was going mad trying to get them off to school. The regular American breakfast scene.

And in the midst of all this hubhub, out of the blue, came the still, small voice of Oppenheimer, saying, unasked, "You know, if anyone asked me why I left teaching at Cal Tech and came to do research at Princeton, I suppose the answer was that at Cal Tech there were 500 students to face, who all wanted to know the answers."

I said, "I suppose the answers to these questions would have been rather bitter."

Oppenheimer said, "Well, as I see it, the world is moving in the direction of hell, with a high velocity, and perhaps a positive acceleration, and a positive rate of change of acceleration; and the only condition under which it might not reach its destination is that we and the Russians be willing to let it go there." Every move we make in fear of the next war in fact hastens it. The old deterrence theory. We arm up to control the Russians, they do the same. Anxiety, in fact, brings about the thing its fears, creates its own disaster.

Goleman: So, just let it happen?

Bateson: Well, be bloody careful about the politics you play to control it. You don't know the total pattern; for all you know, you could create the next horror by trying to fix up a present one.

Goleman: The patterns you talk about in which we are enmeshed seem much larger than we can grasp.

Bateson: There is a larger mind of which the individual mind is only a subsystem. This larger mind is perhaps what some people mean by "God." But it is immanent in the total interconnected social system and includes the planetary ecology.

Goleman: It seems to be almost futile to try to perceive, let alone control, this larger web of patterns and connections.

Bateson: Trying to perceive them is, I'm sure, worthwhile. I've devoted my life to that proposition. Trying to tell other people about them is worthwhile. In a sense, we know it already. At the same time, we don't know. We are terribly full of screaming voices that talk administrative "common sense."

Goleman: Rather than . . ."

Bateson: Wisdom. If there be such a thing.[47]

47 Gregory Bateson, interviewed by Daniel Goleman, "Breaking Out of the Double Bind," *Psychology Today*, August 1978, p. 51.

Tacit Knowing as a Rationale for Liberal Education

HARRY S. BROUDY

University of Illinois, Urbana

The discussion of Michael Polanyi in this article is limited pretty much to the potential contribution of tacit knowing to a rationale for general or liberal education.[1]

It may seem odd to be searching for such a rationale when, ever since Aristotle, everyone has "known" that beyond specialized training for an occupation there is education for man as man, that is, cultivation of those powers man shares with no other species: clear thinking, enlightened cherishing, and humane judgment. Apparently this rationale is now suspect, in part because some do not believe any education other than specialized training is worth cultivating; in part because on the two most commonly used criteria for the success of schooling, general or liberal studies are a failure. Hence we either give up the ideal of liberal or general education or we dispute the validity of the criteria. I shall try to explicate why and how the faith in liberal education is justified.

The most common criterion of instructional effectiveness is the learner's ability to recall the contents of instruction. This is measured by tests that sample these contents. A student is judged successful if he passes these tests; a course is judged successful if the student in post-school life can still pass a test in it. Since scholastic exercises are not customary in out-of-school life, the criterion becomes the ability to recall the right answer to *any* item that was taught in school. But on this criterion and on occasional tests given in national polls the results are disappointing. Only those who frequently review the contents of such courses or idiot savants

---

1 Although there is a difference between general and liberal studies, it is to their common claim of generalizability that the discussion is directed.

50

can recall more than a tiny portion of what they had studied successfully in high school or college.

Selecting the right response from a set in which it is the *only* right response is a less demanding and somewhat more flexible variant of the recall criterion because sometimes one can "figure out" the right answer by elimination without necessarily being able to recall it. To recognize that "x is y" is not the right answer is not itself always or even usually an act of recall. If, for example, one rejects "1775" as the correct response to the question "When did Columbus discover America?" it is not because one remembers that 1775 is the wrong answer, and it may not be because one recalls that 1492 is the right one. It may be that, given the context of chronology and many related items of information, it is inferred that 1775 could not have been the right date. Yet this "reasoning" solution does not necessarily eliminate the need for recall; on the contrary, one may have to recall a number of facts to eliminate the wrong options. Educated adults probably do better on multiple choice tests than on tests of direct recall, but it is doubtful that they do as well as they did on their end-of-course multiple choice tests.

Ability to *apply* is another recognized and highly esteemed criterion of school learning. If, for example, one can "apply" knowledge of physics and chemistry to the diagnosis and remediation of an automotive malfunction, then we say with approval that the study of physics or chemistry was successful. Unfortunately, outside of one's field of specialization, such application is rare. For one thing, application requires not only the *recollection* of relevant facts and theory, but familiarity with the objects in the field as well. For another, a general theory, as Polanyi has pointed out, does not contain within itself indications as to the uses to which it might be put — the principles of physics do not embosom an automobile or any other devices for locomotion. Finally, even after the connection between a field of knowledge and a human purpose is discerned, there remains the need to find a technique or device to operate on a particular set of situations.

Not all specialists, for that matter, apply a theory. An automobile mechanic, for example, usually identifies standard predicaments and matches them with standard solutions. This resembles recall rather than applicative reasoning. Only when standard solutions fail does the need for a more theoretical analysis become apparent — at which point the mechanic shrugs his shoulders and refers the difficulty to the foreman, who, if frustrated, may turn it over to the automotive engineer. Most of what passes for application by a nonspecialist is more properly called interpretation, of which more will be said shortly.

So if the replicative and applicative uses of schooling are taken as criteria, general/liberal education is not a conspicuous success. What, then, can one say about the broad life outcomes traditionally claimed for schooling? Either the claims are fraudulent, or they are the products of factors other than schooling. A third possibility is that a content learned explicitly, although not recollectable, can function tacitly.

If the last option is chosen, a number of questions have to be dealt with. First of all, how defensible is the hypothesis of tacit knowing? I shall have little to say about this, save to suggest that in addition to the evidence from subception, the use of probes, the analyses of scientific discoveries, and other operations discussed by Polanyi, there is reason to believe that persons who have studied certain disciplines the details of which they cannot recall nevertheless perform differently on reading and discussion tasks involving concepts from these disciplines than those who have not studied them.[2]

The attempt to evade the criteria of recall and application challenges the positivistic theory of knowledge that requires the reduction of all meaningful assertions to propositions about publicly verifiable behaviors. The accountability movement in schooling leans heavily on the dogma of behavioral objectives and insists on tests for the presence of the stipulated behaviors after instruction. The implication of such a theory is that what cannot be so tested is not worth learning in the first place. Polanyi's work in identifying the tacit or personal component in all forms of cognition, including scientific discovery, is therefore a welcome resource for justifying general education.

Then there is the question of how an explicit input studied, let us say, in the sixth grade, is transformed so that it functions tacitly fifteen or twenty years later, when it may no longer be recalled as learned. I must plead ignorance of the psychological processes involved. Instead I shall offer a hypothesis that relies more on conceptual analysis than on psychology, namely, that certain uses of schooling, the associative and interpretive, do not require the precise reinstatement of content that had been studied formally; indeed, that for such uses full recollection of learned inputs might be a hindrance rather than a help. I shall argue that cognitive, imagic, and evaluational schemáta develop as a consequence of formal schooling, and that these are used tacitly by the Self in all experience, but especially in interpretation and association.[3]

2 I have discussed some research possibilities in this field in "The Life Uses of Schooling," in *Seventy-First Yearbook of the National Society for the Study of Education*, Part I (Chicago: NSSE, 1972), pp. 219-39.

3 H.S. Broudy, "Research into Emagic Association and Cognitive Interpretation," *Research in the Teaching of English* 7, no. 2 (Fall 1973): 240-59.

Further, if the tacit-knowing hypothesis is at all probable, what does it signify for curriculum, modes of teaching, and testing in general education? One may wonder whether explicit school inputs for tacit outcomes are necessary at all. It sounds as if the school were deliberately teaching for forgetting. Or, to put it differently, why not practice these associative and interpretive operations explicitly rather than rely on mysterious transformations of explicit inputs into tacit outputs? To this question one can only reply that the very notions of interpretation and creative association preclude automatic recall as equivalents.

Finally, one may ask: How reliable is "knowledge" that one cannot make explicit on demand and put to the tests of logic and fact? Is all implicit content necessarily false? If a fantasy leads to a true insight, is its truth impaired by the faulty source? Or does it perchance validate the source? These questions lead to a consideration, to be discussed later, of the difference between truth and credibility.

ASSOCIATIVE AND INTERPRETIVE USES OF SCHOOLING

Although Polanyi holds that "A *wholly* explicit knowledge is unthinkable,"[4] the replicative and applicative uses of schooling emphasize explicitness far more than the associative and interpretive uses. I shall argue that these latter uses are the goals of general/liberal education, and that these uses are difficult to "explain" satisfactorily without the hypothesis of tacit knowing.

By the *associative* use of schooling is meant the connection of an item of experience with concepts, images, relations, encountered in formal study. Sometimes the association can be described and explained by the laws of association (resemblance, recency, contiguity, etc.); sometimes explanation requires psychoanalysis, and some associations apparently are inexplicable by any means. The nexus between stimulus and the association in the present state of our knowledge is largely indeterminate.

By *interpretation* is meant the translation of experience or discourse from one set of concepts to another, from one context to another—for example, the interpretation of a tornado by the concepts of physics, the interpretation of inflation by translation into the concepts in economic theory. An interpretation of X may offer a meaning of X, or draw inferences from X, or explain X. It is expected that formal schooling will provide concepts from religion, philosophy, history, and the sciences, as well as the images created by the fine arts, that can be used as vehicles of interpretation.

It will be objected that all four uses are related and cannot be sepa-

4   Michael Polanyi, "The Logic of Tacit Inference," *Philosophy* 41, no. 155 (January 1966): 7.

rated. To this one can retort that they are in fact only too easily separated. Some recall is a necessary condition for the other uses, but it is not sufficient condition to evoke them. Similarly, some recall, association, and interpretation are necessary for application, but are not sufficient to bring it about. Interpretation requires some recall and association, but the converse may not be true. All I wish to claim at this point is that liberal education is both a necessary and sufficient condition for the associative and interpretive uses of knowledge; that it is neither a necessary nor sufficient condition for the replicative use, and a necessary (as interpretation) but insufficient condition for the applicative one.

THE TACIT-KNOWING HYPOTHESIS

According to Polanyi, in the acts of perceiving, judging, and understanding there are two components: the explicit or focal and the implicit (tacit, peripheral, or subsidiary). There are many examples of this dual functioning.[5] In every perceptual field there is a figure at the center of attention and a ground of which we are only peripherally aware. We call figures ambiguous if figure and ground shift too readily. In stereoptical phenomena the two slightly differing views of the object are fused in perception, but one can shift attention to each of the dual views. However, it is difficult, if not impossible, to pay equal attention to both figure and ground at the same time. We know what is at the focus of attention, Polanyi holds, by means of what is sensed or perceived subsidiarily. Thus one might say that all knowing entails a context that operates in a subsidiary way to give meaning to the explicit content that is at the focus of our comprehension.[6]

Polanyi distinguishes between self-centered integrations, in which the subsidiary clues are not interesting in themselves—for example, words, maps, mathematical formulas—but merely bear on their focal meaning, and those meanings in which the subsidiary clues are of interest in themselves, so much so that the meaning goes *from* the focus, for example, the flag, *to* the complex of concepts and feelings of which the flag is the symbol.[7] The direction of meaning is thus reversed. In metaphor the

5 For a list, see Michael Polanyi and Harry Prosch, *Meaning* (Chicago: University of Chicago Press, 1975), p. 71. More accurately, there are three, the Self being the third.

6 Polanyi notes that in a deductive inference we combine two focal objects so that a subsidiary tacitness would not be required, and I would think that a recall of a school input as explicitly learned might also be an exception to the universality of the tacit component. However, meaning entails more than recall, and when an item is recalled because it is thought to be relevant for purposes other than recall, then it too requires a context that gives it sense (ibid., p. 40).

7 Ibid., pp. 70ff.

meaning flow presumably is in both directions at once. Polanyi needs these distinctions in order to explain meaning in the arts and certain types of symbolism, or what he terms contrived meanings as distinct from "natural" coherences. The distinctions are also important for justifying liberal education, because the contexts supplied by schooling are both conceptual, as in the sciences and science-like disciplines, and imagistic, as in the arts. The latter serve as the nuclei for concepts in general, but can be used to construct a realm of nonfactual reality, the reality contrived by and for the imagination. Imaginative reality is the substance not only of the arts, myth, and ritual, but of ideals, aspirations, cosmologies, and theologies. The latter resources are usually regarded as produced by the humanistic studies.

I am not at all clear as to how accurately I have used Polanyi's theory of tacit knowing, and my confidence is not bolstered by the exfoliation of meaning types in chapters 4 and 5 of *Meaning*. I find myself saying that school studies a, b, c, are known subsidiarily in interpreting a problem (F) focally. But then I want to say that focal knowledge of a theory (F), for example, oxidation, explains a variety of combustion phenomena x, y, z. Thus Polanyi says that we know universals by dwelling in the particulars, I take it, as subsidiaries, but the tacit knowledge of a universal gives meaning to a set of particulars not yet classified. (Cf. footnote 14 referring to the passage quoted on page 454 of this article.)

As regards the rationale for liberal studies, the important meaning of *tacit* is that it denotes an item not *now* explicitly in the center of attention, although when being studied it was at the center of the pupil's attention. However, tacit covers theories, world views, and schemata of all sorts insofar as during an interpretive act they are "the spectacles" through which we see but which we do not see.

Is the hypothesis of tacit knowing probable? To me, the evidence put forward by Polanyi is persuasive, and it is supported by informal observation of the performance of students on tasks that involve concepts and images ordinarily not acquired outside of school. Where disciplines have not been studied formally, gaps in the subsidiary context prevent the focal material from being understood. More systematic research, it seems plausible to believe, would produce more and stronger evidence of this sort. If the hypothesis is correct, then we should expect certain difficulties in schooling itself, if context-building materials for subsidiary functioning were deficient. For example, it would explain failures in reading comprehension despite competence in the mechanics of reading.

If, as I believe, the hypothesis of tacit knowing is defensible, then schooling for the purpose of building tacit resources is justifiable. Indeed, it might be argued that the goal of general or liberal education is to fund the mind explicitly with contents that in time will become tacit resources for the building of contexts.

CONTEXT-BUILDING RESOURCES

1. Images of all sorts in all modalities are accumulated from the earliest hours of life. In time they are clustered by random connection, by the laws of association, and by factors of which we know little. Fantasy, fairy tales, the popular and serious arts, may contribute to and organize the imagic store. Imagination, by creating and combining images, enlarges the store, and the arts enlarge and refine it. Liberal studies have their part in this enlarging and refining process. This store provides content and form for the apprehension and construal of experience. In this activity, we use the imagic store tacitly, not by systematically scanning the total inventory of images, but rather by bringing selected clusters and subclusters of them into consciousness.[8]

For example, suppose someone were to say, "That man has a weak chin; don't let him marry your daughter." Presumably clusters of images associated conventionally with "weakness" constitute the compressed evidence that leads to the conclusion about marrying daughters to weak-chinned men. The number of inferences from aesthetic clues to matters of fact—rarely verified—is both impressive and frightening.

But art, especially serious art, is noted for unconventional associations. The poet uses figures of speech; the painter distorts images of actual objects so that they are perceived as expressive images. Art, it has been said, makes the strange familiar and the familiar strange. Serious art calls for a rich imagic store in order to be perceived, but, having been perceived, it enriches the imagic store: first, by increasing its content, and, second, by maintaining its fluidity. The combination of content and fluidity is the matrix of the creative imagination.

Inferences from aesthetic clues to matters of fact are notoriously deceptive, but there is a species of inference from images that is "verified" by the reality that imagination creates. Ideals, aspirations, and all assertions about possibilities are products of the imagination. This does not mean that they are meaningless, dogmatic positivists notwithstanding; rather it means that imagination can be captured by an idea, an image of

---

8 For those who make the distinction between surface and deep structure, it might be said that the deep structure supplies the meaning tacitly. The point is raised by Gerald L. Bruns in his review of Jean Paris, *Painting and Linguistics*, Praxis/Poetics Series, no. 1, Carnegie-Mellon University (Pittsburgh: The Colonial Press, 1975), in *The Journal of Aesthetics and Art Criticism* 34, no. 4 (Summer 1976): 508.

possibility that, on occasion, human beings actualize. "I know that my
Redeemer liveth . . ." syntactically resembles an assertion of empirical
fact, but the evidence for its truth is not supplied by exhumation or an
empty tomb. It is what Sören Kierkegaard called an example of truth as
subjectivity, that is, an assertion verified by the behavior and demeanor
of those who lived or died as if it were literally true. The belief becomes
act and verifies it. Whereupon the act becomes an *addendum* to the
human reality.[9]

The role of education in furnishing resources for imagination and the
construal of images is illustrated by George Steiner's classification of the
formidable difficulties encountered in reading a poem. Contingent difficulties, he notes, are those created by a gap in our knowledge of some
term or phrase.

> In the overwhelming majority of cases, what we mean by saying "this is
> difficult" signifies "this is a word, a phrase, or a reference which I will
> have to look up." In the total library in the *collectanea* and *summa
> summarum* of all things, I can do just that. And find that a *ptyx* is a
> conch.[10]

Modal difficulties refer to the quality of sensibility.

> Who now reads, who experiences at any adequate depth of response
> the tragedies of Voltaire . . . or the high dramas of Alfieri that came
> after? . . . A substantial measure of European literature from the six-
> teenth to the nineteenth centuries drew constantly and with intimate
> recognition on the epic poetry of Boiardo, Ariosto, and Tasso . . . To
> mid-twentieth-century literacy this entire syllabus of sentiment and al-
> lusion is either a closed book or the terrain of academic research.[11]

A third kind of difficulty, which Steiner calls "tactical," results from
the "writer's will or failure of adequacy between his intention and his

---

9 I do not subscribe to the view that the creation of an imaginative reality by the artist requires
as much relativism as some would claim. The spatio-temporal world need not be each individual's
construct from moment to moment in order for the artist to be creative. The possible combinations
of images are not determined, even if we do not *construct* the world from which these images are
received. The revelation by Carl Sandburg that "the fog comes on little cat feet" does not change the
anatomy of either cats or fogs, from the observation of which comes the metaphor, but it may contribute a new item to the imaginary reality, viz., a foggy cat or a catty fog. For a contrary view see Ina
Lowenberg, "Creativity and Correspondence in Fiction and Metaphors," *The Journal of Aesthetics
and Art Criticism* 36, no. 3 (Spring 1978): 341-50.

10 George Steiner, "On Difficulty," *The Journal of Aesthetics and Art Criticism* 35, no. 3
(Spring 1976): 263-66, 267.

11 Ibid., pp. 269-70.

performative means." Steiner cites as one cause the need of the author to conceal his meaning in order not to arouse political suspicion and ire.

Finally, there is ontological difficulty that confronts us with questions about the nature of speech and poetry as modes of being.[12]

Although Beardsley finds flaws with Steiner's classification,[13] and although Steiner was addressing himself primarily to the interpretation of poetry and literature, the implication for education is clear. Education, especially general or liberal education, has the task of providing at least some of the imagic-conceptual resources for overcoming these difficulties. And in a similar view Bosanquet says:

> All the material and the physical process which the artist uses — take our English language as used in poetry for an example — has been elaborated and refined, and, so to speak, consecrated by ages of adaptation and application in which it has been fused and blended with feeling — and it carries the life-blood of all this endeavor in its veins; and that is how, as we have said over and over again, feelings get their embodiment, and embodiments get their feeling. If you try to cut the thought and fancy loose from the body of the stuff in which it molds its pictures and poetic ideas and musical constructions, you impoverish your fancy, and arrest its growth, and reduce it to a bloodless shade.[14]

2. Experience is also organized around concepts as nuclei. Concepts as class names are universals, and Polanyi argued that the classic problem of the nature of universals (how one term can apply to a varied collection of individuals) is solved if

> in speaking of man in general we are not attending to any kind of man, but relying on our subsidiary awareness of individual, for attending to their joint meaning. This meaning is a comprehensive, and its knowledge is wiped out by attending to its particulars in themselves. This explains why the concept of man cannot be identified by any particular set of men, past or future.[15]

The most refined concepts and classifications are supplied by the intellectual disciplines — the ones studied in school. Each discipline is made up of entities, relations, facts, laws, and modes of inquiry peculiar to

12 Ibid., p. 273.

13 Monroe C. Beardsley, "Some Problems of Critical Interpretation: A Commentary," *The Journal of Aesthetics and Art Criticism* 36, no. 3 (Spring 1978): 354ff.

14 Bernard Bosanquet, from *Three Lectures on the Aesthetics*, 1915, quoted in *A Modern Book of Esthetics,* ed. Melvin Rader, 4th ed. (New York: Holt, Rinehart & Winston, 1973), p. 209.

15 Polanyi, "The Logic of Tacit Inference," p. 11.

itself. They make up its distinctive structure. This structure remains after most of the school lessons that were used to explicate it have been forgotten. Each discipline leaves a residue that, like a stencil or a honeycomb, reveals a distinctive design when placed on experience.

The point to be stressed, however, is that the school should not stock the imagic-conceptual store with the expectation that each and every image can be retrieved at will. Some blend into each other; others are distorted, some repressed. But the schemata persist, so that roses, weak chins, moons, melodies, and certain color patterns prod them into providing contexts for association and interpretation. The result may take the form of a new image or an inference or a value judgment. Speech patterns, personality stereotypes, character patterns, are typical image clusters. The primordial archetypes that Jung believed inhabit the collective unconscious and the great myths and legends constitute another set of imagic clusters. Without them, virtually all discourse, let alone the arts, would be meaningless.

These structures or stencils serve as subsidiaries for the interpretation of the objects at the focus of knowing and understanding. We have to suppose that the school input consisted of explicit attention to the details of the separate disciplines in order to elicit these structures. The structure, to use Polanyi's term, was apprehended by means of the details. Later the structure itself became a subsidiary for supplying a context of meaning to a problem, a piece of discourse, and so forth. It is not anomalous to say that the details must fade into relative oblivion for the structure to function interpretively. And it must be reiterated that attempts to bypass the study of the details in the first instance in favor of studying the structure directly may not be productive, as many schemes of general education that have tried to take this short cut have demonstrated.

THE SELF AS KNOWER

The relation of a subsidiary to a focus is formed by the *act of a person* who integrates one to the other.[16]

For Polanyi, the process of knowing involves a triad: subsidiary, focus, and the person. I have suggested that the imagic-conceptual resources provided by schooling through the study of the disciplines serve as resources for the subsidiaries, that is, as contexts for meaning. But the person as *actor* or agent using knowledge is more than a mechanical retriever from a repository of images and concepts. The "more" is a value schema

16   Polanyi and Prosch, *Meaning*, p. 38.

that categorizes and assesses the situations of life by their import to the person.

Schools influence these value schemata by example and exhortation, but their distinctive contributions come from the disciplines that make up the curriculum of the liberal studies. For the disciplines *are* themselves value exemplars. In time, if schooling is successful, we dwell in these values; to use Polanyi's term, they are the probes by which we explore the domains of value.

> A theory is like a pair of spectacles; you examine things by it, and your knowledge of it lies in this very use of it.[17]

Like the spectacles, the formal study of fact, value, and image creates subsidiaries that we know by using them and not by looking at them directly.

However, it would be presumptuous to claim for any set of studies exclusive influence on the volitional structure of the person. But liberal education need not claim exclusive or even predominant influence. The claim need go no further than that these studies make a distinctive difference in the person's evaluational pattern, and that they do so tacitly, if not explicitly.

I believe this claim is reasonable and consonant with the general expectation that the educated person, especially one educated in the liberal studies, will be loyal to standards of thought and conduct well above those of his uneducated fellowmen. But are the verities of the disciplines relevant to a modern complex, interdependent, technologically sophisticated world? Can the student or adult be influenced — tacitly or explicitly — by the exemplars of bygone cultures? Are they relevant for a career? And vocational relevance seems to be crucial for the college student of the late seventies.

Some liberal arts faculties are strenuously trying to discover or invent such relevance in the liberal studies. To be sure, some general studies, including clarity of communication, critical thinking, basic sciences, are relevant to vocation, and they are so recognized in the preprofessional requirements for admission to professional schools. The more fundamental question for the liberal studies is whether they can sustain a rational stance toward life in a society that in many ways has made the attempt to be rational suspect.

The suspicion has been growing as social problems exceed our efforts to understand their causes and confound our efforts to remedy them. Em-

17   Ibid., p. 37.

pirical science probing into the ways of things should enable us to deal objectively with our predicaments in providing health, wealth, and happiness for our people—even though their numbers reach into the billions. However, the rational stance, which consists of a reliance on objective truth as discovered and enunciated by experts as a basis for choice, is becoming more and more difficult to maintain. Accordingly, there is a shift from theoretical to existential thinking; from the truth of an assertion to the credibility of the assertor. Choice and commitment are grounded less in conclusions from science and logic than in moral gambles. In what sense can one expect a liberal education to function in such gambles?

EXISTENTIAL THINKING

Although the notion of existential thinking is taken from the literature of Existentialism, it need not wallow in the more lurid depths of that movement, either in the form of religious *Angst* or social and moral anarchy.

Existential thinking stresses the significance of assertions for the commitment of the thinker. Objective truth is certified either as a necessary conclusion entailed by true premises or as a generalization derived from empirical inquiry. Existential truth cannot be necessary truth in the logical sense, because it refers to particular persons acting or thinking about particular, contingent predicaments. Nor can the existential thinker rely too much on the probabilities of science. First because, except in very rare cases, individuals cannot verify the findings of the scientist in practice, even though the verification is possible in principle.[18] Second, for a truth on which a person's commitment is to depend, probable generalization is not enough; action is particular and definite; nothing is more irrelevant to a person's actual dying than the statistics on the life expectations of a given population.

A more systemic difficulty stalks the ideal of rational action based on empirical knowledge. There seems to be a limit not only to our control over events and their consequences but even to our understanding them. We are reluctant to admit this because of our faith in technology. We cling to the hope that further developments in communication, data processing, and health research will give us control over the greater and greater amounts of complexity that they have created. Up to a point, this faith is justified, but technology is neither impotent nor omnipotent, and we may have gone beyond that point. We can sense this when the following conditions obtain:

---

18 For example, how many of us can verify the assertions made by experts on inflation, the SALT talks, or the mechanical safety of automobiles?

1. Measures carefully designed to promote good or prevent evil create more difficulties than they solve, for example, the attempt to manage automobile traffic.

2. The cost of administering a program approaches that of the benefits derived from it.

3. The costs of monitoring a program against the ingenious efforts of those who are prepared to subvert it, legally or otherwise, approach or exceed the benefits of the program.

4. The procedural and administrative arrangements in an institution become ends in themselves with large numbers of functionaries devoted to serving these ends.

In such circumstances the individual's attempt to make rational choices founders on sheer inability to estimate consequences on the basis of either fact or principle. Our intellectual resources are inadequate to the first, and our attempts to assess the moral quality of a measure are stymied by the fact that every measure provides benefits for some at a cost to others. Measure X improves the environment, but throws thousands out of work. The attempt to provide free medical care to the indigent drives up medical costs to the point where only the indigent and the rich can afford them. The list is very long, and the intelligent, well-intentioned citizen may be forgiven for concluding that trying to be intelligent about social and moral problems is presumptuous and futile.

The upshot of these comments is that in a modern world thinking becomes increasingly existential and depends on credibility more than on objective truth. Rationality in the conduct of life is not based primarily on the empirical truth about a situation but on the credibility of the person or institution advocating a policy for dealing with the situation. In other words, the fiduciary component in empirical rationality, as Polanyi so often insisted, is not only unavoidable, it can be decisive. It is even more so in existential rationality. It need not be blind faith, however, for although grounds for credibility are moral and psychological as well as logical, extralogical grounds are not necessarily irrational.[19] On the contrary, it may be more rational to act on the assertion of a speaker who is sincere and not self-serving than on assertions that, even if objectively true, are being used for purposes to which one would not want to be committed.

19 Tertullian's "Credo quia absurdum" is one of the more lurid conclusions referred to above.

GROUNDS FOR CREDIBILITY

The fiduciary base of the individual is fractured by the disagreement of experts as to the facts of the case, for example, the energy crisis, and the consequences of various alternatives. It is further eroded when parties to the controversy have vested interests in the acceptance of one view of the situation rather than another. Thus it is important to know *who* is paying an oil expert or an economist before one can assess the credibility of his analysis of the energy situation.

How does one decide which of the conflicting scientific or expert views on the energy crisis to believe? It is on the basis of knowledge or faith? About all even the educated layman "knows for a fact" is that X and Y are officially certified as experts. He has "faith" that the certification system is based on expertise in a conglomerate of disciplines—chemistry, physics, thermodynamics, geophysics, petroleum engineering—and is assessed by members of the guilds charged with developing, refining, and judging these disciplines. Similarly, faith in a conglomerate of theories, experiments, and methods justifies acceptance of the assertion that the sun is 93 million miles from the earth. In a science-based technological society, the fiduciary base for thinking and living is far more extensive than knowledge.

And yet our faith, if we are educated, is not wholly groundless. We may not be able to pass examinations on the sciences we studied in school and college, yet those studies now provide the contexts in which the energy crisis is expressed and debated. Would we construe the problem in the same way had we not studied and "forgotten" these and kindred disciplines? What would constitute our fiduciary base without an imagic-conceptual-value store to which these and other studies have contributed? It is this tacit context that differentiates between someone who believes that the sun is 93 million miles from the earth because he has read it and believes what he reads, and the person who, having studied the sciences, believes the statement and understands what the establishment of its truth would require. We call the latter, but not the former, an educated judgment.[20]

Or as Polanyi put it:

I have shown how our subsidiary awareness of our body is extended to include a stick, when we feel our way by means of the stick. To use

[20] Sören Kierkegaard tells of a patient in a mental institution who was restrained by a ball and chain on his leg. Whenever the ball struck his ankle, he announced that the world was round. This, we would agree, was an objective truth but not an educated statement of it or, as Kierkegaard would say, it was an instance in which objectivity was not the truth.

language in speech, reading and writing is to extend our bodily equipment and become intelligent human beings. We may say that when we learn to use language, or a probe, or a tool, and thus make ourselves aware of these things as we are of our body, we *interiorise* these things and *make ourselves dwell in them.* Such extensions of ourselves develop new faculties in us; our whole education operates in this way; as each of us interiorises our cultural heritage, he grows into a person seeing the world and experiences life in terms of this outlook.[21]

Existential thinking, concerned as it is with grounds for commitment, conjoins thinking about matters of fact with judgments of value. And if the fiduciary base for empirical conclusions presents problems, the base for moral judgments is about as stable as a waterbed floating in a pool of mercury. Diverse philosophical systems, religious beliefs, *Weltanschauungen* of the East and West, provide possible contexts for value judgment. Education through the study of the various humanistic disciplines stocks the fiduciary base for moral commitment. Edith Bunker's judgments about what is right and wrong enjoy a high order of credibility, but if one asks what justifies her credibility with millions of television viewers, it would not occur to anybody to say that it was her study of philosophy, religion, or the arts. A college graduate may express judgments identical with Edith's, but the context in which he makes them should be very different; it is supposed to emerge from studies, the details of which he cannot recollect but which Edith presumably never undertook.

Just as the study of the scientific disciplines creates the fiduciary context for judging the truth claims of empirical statements, so the study of the humanistic disciplines supplies the fiduciary context for educated acceptance of statements about value. These disciplines represent the critical tradition in the scientific and value domains. To regard the humanistic tradition as a static collection of dogmas is a misunderstanding. When a work of art or a classic in literature survives for centuries, it is not because it has been protected from criticism, but because it has survived it. The greater the reputation of a work, the more intense the scrutiny it undergoes from the critics and scholars in every epoch. Its survival is evidence of its inherent strength and quality, and in this sense it deserves to survive. When, as Polanyi would say, we "dwell" in this tradition, commitment is no longer arbitrary.

Tradition is a troublesome category for education. It fosters the notion

21 Polanyi, "The Logic of Tacit Inference," p. 10.

that innovation and creativity are revolts against tradition. There is an unbuttoned view of pedagogy that encourages this delusion in the face of the fact that even genius stands on the shoulders of its predecessors to get a loftier view. The frontier of every discipline is the frontier of a tradition.[22]

Advocates of liberal studies would like to argue that these traditions structure the thought and commitments of the Self with respect to both truth and credibility. But, as has been noted, it is virtually impossible to trace the effects of particular school studies on adult activities. The theory of tacit knowing enables us to understand how the school studies become organized into traditions, and how the traditions function tacitly to structure the Self.

A more persuasive argument would be possible if it could be demonstrated that differences in associative and interpretive uses of knowledge in adult life can be related to school studies. Does a reader who has never studied economics interpret an article on "stagflation" in the same way as one who has studied the "dismal science"? Does a physician who no longer can pass a college test on biology or chemistry interpret an article on drugs or nutrition in the same way as does one who has never studied these disciplines? Does such study differentiate the diagnosis of disease by a modern physician from that of a witch doctor?

Informal studies and observation indicate that there is a difference. As Steiner indicated in the article quoted above, some obstacles to access to poetry are erected by previous poetry. Those who have never studied Latin are unlikely to use images related to Latin roots in their interpretation of reading materials. All this seems plausible enough. But that is not the objection raised by opponents of liberal studies. They argue that items one cannot recall at will do not function at all, and therefore are not worth studying in the first place. They judge the functionality of the physician's study of chemistry not on his adult associative and interpretive activities but on his performance (real or putative) on a test of recall. The study of Latin was exorcised from the curriculum not on the basis of the interpretation of poetry but on its failure to increase scores on tests of English vocabulary and the incontestable fact that we no longer speak or even read Latin in daily life.

22   Whatever else may be said about Thomas Kuhn's paradigms in the sciences, it is profoundly true that, as far as education and the practice of inquiry are concerned, most workers and students have to go through the paradigmatic studies, problems, and methods before they reach the frontier. Only the genius, having reached the frontier, can achieve the revolution of theory that forces the adoption of new paradigms. Thomas Kuhn, *The Structure of Scientific Revolution* (Chicago: University of Chicago Press, 1962).

Systematic research in this field should use schooled and unschooled adults. Initial subject matter tests might be given to provide a baseline for recallable content. Test tasks should be written at the level of the educated adult as found in the metropolitan press or nontechnical magazines. Careful analysis of the comprehension-interpretation responses of the subjects should give some indication of the tacit functioning of the school studies. Especially instructive would be the identification of the concepts or relationships that stop, interfere with, or distort the responses of those who had not studied them formally.

Direct evidence is harder to get. The very nature of tacit knowledge precludes a one-to-one matching of an explicit school input and a tacit use in a test situation. Contexts are broader and more indeterminate than situations. How explicit items will coalesce or skeletonize into theories or value schemata that provide contexts will always retain some degree of this indeterminacy.

Furthermore, we have no way of determining why certain items once studied cannot be recollected, while the transformation of the contents of the imagic-conceptual store remains more or less of a mystery.

Liberal education owes its durability, despite its inability to make its case on explicit casual connections, to a faith that is sustained in part by the tacit operations of formal schooling, but the roots of which lie in a powerful tradition that also functions tacitly.[23]

23 The acceptance of tacit knowing as a foundation for the rationale of general/liberal education does not entail a complete relativism or constructivism in the theory of knowledge. Granted that theory is context bound and that observation is theory bound, that all discourse is language bound, and the inevitability of the egocentric predicament, it is only the hypothesis that there is a reality in some sense independent of all these interventions and screens that gives point to the knowledge enterprise, whether scientific or philosophical. The point of the diverse descriptions of the elephant given by the blind observers would be lost if there were no elephant. Nevertheless, the ontological issue can be bypassed to some extent in the rationale problem of general/liberal education precisely because it is the kind of education that purports to help us move about with facility and some precision within the various realms of discourse. And although ultimately serious discourse is about reality, much of what we call educated discourse proximally is about discourse itself.

Democratic Values and Educational Aims

R. S. PETERS
University of London

EDUCATION

It is often said that "education" is an essentially contested concept.[1] Like "morality" and "democracy," it marks out features of life that are deemed desirable, but there is no one standard usage that can be taken as a model of correctness. So different groups compete endlessly for their particular interpretations. If they attempt any kind of definition they must necessarily produce what Stevenson nearly forty years ago called a "persuasive definition."[2] Selected conditions are linked with a recommending type of word and by this indirect method certain policies or ways of life are given the stamp of approval.

There is much to be said for this contention; for the term *education* is used valuatively, but vaguely with lack of precision regarding its area of application. From this it might be mistakenly suggested that all that needs to be done is to pick out certain criteria that seem central to one's understanding of education and lay these down as a stipulatory preliminary to the issues to be discussed. This, I think, would be a pretty pointless and presumptuous procedure. To start with, the concept of education may be contestable, but it is not completely so. We cannot call anything we like education — for example, scratching our heads. At least it denotes some kind of *learning* — and not any sort of learning either. At one time education was more or less synonymous with the learning involved in upbringing and, according to the Oxford English Dictionary, was used of animals — even silkworms. As with many concepts, however,

---

1 See W.B. Gallie, "Essentially Contested Concepts," *Proc. Aristotelian Soc.* 56 (1955-56); and A. Hartnell and M. Naish, *Theory and Practice of Education*, vol. 1 (London: Heinemann, 1976), pp. 79-94.

2 C. Stevenson, "Persuasive Definitions," *Mind*, 1938.

changes have taken place that mirror changes in economic and social life. Although, on occasion, the term *education* may be used to speak of the upbringing or schooling of children in a noncommittal way, it is also used with more specific suggestions. We can now say that a person has been to school but is not educated or that his upbringing was not particularly educative. Dogs bring up but do not educate their young.

What more can be said that is not contestable about these extra suggestions intimated by this conceptual shift? For the interesting point about contestable concepts, so it seems to me, is the point at which they become so. The clue to the conceptual shift in question is surely the development of industrialism in the nineteenth century. It came to be realized that it would be a benefit if the average man could read, write, and perform elementary calculations. Many skills and roles, too, required a modicum of specialized knowledge if they were to be performed efficiently. What is now called "training" became widespread, often backed up by religious instruction to "gentle the masses." By training is meant knowledge and skill devised to bring about some specific end; it began to be contrasted with education, which was used to speak of the beliefs, attitudes, and outlook of a person qua person and not just in his capacity as a skilled man or the occupant of a specific role. Education thus became associated with developing the "whole man" mainly by various forms of cognitive growth. Upbringing has neither of these suggestions. It is compatible with training a person to occupy a role, and with a narrow outlook as well.

This connection between education and the many-sided development of a person qua person has occasioned, in my view, two characteristic mistakes. On the one hand there are theorists like Langford[3] who equate education just with becoming a person. But education surely cannot mean as little as this; for in a straightforward sense many persons are uneducated, and, if this type of linguistic argument is thought objectionable, surely those who go to secondary schools and universities to continue their education are persons already, unless all sorts of valuative criteria are built into the concept of a "person." On the other hand there is Carl Bereiter,[4] who, building his case on the distinction between training and education, holds that the schools have no right to educate; for this involves the moulding of the whole personality of the individual. But education surely cannot mean as much as this; for a major feature of a person's personality is his temperament, which is singularly resistant to

3 See G. Langford and D.J. O'Connor, *New Essays in the Philosophy of Education* (London: Routledge & Kegan Paul, 1973), chap. 1.
4 C. Bereiter, *Must We Educate?* (Englewood Cliffs, N.J.: Prentice-Hall, 1973).

learning. Insofar, then, as education centrally implies learning, it cannot transform a person's *whole* personality.

What then can it develop over and above those minimum features necessary to become a person, but falling short of the transformation of the whole personality? Education surely develops a person's *awareness* by enlarging, deepening, and extending it. Its impact is cognitive, but it also transforms and regulates a person's attitudes, emotions, wants, and actions because all of these presuppose awareness and are impregnated with beliefs. Also, insofar as these are altered by learning, this comes about through the person's attending to, noticing, or understanding some feature of a situation that he copies or makes his own. And these are all forms of cognition. Of course attitudes, emotions, and wants can be altered and induced by drugs, by physiological changes, and by interferences with the brain. But these changes are not the product of learning; for learning implies mastering something or coming up to some standard as the result of *experience*. And the cognitive aspect of experience is fundamental in learning.

The connection with "wholeness" stressed by Bereiter is explained by the fact that being educated is incompatible with the narrow outlook associated with being just trained for a particular job or in a particular form of awareness, though, of course, training in a skill or for a role may well form part of—even the pivotal point of—a person's education. I have sympathy, therefore, for the view expressed by a speaker at a recent conference, at which the claims of vocational training were being pressed, that the purpose of education is not to prepare people for jobs but to prepare them for life. This, however, is misleading if taken literally, for (1) presumably he meant something like a worthwhile life, not just keeping alive; (2) as Dewey so forcefully argued, education is not just a preparation for living but is continuous with it, in that we should always be prepared to learn—as William Morris put it "Learn to live, live to learn"; (3) "life" needs further specification when contrasted with jobs. It is helpful in that it stresses that education should not consist of the accumulation of "inert ideas" that have no application to people's lives, but it does not in any way specify the areas of application. Toward what situations, then, is the development of awareness to be directed if a person's role or occupation is not to be emphasized? The answer can only be "the human condition." By that I mean, first, those features of the natural world that impinge on man and those that he shares with the natural world as part of the kingdom of nature. In the former category would be included phenomena such as the seasons, storms, tides, electricity, frost, fire, and so forth; in the latter, birth, death, procreation, ageing, and disease. Then, second, there is the interpersonal world of human affection and hate, of dominance and dependence, of friendship and loneliness. Finally, there is the economic, social, and political world of poverty and affluence, authority and violence, crime and punishment, consensus and dissent. Whatever a man's occupation, it is predictable that he will be confronted with phenomena such as these. Insofar, therefore, as education is concerned with learning how to live, his beliefs, attitudes, desires, and emotional reactions in these spheres will have to be developed and disciplined in various ways.

But in what ways? In trying to answer this question we have surely arrived at the contestable aspect of this more specific concept of education. For filling in the respects in which a person's awareness should be enlarged, deepened, sensitized, disciplined, and so forth, depends first on the values with which a society confronts these various aspects of the human condition and second on the emphases selected by its educators. These emphases, as Dewey maintained, constitute aims of education, which can become part of a person's or group's concept of education, in that education means processes of learning directed toward states of mind that are thought valuable, and these specific valuations can be built into the concept. Downie and Telfer, for instance, maintain that knowledge of various kinds is the distinguishing feature of an educated person.[5] I myself, in previous writings, assigned a similar role to all-round knowledge and understanding. But this is manifestly contestable, even within our own society. For though this is *an* aim of education, it is surely a narrow one. Many people, for instance, think that forms of awareness such as the aesthetic and the religious ought to be developed; but to talk of "knowledge" in these spheres is scarcely appropriate. Also in moral education, for example, what people do, their attitudes, actions, and habits, are as important as what they know and believe. Then there is the whole area of emotional development, with which education is surely concerned. Of course beliefs, and sometimes knowledge, are constituents of actions, attitudes, and emotions. But they are not the only constituents; so to confine education to the development of knowledge is to impose an unwarrantable restriction on it.

AIMS OF EDUCATION

It was suggested that aims of education can be regarded as aspects of the values of a society that an educator considers necessary to emphasize at a

---

5 R.S. Downie, E.M. Loudfoot, and E. Telfer, *Education and Personal Relationships* (London: Methuen, 1974).

given time. This suggests two formal points about aims. First they must point to features of development that are thought to be desirable. Second they must pick out reasonably specific goals, like targets. They lack the generality of ideals. They are also—and this is a third formal point—unlike ideals in that, whereas ideals suggest unattainability, for example, truth, universal happiness, the classless society, aims point to goals that are attainable, but with difficulty. If they are aims of education they must therefore be more or less attainable by some processes of learning, though with difficulty, for example, personal autonomy, concern for others, and so forth.

This third point is rather an important one in that it imposes limits on what can feature as aims of education. Happiness, for instance, is almost universally yearned for as a state of mind in which one can accommodate oneself to the human condition. But could it realistically be aimed at by educators? There are three problems about this. First, education is not a necessary path to happiness, for many uneducated people are perfectly happy. Second, happiness is a complex state of mind depending at least upon having desires that are fulfilled and the planning and scheduling of their satisfaction so that they do not conflict, lacking fears for the future and regret or remorse about the past, and having general expectations of life that are matched by circumstances. The subjective side of happiness might be improved by education, but this is very difficult to do for someone else in a teaching-learning situation, unless one knows the other person very well, because desires and expectations can be highly idiosyncratic. But third, and more important, happiness depends also on objective conditions having to do with circumstances, which may change because of events for which the individual may not be responsible, and there is nothing much that education can do about these.

It might be said that a man who is made redundant through no fault of his own, loses his wife, or has a heart attack should be able to cope better with such adversity if he is educated than if he is not. This may be so, but it is a speculative suggestion. For how a man copes with such adversity is a very individual matter depending as much on his temperament as on the quality of his awareness. Also, an educated person is likely to have higher expectations of life and of himself; so the discrepancy between his expectations and his changed circumstances is likely to be greater. And insofar as he does cope, the most he is likely to do is to minimize the misery rather than to restore his happiness. And this would be my general conclusion about the relationship of education to happiness. Education, by developing a person's awareness in various ways, may rid him of forms of ignorance, irrationality, and insensitivity that stand in the way of his being happy. But because of its highly idiosyncratic character and because of the large element of luck lurking in its objective conditions, education cannot predictably promote, let alone guarantee, happiness.

If we turn from such formal points about aims to questions of their substance, we have first, so I have argued, to make explicit the values of the society in which education is taking place, and then state specific aspects of these values that we think need emphasis. Alternatively we could disapprove of certain of these values and state as aims of education what we think needs emphasis as correctives to what is commonly accepted. In either case the articulation of such values must be a preliminary to the formulation of aims. Ideally, in order to avoid the charge of arbitrariness, justifications should be offered for the values as well. But in a paper of this length I fear that that will not be possible. So I must approach aims of education by briefly sketching the basic values distinctive to the type of democratic society in which we live.

DEMOCRATIC VALUES

Democracy is itself a contestable concept and I do not propose here to discuss possible interpretations of it—for example, Dewey's conception of a way of life that maximizes shared experiences and openness of communication between groups. Rather I shall adopt the interpretation of it, which seems to fit this country, that I previously elaborated in *Ethics and Education*.[6] In this central importance was given to a way of life in which matters of policy are resolved, wherever possible, by discussion, *parliament* deriving from the French word for discussion. To decide things by discussion requires truth-telling, respect for persons, and the impartial consideration of interests, as underlying moral principles. But it also requires the institutional underpinning of a system of representation, public accountability, and freedom of speech and assembly. If these are to be more than a formal facade that can be manipulated by interest groups, something approaching Dewey's passion for "shared experiences," together with concern for the common good, is also required to encourage widespread participation in public life. This suggests a revival of the almost forgotten ideal of fraternity to vitalize public projects as well as the ability to discuss and criticize public policy. Such criticism should be well informed and a rational attitude is required toward authority and its exercise.

Democracy, in brief, is a way of life in which high value is placed on the development of reason and principles such as freedom, truth-telling, impartiality, and respect for persons, which the use of reason in social life

6   R.S. Peters, *Ethics and Education* (London: Allen and Unwin, 1965), chap. 11.

presupposes. This development of reason would be unintelligible if value were not also accorded to the overarching ideal of truth.

In spite, however, of this firm commitment to specific values in a democracy, it will be noted that they are predominantly of a procedural sort. By that I mean that they make demands on how social, political, and personal life ought to be conducted. They do not provide a blueprint for an ideal society or indicate what sort of life is most worth living. Indeed there is a sense in which democracy manifests a certain skepticism about values in that no single conception of the good for man is acknowledged, and fallibility rather than certainty tends to be emphasized in the realm of truth. No Platonic seers are acknowledged as final authorities on such matters; they are left to public debate and individual decision. But this kind of pluralism in certain realms of value is possible only because other values such as toleration, respect for persons, and impartiality are accepted as constitutive of the form of life in which it can flourish.

If we look at the set of values linked together in this conception of the democratic way of life we can, for purposes of exposition, distinguish three groups. First there are those such as concern for others, impartiality, and respect for persons that underpin procedural consensus. Second there are values connected with truth, which provides point for discussion and the attempt to decide matters by reason. Third — and this is really a requirement of respect for persons — there are the values associated with the pursuit of personal good. The democrat may have definite views about what constitutes this good but respect for persons requires that he should not impose it on others, nor despise others if their choice of a way of life seems bizarre. Before articulating aims of education arising from these values, however, it will be necessary to flesh them out in a little more detail.

INTERPERSONAL MORALITY

Although a person who accepts the procedural principles of impartiality, concern for others, and respect for persons will refrain from imposing some conception of personal good on others, there are two spheres in which his principles do not require such a laissez-faire attitude. The first is that of the necessity for a basic body of lower-order rules — for example, of noninjury, keeping contracts, respect for property whether private or public — without which a democratic society could not continue. Such basic duties can be justified by reference to the procedural principles and must be insisted on as moral duties; for the police cannot be omnipresent to enforce them as laws.

Second, underlying the search for personal good and the restrictions placed on it by considerations of its effect on others, there is a minimum conception of welfare demarcating the common good. By that I mean that, whatever a person's conception of good, there are certain basic conditions of welfare, the absence of which will militate against his attaining it. These would include health, both physical and mental, housing, adequate income, heat and light, transport, and so forth. But over and above this comparatively noncontroversial level of minimum conditions of welfare, can anything further be said about the individual's good? For in dealing with others as well as in considering our own lives we operate with more positive conceptions.

PERSONAL GOOD

Happiness might be regarded by many as the obvious positive constituent of personal good. But it has already been ruled out as being suitable to generate aims of education, mainly because of its connections with circumstances over which neither the individual nor the educator has much control. The next obvious suggestion, therefore, would be to cut loose the connection with circumstances and settle for individual satisfaction and self-fulfillment. But straightaway there emerges Bentham's problem of comparing the joys of poetry with those of push-pin, which was personalized by J. S. Mill in his defense of the "quality" of pleasure of the perplexed Socrates against that of the satisfied fool. Mill, I think, was right in appealing implicitly to some standard other than a purely hedonistic one in his emphasis on quality. For it is difficult to construct a convincing defense for Socrates purely in hedonistic terms. From the point of view of enjoyment and the mitigation of boredom, a strong case can be made, as by Dewey, for a life permeated by an enlargement of the various forms of awareness, especially the capacity to solve problems and to pursue interests, such as science and art, that are open-ended in that they constantly open up new interests and problems. A life of change and challenge is advocated in which there is plenty of scope for the imagination, for the joys of mastery, and the use of intelligence in shared experiences. The trouble is, however, that this defense relies on the variables of duration and fecundity in seeking satisfaction. It might have no appeal to one who relied more on the variables of certainty, intensity, and propinquity. For him a life riddled with the certain if humdrum pleasures of following well-established routines with occasional plunges into more earthy and intense, if short-lived, types of satisfaction might seem more attractive. If the Dewey type of life, in which education is constitutive of personal good, were to be more decisively defended, its advocate would have, as Mill put it, to take his stand on higher ground. He would have, for instance, to appeal to additional values such as truth, or aesthetic values, or to the elimination of injustice, to which such a life might be devoted. But here again it would be difficult to decide which values, defining the higher ground, are to be deemed more important.

All such conceptions of the good life, however, might be criticized on the grounds that they are too individualistic, though this was not actually true of Dewey who stressed the value of "shared experiences." But even Dewey's ideal of "growth" through problem solving took too little account of the basic facts of our social existence. Most of the actions we perform, and activities in which we engage, arise from our "station and its duties." We are not free-floating atomic individuals restlessly searching for avenues of self-fulfillment. Rather there are well-trodden paths that we have to tread with others as teachers or bank clerks, fathers or mothers, secretaries or chairmen, landlords or tenants, customers or salesmen. Insofar as the individual is going to "fulfill himself," he must do so as a social being through the efficient, sincere, and at times critical attention to obvious duties that confront him every day, whatever he does about more individualistic forms of satisfaction.

Such criticisms, like those of liberty from the standpoint of fairness, reflect the constant tension within democracy between the individual and social points of view. But, whichever emphasis is favored, respect for persons surely demands that the individual should be encouraged to make something of himself, to find some role, occupation, or activity with which he can identify himself and achieve some kind of self-fulfillment. It also demands that, given the range of options open to him, his capacity for choice should be developed so that ideally he will achieve some degree of autonomy and commit himself authentically to tasks that he genuinely feels he ought to perform or to activities that he genuinely wants to pursue, as distinct from devoting himself to externally imposed duties and secondhand interests that are merely socially expected. The clash, too, between principles such as liberty and equality and the controversies about practices such as abortion and euthanasia above the level of basic moral rules will also require a similar move toward some degree of autonomy.

Authenticity and genuineness are only one facet of autonomy, which emphasize the self or *autos* aspect of it; there is also the more reflective aspect connected with the *nomos* that is to be adopted. This presupposes the weighing up of alternatives in the effort to determine what is true, right, appropriate. With the mention of truth we arrive at the third type of value of relevance to education in a democratic society.

TRUTH

The value of truth is emphasized in democracies that uphold the use of reason in social life and personal autonomy as an educational aim, though this should not be pursued completely at the expense of fraternity. Hence the salutariness of Dewey's stress on shared experiences. For truth is pursued mainly in discussion, individual reasoning being largely, as Plato put it, "the soul's dialogue with itself."

But in what way will the value of truth be relevant to education? Obviously it will not be just a matter of acquiring information, of attempting to memorize as many true propositions as possible; for the quickest way to do that would be to get hold of a telephone directory or an encyclopedia and learn its contents by heart. And this might have a minimal bearing on the human condition. Nor will it usually take the form of the dedicated search for explanations in a particular area, like the scientist, or the ruthless and relentless self-examination and questioning of everything of a Socrates, though democracies encourage such relentless probings and challenges to orthodoxies of every sort. These are ways of like to which some feel called as a continuation of their education. Universities cater to such unusual people, but for the average man in his education the value of truth does not require that he become a research worker or a Socrates.

Something much more mundane is demanded. Both in his work and in his leisure time the individual brings to his experience a stock of beliefs, attitudes, and expectations. Most of these rest on authority; he has picked them up from a variety of sources. Many of them are erroneous, prejudiced, and simpleminded, especially in the political realm, where evidence shows that opinions depend overwhelmingly on traditional and nonrational allegiances. One of the aims of education is to make them less so. The citizen has to be taught to look for evidence for his beliefs and to be critical of what he hears from others and acquires through the media. Of particular importance in education, as I have already suggested, will be those beliefs about the attitudes toward the human condition that will confront any man, whatever his occupation.

To expect any final truth about such matters is a chimera; but at least the individual can improve his understanding and purge his beliefs and attitudes by ridding them of error, superstition, and prejudice. Also, through the development of imagination and understanding, he can come to view the human condition in a very different light. New opportunities for action may open up as his view of people, society, and the natural world changes; his emotional reactions may be transformed as he gets a glimpse of the world as someone else sees it; gardening, which was a monotonous chore, may light up because of the new understanding he brings to the soil, plants, and shrubs; and he may be fired by the thought of participating in the change of institutions that he had previously regarded as fixed points in his social world. Thus a mixture of intellectual probity and imaginative curiosity can gradually transform a person's outlook on nature, other people, and social institutions. It should bring with it the intellectual virtues of consistency, hatred of irrelevance, clarity, precision, accuracy, and a determination to look at the facts.

AESTHETIC AND RELIGIOUS VALUES

There are other values, especially aesthetic and religious ones, that are central to man's attempts to make sense of and give sense to the human condition, and hence to education, but that are not particularly distinctive of the democratic way of life. By that I mean that though religions and various forms of art flourish and are encouraged in democracies whereas they may be persecuted and severely censored in totalitarian or collectivist societies, they are possible perspectives on life that a democrat may adopt, rather than values he must accept insofar as he is committed to the types of procedure constitutive of a democratic way of life. Because, however, education demands the development of various types of awareness, individuals in a democracy should be given some form of initiation into these perspectives on the human condition in the hope that many will develop insights and sensitivities that may become of increasing significance to them. For they are persons as well as democrats, and their lives will be impoverished if they have no sense of the beauty of the' world or of man's strivings to give concrete embodiment to intimations about the human condition that he cannot explicitly articulate. Similarly they will be scarcely human if they have not reflected on the place of man in the natural and historical orders. In many the contingency, creation, and continuance of the world, which are beyond the power of man to comprehend, give rise to awe and wonder. The human condition is viewed in a wider perspective, under "a certain aspect of eternity," and ways of life are generated that transcend and transform what is demanded by morality and truth. Others are content to operate within the limits of human understanding and are unmoved by reflection on the order of the world that makes such understanding possible. But both types of reaction are available only for those who have had their awareness extended in this dimension by education.

In a democracy this liberal view of the role of aesthetic and religious values in education is taken because of the importance ascribed to freedom and toleration and because of the reluctance to deprive the individual of possible ways of making something of himself provided by his cultural heritage. Having accepted the importance of aesthetic and religious values in education I will leave them on one side and refrain from exploring the specific aims they might generate. This is partly because of their complexity and the difficulty of being very determinate about them in a short space, but mainly because, as has been pointed out, they are not distinctive of the democratic way of life. To these central values and the aims of education generated by them I now return.

DEMOCRATIC VALUES AND AIMS OF EDUCATION

Ever since the First World War, and the rise of totalitarian and collectivist regimes subsequent to it, it has been characteristic of democratic theories of education to postulate the self-realization of the individual either as the aim or as the most important aim of education. Certainly this is an aim of education that needed emphasis, in spite of obscurities surrounding the type of self that was to be realized. But in view of the injustices and sense of rejection of the "unrealized" that have been among the unintended consequences of this emphasis, it is important to return to the form of life that makes this aim possible and to place it in the context of other aims generated by the values immanent in this form of life.

INTERPERSONAL MORALITY

Encouragement for the individual to make something of himself is feasible only in a society in which respect for persons and its offshoot, toleration, are widespread. These, together with impartiality and concern for others, are the fundamental principles of the democratic way of life, in which as much as possible is decided by discussion rather than by authoritative fiat. The first priority, therefore, in a democracy is to aim at the development in its citizens of what Lawrence Kohlberg[7] calls a "principled morality." But, educationally speaking, the road to this is a long one. The individual has to pass from an egocentric stance toward social rules to a conventional or "Good-boy" type of morality before he can emerge to a more autonomous type of morality in which fundamental principles are appealed to in dealing with dilemmas and discussing the morality of controversial practices such as abortion and the closed shop. Because, logically speaking, an individual cannot, by an appeal to principles, come to adopt a code of his own unless he has, at the conventional

7 L. Kohlberg, "From Is to Ought," in *Cognitive Development and Epistemology*, ed. T. Mischel (New York: Academic Press, 1971).

stage, internalized some system of rules to criticize or accept, and because achieving autonomy is very much a matter of degree, it is essential both from the individual's and from society's point of view that the individual is firmly bedded down in a basic code covering duties like those of noninjury, respect for property, whether public or private, promise-keeping, truth-telling, and so forth, at the conventional stage. For the enforcement of law cannot be omnipresent and, unless the observance of such basic duties is the general rule, no society, let alone a democratic one, could hold together for long. The problem is to teach this basic body of rules in a way that encourages the individual to move toward a more rational, principled type of morality.

This line of development from a conventional morality to a more rational one, in which some degree of autonomy is achieved, is the line of development sketched by Piaget and Kohlberg and adopted by many concerned with moral education. My viewpoint differs in two important respects.[8] First, compassion or concern for others should be given an importance equal to that accorded by Piaget and Kohlberg to the development of reason. Second, more emphasis should be placed on the crucial stage of conventional morality. Also, though Kohlberg, in places, makes mention of the importance of ego-strength, too little attention is paid to the virtues of the will such as perseverance, courage, and integrity, which are necessary for the translation of principles into practice.

KNOWLEDGE AND UNDERSTANDING OF THE HUMAN CONDITION

Whether an individual is concerned about the plight of others or occupied with fulfilling himself in his pursuit of personal good, he must have some knowledge and understanding of the various aspects of the human condition. This utilitarian case for knowledge and understanding is reinforced by the value of truth, which suggests a noninstrumental condemnation of ignorance, error, prejudice, and superstition. In what areas of life is such knowledge and understanding essential? Basically in those three spheres of being previously picked out as characterizing the human condition, namely the natural, interpersonal, and sociopolitical worlds that human beings inhabit.

It goes without saying that, in an industrial society, an individual is severely handicapped if he lacks the basic skills of literacy and numeracy. For these are necessary for being at all at home in all three types of world. Urbanization, however, has created a shield between modern man and

8 See R.S. Peters, "The Place of Kohlberg's Theory in Moral Education," *Journal of Moral Education* 7, no. 3 (May 1978).

many of the features of the natural world with which his less literate forefathers had to come to terms. But science and technology, which have been largely instrumental in creating this artificial environment, have brought in their train a host of new things to understand. So modern man, in confronting the natural world, has to understand something of gas, electricity, and pollution, as well as more enduring phenomena such as fire, snow, the seasons, and the properties of the soil. He must also develop a modicum of practical knowledge in dealing with them. For there are countless contingencies in an industrial society ranging from repairs to the water system to first aid to the injured, to deal with which expert help is not always readily available. Under our present system of schooling it tends to be only the nonacademic child who gets any systematic training in such practical skills. There has been too little thought about the role of practical knowledge in education that is not part of training for a particular job.

As a member of the natural world, too, the individual must have some understanding of how his body works, of procreation, aging, and disease. The intimate connection between body and mind is being spelled out in more and more detail by physiology and brain chemistry. Awareness is subtly affected by the circulation of the blood, by glandular secretions, and by the metabolic rate of the body. So not only is instruction in diet, hygiene, and the avoidance of disease essential; the body must also be cared for by physical exercise of various sorts. It is rather out of fashion in physical education circles to emphasize the importance of physical fitness and the general dexterity and control of the body developed by various exercises, swimming, and games. They tend to be defended because of their aesthetic features, as if footballers were like ballet dancers. Or their character-building aspects are cited. But their basic rationale in terms of care of the body is seldom stressed. Little is made, too, of the enjoyment many derive from them, which can provide a lifelong interest.

In the interpersonal world the individual has to learn to understand and adapt to others as they perform their various roles. But he also has to discern the individual at the center of these socially expected routines with all his inner motives, aspirations, and idiosyncratic perspectives on the world. Such understanding is not easy to achieve, yet there are psychiatrists who argue that many of the milder forms of mental illness can be traced back to systematic misperceptions and misunderstandings of ourselves and others, and of consequent failures to form satisfactory relationships. The positive value of understanding others in cooperative projects, community life, and forming friendships is obvious enough. Also, interpersonal morality presupposes an accurate assessment of motives and intentions if moral judgments are to be realistically based. This form of understanding is central to the education of the emotions, which is one of the most sadly neglected spheres of education.

In the sociopolitical sphere much is demanded of a citizen of a democratic state. He must have a general knowledge of how the political system works, and be sensitive to the social and economic conditions that it has to shape and by which it is shaped. He must be familiar enough with current affairs to criticize policies constructively and to make up his own mind which way to cast his vote. Ideally, too, he should possess the social skills necessary to participate in public affairs at least at the local level.

This, of course, is only a rough and sketchy indication of the types of knowledge and understanding that anyone in a democratic society should possess in order to participate in this form of life, and that is also required by the demands of truth that democracy endorses. But it can, of course, given curiosity, the development of imagination, and, perhaps, what Simone Weil calls "a love of the world" be extended infinitely by study of the natural sciences, geography, history, psychology, literature, and the social sciences. Experience of people, places, and institutions can gradually be transformed by the new conceptual frameworks in which they are located.

It might, however, be argued that this is little more than a refurbished version of Dewey's approach to education — that learning should be related to the solution of some current practical or social problem and that "subjects" should be taught only on this condition. This, in my view, is too narrow a way of formulating the relevance to the human condition that I take to be the hallmark of the type of learning that we call education. To start with I am suggesting that people should be introduced to knowledge about matters that will predictably be of some significance to them at some time in their lives as persons; I am not saying that they should be introduced to it only when confronted by a practical problem to which it is relevant. One of the hallmarks of a good teacher is to stimulate new interests, not just rely on existing ones.

Second, much of the knowledge of the human condition is not of immediate practical use; rather it transforms a person's conception of the general context in which life has to be lived. The Copernican theory, which shattered the belief that the earth was the center of the solar system, was of profound emotional significance to human beings; this was far more important than the marginal improvements it permitted in navigation. Similarly, the emotional significance of the theory of evolution was of far more significance to the average man than its practical outcomes, and Freud's claim that the thought and conduct of the grown man are influenced by unconscious infantile wishes is of more significance because of its transformation of man's conception of himself than because of its faltering and often fruitless practical outcomes in therapy. Much of education is concerned not with answering practical problems but with mapping the contours of the general conditions within which such problems arise.

Third, many problems are wrongly so-called; for a problem is something that, in principle, admits of a solution. Many situations with which the individual will have to deal cannot be so optimistically described. They are predicaments that he somehow has to learn to live with, such as the inevitability of death, the birth of a badly deformed child, a heart attack or unexpected redundancy in middle age. Understanding and the reorientation of attitudes can do something to help the individual to live with such predicaments, though, as was argued before in discussing happiness, it is optimistic to expect too much. But they cannot be "fixed up" by technology.

Finally, the case for knowledge and understanding does not rest purely on their relevance to practical and social problems and their emotional significance to anyone in trying to discern the contours of the human condition. There is also truth, which is conceptually connected with knowledge, and a value in its own right. By that I mean that, other things being equal, being deluded, in error, or prejudiced are just bad states of mind to be in. For belief is the state of mind appropriate to what is true, and though true beliefs usually help us to further our practical purposes, their value does not derive from this source alone. Truth just matters, irrespective of its payoff.

THE SELF-FULFILLMENT OF THE INDIVIDUAL

What is to be made of the traditional aim of democratic education — the growth, self-realization, or self-actualization of the individual? There is an initial obscurity about it, for some theorists have a definite view of the sort of self that ought to be realized, whereas others regard it as a very individual matter. Carl Rogers, for instance, finds that, given appropriate circumstances, individuals move toward genuineness, acceptance of self, openness to others, and self-direction. But the qualities characterizing Rogers's "self" are almost identical with those advocated as values immanent in his client-centred therapy; it seems improbable that they are the products of some spontaneous unfolding of dormant potentialities. Those, on the other hand, who stress individuality and the many avenues open to the individual in his search for self-fulfillment must rule out certain avenues that are manifestly immoral and stress the development of autonomy without which the individual cannot choose which avenues to explore. And these requirements presuppose a lengthy period of moral education dealt with in the first aim, and the development of a widely informed imagination dealt with in the second aim.

These brief reflections suggest that self-realization involves authentic commitment by the individual to modes of conduct, beliefs, attitudes, and activities made available to him by the types of learning falling under the first two aims of education. It is an offshoot of these two basic aims. It has, however, two dangers. The first is that it may encourage too self-conscious a search for avenues of fulfillment. Those who achieve some kind of self-fulfillment are usually absorbed in various activities and duties with which they identify themselves wholeheartedly without much thought of realizing themselves. Second, like the old quest for individual salvation, it may degenerate into a lonely quest at the expense of fraternity and a sense of community. Dewey, in his emphasis on shared experiences, was acutely aware of this too individualistic perversion of this democratic aim. So is Rogers with his stress on personal relationships as the essential context for the development of the self. Given these qualifications and caveats, a place must surely be made, grounded on respect for persons, for the self-fulfillment of the individual as an aim of education. Opportunities should be provided for all to participate in activities and pursuits and to undertake responsibilities with which they can identify themselves and attain some kind of mastery. These may be shared experiences such as science, social reform, or sports, or more individual activities such as cooking, gardening, or astronomy. If there is some kind of identification of the individual with the pursuit or duty, it will give the individual an introduction to nonalienated learning. It will do something to generate self-esteem, which is central both to character and to motivation, and will bring with it virtues of the will, especially attention, concentration, and perseverance, to which, in my opinion, too little attention is paid in our present educational system.

PREPARATION FOR WORK?

I have made the point that, in democracies, there is a constant tension between the pursuit of personal and public good and that this manifests itself in the types of emphasis that emerge as educational aims. One criticism that is current at the moment, of the emphasis on individual self-fulfillment, is that it has been to the detriment of the economy. Insufficient attention is being paid to preparing the citizen for an occupation. There is nothing specifically democratic about this aim, but as it is *also* argued for as an obvious avenue of self-fulfillment for the individual, and hence an offshoot of the aim, it is worth ending with a few brief comments about it. These comments may be superfluous in ten years' time; for if technological change continues in its present direction, the demand may well be that education should do more to prepare people for leisure. The present demand is often misleadingly expressed in terms of preparation for work; for leisure-time activities like making cupboards, playing the violin, and growing roses involve work just as much as do tool making, scientific research, bricklaying, and running a school. So if what is really meant is "work," this has already been covered by aims two and three.

Manifestly, however, people who stress the importance of preparation for work[9] are not talking about work but about jobs or occupations. And many jobs do not involve work but what Hannah Arendt called "labor."[10] This distinction is difficult to demarcate briefly, but roughly it is between activities in which the individual employs some kind of skill to create a relatively durable product that he can see to be the result of his own efforts, and those in which he employs little skill in contributing to some process whose end product he may never see or for which he feels little responsibility or in which what he helps to create is more or less immediately consumed or destroyed. The rewards of labor are extrinsic. The lavatory attendant goes through endless routines of changing towels and toilet rolls, and sweeping the floor, with thoughts in his head about the pay packet at the end of the week. Work, on the other hand, though it may have extrinsic payoffs, is done basically for the enjoyments intrinsic to it. Thus labor involves what Marx called "alienation"; the individual cannot identify himself with what he is doing. He is at home when he is not laboring, and when he is laboring he is not at home.

Preparation for jobs, therefore, raises complex questions. Insofar as a job involves some specific sort of work, there is no reason why the individual should not opt for preparation for it at school if it is likely to provide a concrete motivational focus for his education as well as to aid the economy. But this is to be encouraged only on two conditions. First, it should not just be narrow training. It should also serve as a way into the understanding of principles of more general application and as a focus for more general matters of human concern. Second, it should not take place too early because of the danger of prematurely determining an individual's life chances. It might be argued, too, that a greater use of released time would be a better way of catering to this demand than a

---

9 See, e.g., M. Warnock, *Schools of Thought* (London: Faber & Faber, 1977), chap. 4, pp. 143-51.

10 See H. Arendt, *The Human Condition* (Chicago: University of Chicago Press, 1958), chaps. 3 and 4.

widespread attempt to bring the factory and office into the school, especially as techniques in industry change so rapidly.

But what is to be said about preparing people for labor? For it surely is not the business of education to prepare pupils to tolerate boredom and frustration, even though this is what some schools unwittingly do by the alienation of pupils from the learning to which they are exposed. Yet there are countless jobs in an industrial society that fall into the category of labor, for which little in the way of special preparation is required. This widespread problem is surely one for politicians, unions, and employers to tackle — for example, by rearranging labor so that more of it approximates to work, by worker-participation schemes, and by more flexible hours that permit employees to plan their day so that more activities involving work can be fitted in off the job. Education can, of course, improve the quality of personal relationships of those who labor; it can encourage a spirit of service to the community, equip people for more constructive use of their leisure, and encourage a sense of outrage at depersonalizing conditions of employment. It can, too, discourage the tendency to identify a person with the job that perforce he or she may have to perform. But it cannot transform labor into work and can only gradually contribute to changing a society that tolerates such widespread alienation. Unfortunately the influence is too often the other way round. For in many schools mindless rote learning in order to pass examinations mirrors the alienated labor of the factory floor.

CONCLUSION

This brief catalog of aims may sound a bit mundane and unexciting. How much more inspiring it would be to proclaim with Dewey that "education is growth" or with Whitehead that it is "the art of the utilization of knowledge" or with Hegel that "education is the art of making man ethical." But all such concepts of education are contestable, for what has happened is that an aim of education has been taken as *the* aim and incorporated into the concept of "education." It is easy to see how this happens, for education is a teleological type of concept in that it indicates processes of learning directed toward some end. Particular ends that require emphasis can then be singled out to the exclusion of other possible ones and the result is a stipulative definition.

I have tried to avoid this by sketching what I take to be incontestable about education and then articulating some major aims that could give direction to it. In order to avoid the charge of arbitrariness, I have tried to show the values from which such aims can be derived. They are, of course, eminently contestable because, first, I have confined myself to democratic values; second, my concept of democracy is contestable; and third, I have dealt only briefly with aesthetic and religious values as not being particularly distinctive of democracy. Many might regard this brevity as banal. Finally, though probably all democrats would agree about the importance of morality, and truth, there could be disputes about my interpretation of these values and what aspects of them should be emphasized as aims of education.

Thus, though the aims I have suggested are contestable, they are not just my personal preference, for they have been presented as emphases within a public form of life. Indeed I have followed Plato's contention that there is a fit between a type of state and a type of man. My account, however, of both the democratic state and the democratic man differs radically from Plato's. There is, of course, a general similarity in that, on both accounts, the development of reason occupies a central place in education. But whereas for Plato this is represented as a process by means of which a few arrive at an authoritative vision of the Good, both an agreed end-point and the existence of such an élite are denied by the democrat. Instead stress is placed on the social principles presupposed by the use of reason in social and personal life and the intellectual virtues implicit in the elimination of prejudice, superstition, and error. Democracy is concerned more with principles for proceeding than with a determinate destination and aims of education in a democracy should emphasize the qualities of mind essential for such a shared journey.

A Personalistic Philosophy of Education

PETER A. BERTOCCI
Boston University

I. PERSONALISTIC IDEALISM

The personalistic philosophy of education I shall propose is allied with a system of idealism that was formulated in the United States by Borden Parker Bowne (1847-1910) and critically reformulated by his creative disciple Edgar S. Brightman (1884–1953), who was the first Borden Parker Bowne Professor of Philosophy at Boston University.[1] I use the word "allied" because a philosophy of education cannot be deduced from any metaphysics. At the same time, a philosophy of education, thoroughly developed, will itself move toward a comprehensive theory of man in relation to the Ultimate. As background for the present effort I shall swiftly summarize personalistic idealism.

1. Every form of idealistic metaphysics sees in mind the ultimate structure of all there is. According to monistic or absolutistic idealism

---

1. Among Bowne's pupils and especially distinguished disciples were, besides Brightman, Albert C. Knudson (1873-1953) and Ralph Tyler Flewelling (1871-1960). Knudson, longtime Dean of Boston University School of Theology, articulated a systematic Christian Theology. Flewelling focused on the meaning of the person, finite and infinite, for the grounding and development of human values and democratic ideals; he founded and edited *The Personalist*. Brightman found it necessary to substitute a more temporalistic view of the finite and divine person, and, in order to explain evil in the world not explicable by human freedom, postulated a finite-infinite God. The pupils of these scholars — and they peppered American institutions of higher education in teaching and administration — differed on this last theme in particular even as they continued to investigate issues in religious and philosophical psychology and to expound and strengthen the value-theory and system of moral principles uniquely presented by Brightman in his *Moral Laws*. Any brief list of these disciples would include Walter M. Muelder, L. Harold De Wolf, S. Paul Schilling, Paul E. Johnson, Warren Steinkraus, Robert N. Beck (founder and editor of *Idealistic Studies*), John Howie, Jack Padgett, John H. Lavely, Thomas Buford, Erazim Kohák and William Mountcastle, Jr. Martin Luther King, Jr., was strongly influenced by both Brightman and De Wolf. Bertocci followed Brightman as Borden Parker Bowne Professor of Philosophy until 1975; the Chair as of 1978 is honored by John Findlay. The Personalistic Discussion Group has, since 1938, assembled at the yearly meeting of the Eastern American Philosophy Association (another more recently at the Western Division).

Mind is One; it "includes" persons as modes, centers, or instantiations of It (Sankara, Ramanuja, Plotinus, Spinoza, Hegel, F. H. Bradley, J. Royce, Radhakrishnan, Aurobindo, Mahadevan, Tillich, J. Findlay). Bowne and Brightman, however, while conceiving Nature *as* cosmic Person, resisted (as W. James resisted Royce) any Absolute that in the end loses the moral autonomy especially of finite persons.

2. In essence, persons, however related to physical and biological realms, are creations *ex nihilo* (meaning not "from" nothing) by the uncreated Person who in all his activity respects their moral freedom.

3. Personalistic idealists, however, in contrast to theistic or naturalistic realists, hold that Nature cannot be understood as a Realm of nonmental beings and events independent of mind, finite and Infinite. It is omnipersonal but not nonpersonal. Its order expresses the *standard* dynamic of God's will as the dependable ground for common interaction.

4. Hence, personalistic idealism, theistic and teleological, upholds, in Kantian fashion, the creative response of personal minds in all knowing, willing, and valuing. The cosmic Presence, impersonal in Nature, allows, within limits, for human participation in every dimension of value experience.

5. Both Bowne and Brightman gladly accepted undogmatic conceptions of biological evolution, but both also resisted any simplistic tendencies to think of persons as higher animals. At the same time, while rejecting windowless monads and their preestablished harmony, they build on the Leibnizian emphasis on the telic unity of minds. However, they (Brightman more explicitly) found natural processes too regular to be explained by any hierarchy of essentially nonrational monads (even in the more intriguing view of recent process-philosophers in the Whitehead-Hartshorne school).

6. The personalistic *theistic* idealist, for whom omnipersonal natural processes are expressions of the Person's purposes, finds in this cosmic immanence the necessary but not sufficient ground for the knowledge and values that are minimal for developing His communitarian goal: persons responsive to each other and to their Creator.

7. However, in what follows, I shall set out a temporalistic doctrine of the finite person that does not assume the metaphysics of personalistic theistic idealism. I shall assume, however, that synoptic method and *experiential*, growing coherence constitute the best approach to the organizing of data relevant to man, his values, and his place in the order of things. On this view of coherence, logical consistency is never to be abrogated; it serves, rather, the function of reason (reasonableness) as the person weaves together his sensory and nonsensory data for both theoret-

ical and practical purposes. In this sense, a person's *Lebenschauung* is the basis for further reasoning about his *Weltanschauung*. I shall orient my exposition to the more limited purposes of this article.

II. THE PERSON AS SELF-IDENTIFYING
UNITY OF CONSCIOUSNESS

1.   No reader of Brightman can miss his stress on the person as a conscious, complex unity of experience, capable of self-consciousness and therefore of reason and of ideals. For him there is no denying the "saddleback" specious present each of us finds himself, minimally, to be. Influenced by Bergson more than Whitehead, Brightman revised the Cartesian conception of the soul as nontemporal substance. The undeniable datum as *erlebt* is a telic *now,* a *durée.* This intrinsically unified datum-person, crescent in his own interaction with his ambient, does, from moment to moment, selectively carry its past with him.

More concretely, existing always in a crescent present, I am the activities (with their potential) that constitute me *this* person. Were it not that I can remember, reason, and anticipate on the basis of what I undergo now, I would have no experiential grounds for my linking this saddleback with *my* ambients. Within this endured *now* I find myself referring cognitively to what is other than now-experience and gradually sifting out what is mine and not mine with reasonable probability. A whole theory of knowledge must be skipped here, but in the end a personalist opts for establishing reasonably inferred correlations between his conscious–self-conscious experience and his body, his unconscious, and any environment with which he interacts.

2.   More important here is the conception of personal identity. Following Brightman's lead, I propose that the person is a self-identifying unity whose nature it is to act and be acted upon.[2] The attempt to find unity-in-continuity in personal experience by affirming an *identical* soul-substance, immanent in its activities but not affected by them, involves insuperable difficulty. On the other hand, if indeed the inescapable datum is a self-identifying person, capable of selectively maintaining itself in and through *its* interacting transactions, we can better capture what we actually experience ourselves to be, namely, the quality of existent that, in being himself, becomes. Hence, whatever else, to be a person is to be a self-identifying unity-in-continuity of being-becoming.

Warning: Persons in being aware of themselves come to realize that they do not discover themselves in the same way entirely that they know

2   See Peter A. Bertocci, "The Essence of a Person," *Monist,* January 1978, pp. 28–44.

any other being. Yet they can know nothing else, and could not more fully know themselves, unless they are self-identifying, being-becoming unities-in-continuity. What is the essential scope of the conscious–self-conscious person?

III. BASIC DIMENSIONS OF A PERSON'S ACTIVITIES

Significant differences in the philosophy of education stem from a philosopher's conception of the constitutive dimensional activities of the person. I shall here list those I cannot do without, and focus further attention on several that are critical for a philosophy of education.

1. The unity-in-continuity that defines a person's scope consists in distinguishable (not separate) activities: sensing, remembering, imagining, thinking, feeling, wanting, emoting, willing, oughting, and aesthetic and religious appreciating. The first four enter not only into our knowing *what* is referred to in the variety of sensing experiences, but they also enter into knowing (but not *always* as the *sine qua non*) the nature and contribution of the other activities. Remembering, imagining, thinking, are indispensable to all person-al cognizing and evaluating. The critical, controversial thesis here is that the person is *essentially* these activities with their potential — hence are activity-potentials with their characteristic objects and objectives. However, while maturing, these experiencings of the person are not produced by environment, but are modified within limits by their interaction with their ambients.

2. By now it will be clear that I am not assuming psychological doctrines of the human being that either ignore a person's consciously experienced activities or treat them as phenomenal by-products of unconscious, bodily, and behavioral processes. The person is not a complicated product of biological evolution alone, nor is he a product of *any* "natural" environment alone. However, as he reasoningly inspects his experiencing, he cannot understand its content or its course without inferring relationships between himself and other factors — many obdurate and beyond his control. In brief, the *essential* person is missed if we assume that his activity-potentials are to be understood solely in terms of his organic life, or solely by analogy with the activities of his subhuman neighbors, or of the Divine.

3. Not for a moment would I minimize the importance of social, natural, and divine environment in the growth and pattern of the person's *personality*. But I contend that we have come to neglect the person's activities insofar as we assume that they are derivations of learning in environment rather than constitutive factors in learning that open horizons of fact and value otherwise minimized (if not omitted). A person is a

knowing-wanting-evaluating agent, "a fighter for ends" (W. James). As he expresses and adapts his activity-potentials in environmental situations, he develops a more or less organized personality as *his* acquired mode of response to factors in environments. In the following section I shall expand briefly on four activities within the Gestalt of personal being-becoming that make a difference not only to theory of learning but to the conception of the life good to live and to the aims of education and the organization of personality.

IV. THE WANTING, WILLING, OUGHTING PERSON

1. To begin with, the time is overdue to stop using "feeling" and "emotion" as relatively loose omnibus terms. For example, instead of resorting to "feeling" when we know not how else to stipulate what is going on in us, I would confine this term (and "affective") to hedonic (pleasant) and unhedonic (unpleasant) tones, that is, qualitative factors ingredient to our experiencings. While I would agree that we are the kinds of persons who prefer hedonic rather than unhedonic experiential qualities, this is far from affirming that "life is essentially feeling" (or "emotional"). I am not unmindful that while experiential activities usually have *their* own hedonic or unhedonic tone, they become unhedonic (or vice-versa) in different contexts.

But to propose that persons are so constructed that they are pleasure-seeking beings (or ought to be) betrays faulty insight. Both psychological and ethical hedonism overlook the fact that there is no "feeling" of pleasantness (or pleasure) as such. There are only hedonic qualities that "attend" experienced objects and objectives. The hedonic quality arising in the context of eating-a-pear certainly is not the hedonic tone of eating-an-apple. No way do we live "for pleasure" *as such*, or for a maximum of pleasantness over unpleasantness in any way that will guide us significantly. For there is not "pleasure" apart from what "yields" pleasure, that is, *this* or *that* qualitative hedonic tone. The hedonic tone of dancing is not the hedonic tone of friendly encouragement, and the same goes with all the hedonic qualities arising in the contexts of varied experiencings. As persons we are faced with the contexts within which the hedonic factors themselves need further evaluating in their contexts.

2. In a day when we are so often told that we must "take full account" of the emotional bedrock of our lives, or that man, after all, is an "emotional being," it is amazing what is taken for granted. For example, do we need to generalize from the qualities of some emotions in a way that is blind to the many facets of emotional quality in our experiencing? I leave it to my reader to call up simplistic and conflicting characteristics about

emotions — such as "disturbing," "confusing," along with "purging," "serene" and so on — and to ask whether these begin to do justice to the varied range of emotions and their even wider fusions or blends.

3.   I would propose more specifically what I can only hint at here. Let us stop thinking of emotions as distinct from "basic motives" (urges, needs, wants), for in fact we do refer to emotions as motives "whose power is . . ."! I wish to challenge both the view that "basic" emotions are not themselves our primary motives, and also the view that only those motives and emotions are unlearned whose physiological correlates can be designated.

Should there be a scintilla of wisdom in such proposals, the positive attention demanded by the wider range of distinct primary emotions would make itself felt immediately in our theory of learning and our theory of value. For example, if in addition to the affective-emotive dynamics in hunger, thirst, and "survival," if in addition to the universal or unlearned emotions like anger, fear, and lust, we could take seriously also the (carefully defined) emotional predispositions like tenderness, sympathy, respect (not fear), zest (as in competence-mastery), wonder (as in curiosity), and enlivenment (as in creativity), we would have more and more varied emotive roots for which we would seek appropriate nurture. In his affective-conative dimensions the person would then bring to interaction with his ambients these ranging emotive predispositions that indeed help to define the actual meaning of "urge-to-live" for persons as they experience themselves.

4.   After all, what we mean by "will-to-live," by "survival-value," will continue to remain an empty vacuum unless we designate the scope of affective-conative predispositions that inform the essence of the "fighter for ends." In any case, for the personalist, education always involves fulfilling as far as possible, in interaction with varying ambients, the relatively flexible affective-emotive predispositions that are the selective, the relatively raw, telic material of personal being-becoming.

I must add immediately that while the recognition of the primary emotive spread of a person's life does not by itself settle such ethical questions as egoism-altruism (since one can be very selfish in expressing any predisposition), it does sensitize us to broader demands involved when we speak of the growth in goodness of plastic, telic givens. For now the ethical and unethical parameters of personal existence involve the person as reasoning at least about the relatively raw materials of his sensory-affective-emotive dimensions — as he matures and learns in ambients to which these factors orient him selectively.

5. But if we are to root value-theory in what a person's constitutive activities are, we cannot but intimate at least two other ingredients in the matrix of personal being-becoming that make considerable difference to our conception of the person's moral agency: the person's *willing* and *oughting*.

a. About a person's willing I limit myself to three statements here. First, I believe in (limited) free will for the same initial reason that I believe in "blue" and "anger" — that is, I experience *will-agency* in the matrix of many situations. But, second, in the end I would be inclined to accept the arguments of determinists for not trusting this experience if they could show why any of their claims to the truth or falsity of judgments ought to be trusted. If there is no freedom to judge, if determinism is true, then all our judgments are the *outcome* of causes in our history, and not *conclusions* based on evidence. A judgment claimed to be true is worthy of my consideration because I assume that the proponent, as he reached his conclusion, was free enough to relate the evidence to the hypothesis and free to exclude irrelevant factors and other favored conclusions.

b. Since de-liberation is essential to the reasonably evaluative existence of the person, I all but affirm: *Volo, ergo sum,* in order to emphasize that a person is a moral agent (not a matrix solely of nonmoral processes), capable of thinking and conducting himself in accordance with ideals of truth and value.

c. Third, experience has taught me that my irreducible will-agency is often confronted by obstacles that will not give way before it. Hence, without denying my will-agency, I am led to distinguish it from my *will-power* as it actually is exhibited in choice-situations.

In sum: If I were not capable of will-agency I could not declare myself capable of initiating reason or of continuing to an unwanted yet reasonable conclusion, given the data. So also, my evaluating would be completely untrustworthy; action (rather than reaction) would be impossible. I am an agent-person whose choices neither are made in a psycho-physiological-physical vacuum, nor are the outcome of these processes.

6. I have introduced "oughting" among the activity-potentials of the person. I am pointing to an *erlebt* experience that we have lost from sight for understandable reasons. In theorizing about *what* one *ought* to choose and will, a long tradition has seen the "moral imperative" (or the moral consciousness) as a kind of knowing (i.e., I ought to choose *x*-value, say, justice, or mercy). Other thinkers, convinced that "ought" does not express any kinship with nonnatural or nonhuman values, have conceived

of values (*what ought* to be chosen) as man-made, and then have gone further and reduced the experience of "ought" to a derivative of individual-cultural wanting. The experience I am referring to by "oughting" does not depend on any particular view of values and of knowing them. Neither is it any more reducible to affective-conative experiencing than thinking is. This unique experiencing should no longer elude us.

a.   Is it not peculiar that, for example, two persons, one believing that he ought to choose *x*, the other that he ought to do *y*, in so doing still recognize an activity within themselves that is not experienced *as such* as wanting (or any inclination or disinclination)? Each does not experience (moral) obligation to *what* the other holds to be imperative, but he still experiences the imperative: I ought! But supposing that he changes his mind about *what* he ought to choose. Does his experience of "oughting" change? No, only the "value-goal," *what* he ought, changes.

Moreover, if a person acknowledges that *x* is his best option, and yet does not do what he can to reach it, I suggest that he experiences some "degree" of *moral guilt* (not anxiety). At the same time, if he does what he can but fails, he will be disappointed, he may experience social disapproval and anxiety, but he still experiences *moral approval.*

b.   To identify anxiety with *moral guilt* (not legal guilt), to identify social approval with *moral approval*, is a costly error in the dynamics of personality change. For it encourages undue or misplaced responsibility *and* faulty treatment because of the wrong assumption that that anxiety and guilt can be treated in much the same way.

I am suggesting, then, that any person mature enough to conceive alternatives, who decides that *x*-value is better than *y*-value, *never* experiences "I ought to choose *y*" (even thought it may turn out that he does choose *y*). This peculiar *erlebt* imperative, verbally expressible as "I ought to choose the best I know," I refer to as another constitutive activity-potential: oughting (and *moral approval* and *moral guilt* are inevitable consequences expressive of his evaluation of his moral choice). A person can feel both guilt and anxiety about the course of a self-imposed choice; but he experiences moral approval or guilt (whether or not he experiences anxiety) only if he does not do what he acknowledges to be best.

c.   Part of the noble sadness of life stems from the fact that persons who "ought" different values ("bests" as they believe) often suffer because, be they conscientious objectors or conscientious believers, there are "turning points" at which they "can do no other" as they march to their "inner drummer."

V. THE PERSON AS AN END IN HIMSELF

This very sketchy topography of the person is incomplete, for I have no
more than mentioned aesthetic and religious appreciating, each of which
needs to be seen for itself and in relation to other dimensions of the person. In articulating the conception of the good, I shall not forget them.
But the groundwork for a personalistic theory of the life good to live and
of education is now laid. Along with acknowledgements already made, I
must accept responsibility for modifications of Platonic, Aristotelian,
Kantian, and Christian insights as well as modifications of some tendencies in recent psychology of personality.

1. The Kantian doctrine of treating any person as an end in himself,
and never a means *only*, cannot hold for any conception of human nature. If a person is a mechanical computer, with so-called options prescribed, with no activity of thinking or of agency related to any self-imposed goal, there would be no meaning to "end in himself." I am not for a
moment denying that often the regnant factors at choice-point override
reason and will and acknowledged obligations. The upshot of contentions
already advanced is that were persons not capable of thinking and willing
in relation to the alternatives consonant with their affective-emotive tendencies, they would have no reason for treating themselves as ends; they
could reasonably be treated as things. Only that person can be an *end in*
himself who can be an end *for* himself. This is the baseline of a personalistic theory of the good and therefore of education. It is *not* enough,
even though I, for one, would take it quite seriously in deciding choices
related to ethical respect for persons in "premature" or "postmature"
stages (such as the embryonic, infantile, senile), or so "deficient" that
choices are not open to them.

The human situation does indeed require that we use each other as
means. Yet for me to use any other reason-capable being (I focus on persons here) *as means only* is to overlook the fact that he as a person
deserves the same consideration as I, unless I can show why not. Consequently, the next "bottom line" for persons, as they choose, is that
might, as such, never can settle the problems of choice. Reason-able persons cannot *accept the authority* of power even when they fall before the
blasts of Nature or the cruelty of the authoritarian. The doctrine of respect for persons is rooted, then, in what persons are — at least thinking-
oughting-willing unities. But I still submit that all this is not enough,
however important.

2. A personalist (like many others) remains at a standstill if all he can

say is: Respect persons! For this basic imperative remains empty until he decides what values and ideals are the best for persons. For example, to urge, as is so often done, that persons ought to love their neighbors, or be democratic, or be mature is to remain harmfully ineffectual, until we articulate *an ideal of personality* that ought to be realized as far as possible (meliorism) in the context of the raw materials of personal existence. The personalist looks for authority (for what so many call "being authentic") at least in the dynamics of the person's basic motivational needs and abilities, as they reason together, in their present and foreseeable environments. Let it be clear: To reason about life is not to take the stuffing out of life, but to see what happens when we examine the dynamics of connections within persons in relation to their relevant environment(s). The personalist's next question must be: How shall we reason about the actual good open to persons, by which all educational choices, formal and material, ought to be guided?

3.   *No one experience, no one (emotive) desire or need, no one ability or capacity, is to be given privileged status, or dictate to any other, without further criticism, or without coming before the bench of the rest of our experiences. No experience is guilty unless proven so; but neither is it necessarily innocent.* Experiences live with each other in environments far from neutral to what persons do. "Come, let us reason together," is the source of cognitive authority. But that authority is itself derived ultimately from the fact that, in relating what we are as persons to ourselves and to each other, we can protect ourselves against bias and myopia, as much as possible, by giving no experience and no person *arbitrary* authority.

4.   Thus, inescapable as a person's feelings, needs, wants, or emotions (I shall hereafter use the word "conative" for these) are in his initial and continuing "well-being," all the more ought a person, as soon as possible, to realize that he cannot "find himself" by looking only to them for guidance. If he is to know himself, he must know what he can do about his conative demands within the context of his capacities and skills, in relation to his social and nonsocial environments. Granted, the debilitating fault in so many lives is unnecessary suppression (and, worse, repression, rooted in misconception of what is required). Nevertheless, it is more reasonable to guide not only by: "What do I feel like doing, or am interested in, or want?" but also by: "What can I do?" To be sure, often one has nowhere to turn other than to regnant "interest (s)," or to the most demanding external pressures. But the thesis here is that the "reality principle," indeed, the *"art of the possible, given one's own growth-point,"* yields more insight for planning and action.

Again, despite sometimes raucous disclaimers, most persons, be they more "privileged" or more "underprivileged," are not destroyed by their conflict with "Society"; the fact is that they want more than they themselves are willing to strive for; their anxiety and frustration is the greater because they will not cut the cloth of their lives to fit both their feelings and their wants *and* also their abilities and the trends of their achievements. For example, no amount of "understanding my feelings and emotions" will fill the vacuum left by my inability, and often my unwillingness, to develop the skills within my power.

5.   Finally, then, the personalist, without disregarding the impact of blind chance and undeserved misfortune, still looks for the source of "moral authority" as self-imposed by the person reasoning about the dynamics of his own life in relation to the dynamics of the reasoning of other persons. "Reason" is the person trying to see what the connections may be in the growth of his own potential and that of others at his stage of development in this kind of world. This answer is far from complete; it is more acceptable if our reasoning can now discover an interdependent pattern of values that are minimal requirements of the good for persons.

VI. VALUES AS THE EXPERIENCES OF PERSONS

1.   My central theme, then, will be that as persons reason about the relations among values, they discover a mutually supportive patterning that discourages fruitless conflict.

No one can live simply by the maxim: I want what I want when I want it. And no one can live without being in conflict, without any frustration, anxiety, or suffering; psychic regnancies appear and are challenged from within and without. For a person to discover and develop his own potential means prolonging the hallway of desires and "sacrificing" some values for the promise of others. Hence, the question a person faces is not: Will I be in conflict? but: What conflict will be worthwhile? or What conflict will yield optimum value? But does the human venture justify such assertions?

2.   A value is always a wanted (desired) experience of a person. That is, value occurs when a person *experiences anything he wants* ("disvalue" as any experience is not desired). It is the experiencing of eating a pear, the experiencing of hearing Bach, the experiencing of friendliness, that is the value (or disvalue). Each value, each disvalue, in its context will have hedonic or unhedonic tone unique to it. "Value" and "disvalue," in other words, refer to some personal undergoing, to some *Erlebnis*. No persons, no values or disvalues.

3.   The experiencing of value, however, is not the evaluation of the

experiencing. When we *evaluate* we are inspecting immediate value-experiences as *erlebt* and going on to examine and trace their relations to others, including the evaluations of other persons *in a similar situation*. In other words, in human experience we never start in a value vacuum, from zero value-experience, as it were. Nor do we begin *evaluating* by some point of reference exclusive of the value-experiences themselves. Evaluating finds us already conatively predisposed toward some values and value-patterns.

This contention, debatable to be sure, is basic. Before we start evaluating preanalytic value-experience, our psychophysiological conative tendencies have already been in the business of reaching for, preserving and avoiding, some experiences and not others.[3] Accordingly, we do not, when we *evaluate*, *create* the value-experiencings; we ask questions about them from within our experience simply because we find that the value-experiencings have different qualities, that they conflict or converge with each other, and are otherwise related to each other. Consequently, in evaluating, we have no recourse to other than the nature of the interrelations that take us beyond *erlebt* contexts. For example, a person may enjoy the taste-quality of a certain brand of cigarette and the sociality of smoking with other persons. Let us assume, on the one hand, that he now comes to enjoy the quality "brand-*y*-cigarette" without decreasing wanted sociability, although he still prefers brand-*x*. On the other hand, he finds that he does not approve the image of himself as a chain-smoker, and he gains no comfort from statistics about the relation of cigarette smoking to serious diseases. If another cigarette is marketed that does not taste so good but does not endanger health, he may switch to this brand. His analysis, note, is of actual experiences and of foreseeable, *given* consequences for disvalue or value-experiences.

To generalize: Any value-pattern we discover will be a description about persons in their world, or of the world *with persons left in it*. The ideal of the life good to live will be a consequence of man's relating himself in thought and action to his own activity-potentials and to his environment, as conceived and as it really is. Values and value-patterns are neither *relativistic* nor *objectively independent* of persons. To hold that values and disvalues are *related to* the person's conative-cognitive-volitional nature is to maintain that the person's value-patterns are not the

3   This view of value is very ably set forth in Ralph Barton Perry's *Realm of Values: A Critique of Human Civilization* (Cambridge: Harvard University Press, 1954); Edgar S. Brightman, *Moral Laws* (reprinted by New York: Kraus Reprints, 1968); F.R. Tennant, *Philosophical Theology* (Cambridge: Cambridge University Press, 1928); and Brand Blanshard, *Reason and Goodness* (London: Allen and Unwin, 1961).

product of his whims or desires, but joint products of his nature in interaction with the total environment.

Accordingly, the underlying, recurrent experience upon which this theory of the good builds is that any prima facie value-experiences require *evaluation* by comparison and contrast with other experienced values and disvalues, and by ascertaining whether they are supported by, enhance, or endanger other values. The minimal pattern of *cardinal* values to be proposed takes root in our hedonic-conative-interests, but evaluation takes us beyond these alone to a framework that sustains these (and other) values in the life good to live.

VII. EXISTENCE, HEALTH, AND TRUTH-VALUES

1.   Persons prefer life to death. There would be no problem about the ethics of suicide and other acts of killing were this not so. Yet being alive and staying alive are only the necessary but not sufficient conditions for all other values. Since in being alive a person is already undergoing value-and-disvalue experiences, his question remains: What values are mutually enhancing and sustaining? Even for Hamlet, "to be or not to be" was uttered in the context of his own disappointment with deceit and infidelity and what he should do about heinous injustice. "Survival" for persons who remember, think, and think about the meaning of "living well," the (Socratic) unexamined life, is no addendum to "living."

2.   Consequently, the moment a person *decides* to live, he needs to know what physiological *health*, more than sheer survival, entails. Let him decide to pursue health in preference to illness, or vice versa, and he discovers that both physiological survival and health-values depend on still other values. Health-values not only enhance the likelihood of survival but they lend quality and vigor to day-to-day existence. Note: We do not make up these connections between values and disvalues. Moreover, the undernourished and ill-nourished the world over and of every age are constant reminders of brute physiological givens; yet they also testify to the fact that persons do not live by bread alone. How many healthy retired persons know what it means to "enjoy" bodily health — and all but meaningless existence! Even a little observation and reflection cannot miss the many quiet, "genteel" abortions of *quality in life* that take place when healthy persons of every class endure lives that are empty of so many of the values that could give substance, purpose, and dignity to their survival.

In any case, we are pushed beyond existence-values to health-values and beyond these to still others because even the definition of them, let along the pursuit, reveals that they depend upon other values. And cru-

cial to these are the values of truth (that guide the pursuit even of disvalues), since a person needs to know in what they consist and how they
are related to other values and disvalues.

3.   At long last, truth-values include all the values and disvalues involved in examining and discovering what the nature of the human good
is in relation to the total environment. To know the good does not of itself
assure its realization, but there can be no awareness of the horizon of
values, including the more specifically moral values (our moral dispositions or virtues) without truth seeking. (Here I distinguish [see character-
values, below] within the realm of values *moral dispositions* [virtues and
vices] that depend more on our willing than on our environments.)

There is no escaping the interpenetration of values with each other,
nor of moral dispositions with each other. Thus, *honesty*, the willingness
to convey the truth, and *courage*, the willingness to risk both discovering
and living by whatever truth we have, need each other. And *tolerance*,
the willingness to endure the explorations and affirmations of those who
disagree with one's own convictions, joins these and other values in
creating the atmosphere in which truth-values may increase.

4.   In schooling, particularly, we cannot forget that truth, and the
ability to test truth-claims appropriately, are never simply instruments to
other values. Socrates, himself dying for the value of free investigation,
aware of its unique instrumental value, would, I am sure, defend the actual experience of knowing because examining *as* experienced is
preferable to physical health *as* such. None of us would prefer a healthy
idiot, a moron, or an uninformed and dull person to a curious, problem-
posing, problem-solving, reflective person. Our persistent problem is to
keep truth finding and truth telling linked with the courage to make both
the necessary (not sufficient) conditions in the lives of all.

To summarize: We have already discovered that while value-experiences (such as existence, health, and truth-values) are different from each
other qualitatively, these cardinal values do not exist in separate compartments; they are mutually related or interpenetrating (or com-
penetrating, to borrow Phenix's word)[4] phases in the experience of persons. Because as persons we have no unerring, unlearned conative or cognitive capacities, we cannot survive, let alone with quality, *unless we are
free to observe the qualities of the experiences themselves, and the causal
web within which they exist.* Value-experiences in persons are not "unstructured ecstasies"; our lives, at any level, cannot be a chaos of leaves

4   Philip H. Phenix, *Realms of Meaning: A Philosophy of the Curriculum for General Education* (New York: McGraw-Hill, 1964).

that the winds of impulse and desire drive hither and thither. To live at all is to live "in connections" we can't escape; our problem — the fundamental one in education — is to discover the framework, so to speak, of connections among our value — and disvalue — experiences.

VIII. TRUTH-VALUES AND CHARACTER-VALUES

I have already suggested that once we are aware that truth and health are interrelated with other values, that same realization carries us to still other values, not the least *moral* values, if they and our potential are to be actualized. Because we do not find truth under a stone, or in a book, we realize that even information, let alone broad wisdom, comes only to persons who are willing to sort out their values and discipline themselves by the knowledge they gain. I have already hinted that knowledge, as value or disvalue, cannot exist without virtues, such as courage and honesty. But even these can lead to fanaticism if the conscientious person does not examine the links of "his cause" to other values and virtues and discipline himself thereby. I do not break with the great tradition by now bringing into focus that neglected, if not maligned, concept of *character*.

1.   A person's willingness to discipline himself by his ideals is his *character*. Of course one does not set out to will his "character" into being; this is the class name for the forms of self-discipline (psychologically speaking, willed traits or dispositions) that we call virtues and vices. In a more adequate discussion I would defend "a moral backbone," as it were, of *cardinal* virtues, inclusive at least of such traits as honesty, courage, kindness, gratitude, meekness, humility, fairness (justness), tolerance, and forgiveness.[5]

2.   I am bringing *character* back into the center of the life good to live because we have as teachers been so fearful of "moralism" and the flexing of moral muscles by the individual — although I wonder what else we really had in mind when we spoke of autonomy and "it's up to you, now." In our cool moments we know that there are boulders and potholes on the road to wholesome truth. It is not only "gratification now" that keeps us from the rationalizing that our schooling itself can make us adept at. With all our justified attempts to improve the atmosphere in home and school and community, we know in our hearts that environment and social services alone will not solve the problems. We can provide and should make available medical aid; we can see to it that food and housing are adequate; but a person must himself sit in the dentist's chair, face possi-

5   See Peter A. Bertocci and R.M. Millard, *Personality and the Good* (New York: David McKay, 1963), chaps. 16, 17.

ble "bad news" from the doctor. Again, knowledge is not virtue, but virtue involves knowledge of values if it is to be fruitful.

It might seem that I am about to crusade against "permissiveness" in favor of "conformism." Rather am I concerned to plead that the kind of contribution that "each" value and virtue can make in an individual's life be scrutinized in terms both of its prima facie quality and in terms of the best possible actualization in relation to the optimum values reasonably open to individuals-in-community. Have we failed to emphasize the courage involved in being honest with ourselves as persons and with the community's claims because we failed even in theory to recognize the moral-volitional matrix of personal being-becoming? Denying or ignoring will-agency-in-context, have we stressed "authenticity" without realizing the risk involved both within our own lives and in relation to others who also risk in their search for "identity"?

3. In short, there is no substitute in personal-social affairs for purposeful *com-promise*. But this brings into full play the values of *affiliation*. The person who will not discipline himself for the sake of a mutual trust will not begin to enter into the realms of value that purposeful, appreciative living with other persons brings into existence both instrumentally and intrinsically.

I have been stressing the need for conscious awareness of the values and virtues of truth-honesty-courage and of their minimal imbrication with health and affiliative values. In schooling we need more imaginative ways of articulating their interpenetrating centrality for persons *as agents*. My words may seem to fit adult ventures in truth seeking, but the situations I have in mind involve youngsters who, in exploring their competence, lay bare a universal human predicament. At every level of "maturity," persons who want knowledge and truth may jealously throw roadblocks in the way of other truth seekers. Students, teachers, and social groups can belittle the effort of others; they can pile scorn, persecute each other in subtle and crude ways in and outside of "school."

Honesty with ourselves demands that we consciously realize, as investigators and critics, how much the freedom of any one explorer, scholar, inventor, depends on the understanding tolerance of others, and not the least on the forbearance of equally learned scholars. Yet he who pursues the truth must be willing to be censured and to be criticized; still a society will stagnate if it represses responsible criticism of its present values, laws, and codes. Even society can never affirm that might as such makes right; civility depends on the responsive-responsible members of a community determined to protect investigators' claims to truth until they are tried in the court of reasonableness.

4.   Character, accordingly, is a simple word for a person's complex, learned, moral dispositions to face value conflicts that inevitably or purposely arise in and around his efforts to discover and increase values in his own life and that of others. In this context I heartily endorse Kant's conviction: "Nothing in the world — indeed nothing even beyond the world — can possibly be conceived which could be called good without qualification except a good will!" For Kant saw that the good will is "the indispensable condition of even worthiness to be happy," as well as the condition for the development of other values. And with unerring insight he also saw that the experience of good will, "the summoning of all the means in our power" to do what seems best, "would sparkle like a jewel with its own light as something that has its full worth in itself."[6] But respect for persons as ends, respect for character as the pearl of great price, is not enough. The relative autonomy of will-agency, the consistent respect for persons as ends in themselves, ought to discover the best of which persons are capable.

IX . TRUTH, CHARACTER, AND AFFILIATIVE VALUES

Consider the quality of personality we would have before us if the person is strong in the values of health, truth, and character, but is weak in the value of *affiliation*. Normatively, *affiliation*, with conative roots especially in tenderness, sympathy, and respect, is expressed in active appreciation of, and constructive response to, other persons and their values. The person who cannot care about anyone else, who treats other persons like commodities, as means to his own ends only, may have physical health; he may be strong willed, and he may make it his business not to hurt anybody unnecessarily, but he can hardly claim honesty about the range of values in others that need his support. The psychologist of personality, Gordon W. Allport, has emphasized that the normal development of a mature personality involves the movement from dependence to independence to dependability. This is a fact of experience that is no casual happening: Persons do find most of their values not only rooted in, but rendered more worthwhile by, their associations with others, ranging from the consciousness of caring and being cared for in "the little things" to joy and suffering. Words will not capture what I refer to as unique, irreducible qualities of "belonging in mutual care." The quality of conversation, the development of science, art, industry, the family, church, state — these all depend in large degree on the values that render "affiliation"

6   "Foundations of the Metaphysics of Morals," First Section, ed. and trans. Lewis W. Beck, *Immanuel Kant: Critique of Practical Reason and Other Writings in Moral Philosophy* (Chicago: University of Chicago Press, 1949), pp. 55, 56.

concrete. Indeed, so many of the values of life are created in, and enhanced by, mutual sharing and enjoyment that there is no need to labor the importance of affiliation.

1. Yet, in our own day we are in danger of forgetting that affiliation, including friendship and romantic love, become shallow when sentimentality and mutual parasitism sets in as persons fail to enlarge their value-concerns and reroot their affections. There are special contemporary reasons for our reminding ourselves, and not the least in the area of sex education (never information only!), that two persons will be juxtaposed only in space if other values do not unite their lives[7] in the qualitative rhythms of responsive-responsible caring. Persons who use each other, even in "genteel" ways, in or outside of marriage, never know what confidence and trust are worth.

2. What we are not facing squarely either in schools or elsewhere, in "programs" of sex "education" about "all you need to know about sex," is that persons need to feel cared about for themselves, that they cannot give themselves if they think that their meaning to another is confined largely to a segmental source of pleasure, however discreet. Rollo May, in *Love and Will*, speaking from his psychiatric experience, says that many of the patients he treats are no longer afraid of their bodies—they are afraid to care. Add to this an underlying theme in Erich Fromm's work *The Art of Loving*: No one is emotionally mature who has not moved from: I need you, therefore, I love you! to: I love you, therefore, I need you! And centuries ago, Antigone, in the great play (by that name) of Sophocles, sang out: "I am made for fellowship in love not fellowship in hate." Our deficiency is not so much in pertinent facts but in the value-connections those facts have in both maturing and grown persons.

The evidence for such contentions, again, is not only in our loins but in the larger psychodynamics of our conative dispositions and our abilities. I am proposing that sexual emotion (lust) is not a segregated segment of a person's nature; it can grow in meaning and express the creativity for which his whole being yearns in various ways. Sexual intercourse can also express symbolically the growth in values that define the partners' venture—their failures and successes—in value-realizations, in trustful and cocreative togetherness.

X. WORK AND VOCATION

When Freud was asked what the conditions of mental health are, he replied: "Work and love." For a person, the *quality* of affiliation involved in

7 See Peter A. Bertocci, *Sex, Love, and the Person* (Mission, Kans.: Sheed, Andrews, McMeel, 1967).

his earning a living makes much of the difference between sharing in a common task and "making a buck." The job one has, the work one does "for a living," may well take its place alongside of family-experience as the gymnasium in which most persons shape their personalities.

Again, a person's work and its value in a community may indeed be his economic and social capital; it may evoke admiration, respect, and praise from others, and thus be a source of much social and economic confidence. It can, accordingly, support and express the varied values of health, truth, character, and affiliation. What unemployment means to a person ranges all the way from fruitless idleness to feeling that he cannot make his way in his community. The statistics pertaining to unemployment always need to take on the poignant meaning: Persons suffer value-deprivation as persons, even when they can receive adequate compensation financially, insofar as they and those who love and are loved by them feel uprooted and know not where to turn. A schooling process and a responsible society cannot prepare a person for all economic hardships, but their priorities must include helping him to discover his primary and supportive skills.

1.   Unrealistic as it may seem, at any one point in a person's development, his "job" will be more meaningful as it becomes related to his conscious sense of vocation. A *vocation* gives direction to a person's life as a whole, hopefully actualizing the purpose that allows for fuller actualization of his individuality. To indicate interpenetration once more, many persons have no sense of vocation because they think of jobs in economic-social terms instead of accepting the challenge of a larger task that gives meaning to their values as a whole. When a person can see his job as part of his foreseeable life span in his relation to others, the drudgery that accompanies working out any job is taken in stride as part of "my station and its duties."

2.   Consequently, the schooling of persons cannot be geared to policies aimed exclusively at preparing persons for the jobs that render them more capable of filling *a* niche, as if a vocation must be only an adjunct to *the* job, or as if vocation is avocation (important as the latter is). There is no intent here to minimize the educational policy that provides graded and diversified programs that help the person to discover his competencies and the areas that bring him significant qualitative satisfaction. Too many people who are "making good money" are bored with life; they court mediocrity and then accept it because they do not become aware soon enough that vocation need not be restricted to job and economic status. More and more persons, especially in an economic world in which automation spreads, will need to find their larger vocation in values that

serve other than economic and status needs. Unless daily, including in their schooling, persons can be encouraged to enlarge their horizons of value, they lose any sense of their own potential, let alone of being needed; they develop a psychic emptiness that, alas, will not be overcome by the rounds of "pleasant activities." For example, mothers and fathers (and surrogates) who accept responsibility for all sorts of dull routine may well point out that so often in their own lives this "dull routine" is a component in the work well done in their attempt to actualize their dedication to each other as partners in wholesome, cooperative creativity.

3.　Here is the place to emphasize once more the interrelation of virtues, environment, and the individual pattern of values. For I am not maintaining that the content of happiness, the quality of fulfillment, is unrelated to environment. I agree that the technological age in which we live poses special opportunities for goods and evils. There is no denying, for example, that while courage does not depend on the environment, the courage to marry, or to become a parent, in this age involves harder, more far-reaching risks than it did in another.

Yet my keen awareness of the varying demands on the cardinal virtues (in the situations that persons *cannot escape because they are persons*) for values that will demand compromise but be endangered by opportunism keeps me pressing for a tensive pattern of the most comprehensive actualizing of cardinal values and virtues. This pattern will be what I have called elsewhere an "unfinished symphony of values."

I do not retreat from my stand that while persons develop virtues in order to deal more effectively with their own developing natures and with the changing environments, environment cannot create the virtues and be solely responsible for value actualization. Virtues, in particular, are the person's own creation, if you will, and no one can readily take them from him. Which of us, for example, has not known that unschooled person, one also whose horizon of values is limited by economic and other circumstances, yet who does his work well, who is honest to a fault, who can be trusted to see the effect of what he does on a fellow-workman, his family, and his narrower community at least, whose "thank you" and "I'm sorry" is not perfunctory, who suffers the outrages of pain so that others will not be hurt, who has a sense of humor about himself, who does not take what belongs to others, who keeps his promises, and who is kind to those who need his help? We admire his moral backbone, as we say, and we realize that his are values experienced because he has done the best he can with what is open to him; he has brightened his corner.

XI. THE SYMPHONY, NOT THE SCALE OF VALUES

1.   My omission here of the values of recreation and of aesthetic values would be even more egregious, despite space limitations, could I not refer especially to Harry S. Broudy's *Enlightened Cherishing: An Essay on Aesthetic Education*,[8] in which he unfolds the intrinsic and interpenetrating nature of the aesthetic experience — that harmonizes with much of what I have so far set forth in the "symphony of values." Indeed, his *Building a Philosophy of Education*[9] expands on this ideal of mutual self-fulfillment. Suffice it to say here that we need to insist, in schooling and education, that the prima-facie and criticized values in the ranges of aesthetic experience are no "frosting on the cake" but yield a kind of growth that enhances the quality of all other values. The disciplined expression of aesthetic "cherishing" brings satisfaction merely suggested by the expressions "the good deed graciously performed" and "the ugliness of that perfidious conduct."

2.   I shall, however, emphasize the task, forced upon us by the perpetual need to organize the values of the symphony within the individual life especially. For we have been — in inspecting, scanning, sorting, and sifting — becoming aware of a dynamic network of cardinal values and virtues that express different facets of our maturing and learning beings, and at the same time create problems of harmony. Hence, for any person the moral task is to learn, at different stages of development, how to "orchestrate" the values that make for the most compossible whole within himself in relation to his total situation — and this without forfeiting individuality any more than creative compromise necessitates. In this task of orchestration the issues of the vocation of persons becomes a persistent concern, and we shall end this essay with the values of religion and philosophy of life. But first I cannot stress enough that the conception of (unfinished) symphony of values and their orchestration supersedes that of scale of values (with a higher and lower end). For since persons live in their values from day to day, different motifs and movements of values are especially conducive to their growing-point.

3.   Hence the question always is: Which orchestration of values will not foreclose values unnecessarily? I would urge, not merely "in passing," that the death of quality begins when persons adopt the attitude "any-

8   Harry S. Broudy, *Enlightened Cherishing: An Essay on Aesthetic Education* (Urbana: University of Illinois Press, 1972).

9   Harry S. Broudy, *Building a Philosophy of Education* (Englewood Cliffs, N.J.: Prentice-Hall, 1954).

thing is all right once." This encourages a cheap democracy, or mobocracy, of values. At the same time, the answer is not specialization in one area of values. Such concentrations as "intellectualism," "aestheticism," and "moralism" warn us of what can happen to warp life when a person sacrifices too many other value considerations to high hopes of proficiency or "perfection" in one area.

4. If persons are to achieve optimum quality without sacrificing variety, three things are well nigh certain. First, tension, conflict, and challenge will scarcely be avoided in creating, conserving, and increasing values. Second, at any one point in the development of a symphonic pattern, the problem is to keep the themes in relationships that will be mutually enhancing. Phrases like "nothing too much," "creative counterpoise," "dialectic of values," are different ways of indicating that the human search for quality in value-experience always faces some concrete problem of selection for the sake of ultimate range and unity; risk is integral to this search, and "peace of mind" is inimical to growth. The goal of life, the meaning of happiness, cannot be "serene" fulfillment but a melioristic "creative insecurity."[10] I am not presenting a fixed pattern of values that becomes a kind of harness to which one fits his changes as a person. His task, ultimately of self-education, is the task of finding where he is, and how far he can go, in relation to the total human venture in value-realization.

XII. RELIGIOUS VALUE AND PHILOSOPHICAL ORIENTATION

1. "He who has a why to live can bear almost any how," said Nietzsche. I have been arguing that the why to live is to be found in the dynamic relations among values that we discover in this kind of world, with our kind of activity-potentials. The mysteriousness of existence is its ultimate givenness; for example, that quality in human experience does take some such pattern. A philosophy of life does not solve the mystery. As Whitehead once said, it seeks to "corner it." I am proposing that it is the person as thinker, or evaluator, as actor, who asks whether he is alone in his concern for value-realization. Is the embeddedness of values within persons alien to, or witness to, whatever the ultimate structure of things is?

2. This philosophical question cannot be answered without an examination of another area of value-experiencing, namely the holy or the sacred. The vitality of any religious faith dries up if it is not freshened by such experiences not only of religious "experts" like the mystics in every culture, but also by the "garden variety" of millions who are not religious

10 See Peter A. Bertocci, *Religion as Creative Insecurity* (New York: Associate Press, 1958; Westport, Conn.: Greenwood, 1973).

seers or prophets. At the moment I care not how we *finally interpret* the experience of the holy. But we cannot neglect the fact that those human beings who experience the holy find that this experience is at least as significant for them in their search for value as any other—indeed other values are both challenged and supported by it. And they report that it gives them power such as no other value-experience gives them. Often, the inspiring theme for the orchestration of values depends ultimately on the particular interpretation the experients give to their experience of the holy.

Let me put this theme in another way. The person, in view of his religious experience, has been called a worshiping animal. What he has worshiped has become the source of unity and power in his life—his cosmic vocation. The Object of worship has fascinated him, gripped him, and claimed his allegiance. In its Name he has lived and died; in its Name he has been willing to sacrifice all other values; in its Name he has been willing to extend himself unrelentingly in search for truth, beauty, and goodness, both for himself and others. In its Name—we must face this fact also—men have hurt themselves, persecuted, and destroyed others.

3.   If such a brief description is at all true, it follows that no search for a pattern of values can possibly disregard the "soundings" of the holy and of worship. For the penetration of the holy can destroy a symphony of values, or it can be its dominant creative theme. No responsible educator, therefore, can minimize the importance of the search for, or neglect the task of interpreting, the meaning of religious experience. Not, at least, if he is interested in the dynamics, psychological and metaphysical, of the orchestration of values. If at every stage in education there is concern for, appreciation of, and responsibility for both the parts and the whole of value-experiencing, then education that discourages the disciplines of religious exploration is truncated education.

4.   It will be noted that I have not been speaking of religious cults and denominations. These have both produced their prophets as well as persecuted and killed them. My concern is more far-reaching, especially in a day when religious and philosophical dogmatism of the right and of the left seems bent on spilling the wine that does not fit their bottles. I can here only suggest that, in view of what William James properly called "the variety of religious experience," we recognize (as James himself did) that religious experience does not come with a final specific label and is married to no specific theology.

5.   Thus, whatever one's final conviction about the validity of a specific religious revelation or interpretation, any person within any religious tradition must be cognizant of human disagreements in defining the

faiths by which men live. To be tolerant religiously does not mean that religion, of course "a private matter," can close heart, ear, and intellect to the value orientations encouraged in faiths at odds with one's own tenets. Religious experience must not dictate to the other values of life but partake with them in defining what the worthwhile ventures in life are. Religious sensitivity and conviction remain, after all, a testimony to the essential goodness of life, seen in terms of the structure of faith. One thing all religions do: They keep man from idolizing either himself or any of his institutions; they make him peculiarly aware that he is given much, both evil and good, that he does not deserve.

6. Professor Gordon W. Allport[11] expresses our situation in his discussion of the mature religious sentiment. He recognizes the need for a unifying philosophy of life. He also stresses that an immature religious sentiment keeps a personality from growing and promotes rigidity. But this student of personality finds that a mature religious sentiment connects a person to what he regards as permanent or central in the nature of things without damming up the mainstream of personal experience by unstructured ecstasies. Indeed, because it is part of the individual's search for meaning, the mature religious sentiment will be more than just emotional, more than "cold" reason. It will encourage the person not to allow his life to run off into little rivulets by confronting him with the demand that he take seriously the integrity of his values and their possible integration with a Ground of being. The mature religious personality will indeed know that, since he cannot know all, he must remain in uncertainty even as he learns to act wholeheartedly.

7. To conclude: In the ideal of personality presented here, the overriding sin is to pursue one dimension of values as if it were the end-all and be-all of life. To be creative is to persist in the orchestrating of the value-experiences of life. Only by so doing will a person be *responsive* to the reaches of his own being, *responsible* for communion with the horizons of values in other lives, and gratefully reverent before what Whitehead calls "the tender care that nothing of value be lost." Thus, a personalistic theory of reality is the systematic reflective response to what is reasonably suggested by the fact that persons, in finding their value-creativity in symphonic motifs, at the same time discover that their roots are sunk, not in a universe indifferent to their disciplined needs, but in a Ground that nourishes responsive-responsible community.

11 See Gordon W. Allport's discussion in *The Individual and His Religion* (New York: Macmillan, 1950), pp. 17ff.; idem, *Becoming* (New Haven, Conn.: Yale University Press, 1955); and idem, *Pattern and Growth in Personality* (New York: Holt, Rinehart & Winston, 1963).

Education in Values:
Acculturation and Exploration

ROGER L. SHINN
Union Theological Seminary, New York

Education is both acculturation and exploration. The two are not utterly opposed. Indeed, one of the challenges of education is to relate them so that they strengthen rather than neutralize or oppose each other. Yet there is enough conflict between the two processes to keep education usually interesting, sometimes explosive.

One instrument of education is schools. In the million or so years of human experience with education, schools are apparently a recent invention. They have proved useful enough that industrialized societies rely on them for a great part of education. So important are they that most people, when they hear the word *education*, think of schools. Education, however, is carried on by families, mass media, peer groups, and many other forces — sometimes working with and sometimes against schools, sometimes inside and sometimes outside of schools. Out of deference to habit I shall take most of my examples from education in schools.

Whether we are thinking of schools or other agencies, there is no conceivable way to isolate education from its acculturating and exploratory work in relation to values. Any style of education teaches, for example, that clocks and the peculiar kind of time they register are — or are not — valuable. It teaches that competition is — or is not — desirable. It infuses the attitude that coeducation is exceptional or normal, that the authority of teachers is to be esteemed or disdained, that the traditions of the culture are to be preserved or revised. A value-free education is about as possible as a protein-free diet.

ACCULTURATION IN VALUES

In that education called "elementary," an older generation teaches a younger generation how to stay alive, use language, and relate to other people in the styles characteristic of a particular culture. It teaches ways of winning approval or suffering disapproval. It shapes behavior, habits, and attitudes. In all this it inculcates values. The younger generation is simultaneously doing something more or less similar to the older generation.

Perhaps the most effective value inculcation is so implicit in educational processes that it is scarcely conscious. Attempts to state the goals of education usually omit those unquestioned goals that are rarely verbalized. For example, by observing holidays education distinguishes between the routine and the festive, perhaps even the sacred, elements of life. Any organized educational process inculcates some valuations of promptness, of rhythms of work and recreation, of prestige. Its structures and practices impose notions of acceptable sex roles and racial attitudes. They transmit some sense of the relative values of cooperation and competition.

On the more intellectual level education acculturates people to the prevalent beliefs of a society—or of the groups in a society that control the educational processes. Indoctrination in beliefs has some effectiveness. John Kenneth Galbraith goes so far as to say: ". . . power that is based on belief is uniquely authoritarian; when fully effective, it excludes by its nature the thought that would weaken its grasp."[1] But that statement may betray the bias of the intellectual. Indoctrination in behavior is at least as important. Behavioral patterns determine many attitudes. And, as sociologists are fond of saying, behavioral change often precedes attitudinal change. The point is important because education *almost* always communicates beliefs; it *always*, I suppose, communicates patterns of behavior.

The function of acculturation, always implicit in education, frequently becomes explicit. Societies intentionally pass on their cultural habits, symbols, and ideas—as do ethnic, racial, professional, and religious subcultures within societies. When a society finds the implicit communication of values ineffective, it usually increases the emphasis on explicit means. Thus a news dispatch reports that the U.S. Military Academy at West Point, concerned with "a moral rot that has infected the Army since the Vietnam War," is instituting "four years of courses in morals and ethics." The report continues that such courses were not conducted in the past because "the honor code . . . and other traditional means of discipline" were considered adequate.[2]

1 John Kenneth Galbraith, *Economics and the Public Purpose* (New York: New American Library, Signet edition, 1975), p. 215.

2 Drew Middleton, "West Point Seeks to Eliminate Moral 'Corruption' in Army Enlistees," *New York Times*, August 6, 1978, p. 38.

One of the most obvious—and perhaps least effective—ways of inculcating values is exhortation. Some sociologists think that the American society has a peculiar fondness for this method. Thus Gunnar Myrdal, the Swedish social scientist, has written:

> America, compared to every other country in Western civilization, large or small, has the *most explicitly expressed* system of general ideals in reference to human interrelationships. This body of ideals is more widely understood and appreciated than similar ideals are anywhere else. The American Creed is not merely—as in some other countries—the implicit background of the nation's political and judicial order as it functions. To be sure, the political creed of America is not very satisfactorily effectuated in actual social life. But as principles which *ought* to rule, the Creed has been made conscious to everyone in American society.[3]

Myrdal's statement suggests the problem in the conflicts between the values explicitly communicated in moral language and the values implicitly communicated by "actual social life." This conflict is the "American dilemma," to use his famous phrase. Such a dilemma afflicts all education in values. Learners may receive conflicting signals from parents who exhort them to honesty but tell obvious lies on the telephone, or from schools that verbally exalt intellectual attainment but actually show higher esteem for athletic prowess. Living with such conflicts is part of the educational experience of everyone in modern civilizations.

EXPLORATION IN VALUES

The recognition of conflicts in values makes exploration inevitable. Yet the educational exploration of values is, in most communities of most societies, a more controversial enterprise than acculturation. Exploration implies some challenge to received traditions, or at least some recognition that the traditions are incomplete. Or it involves some exploitation of conflicts within the tradition. Since tradition is inherent in human cultures, any weakening of the tradition appears as a threat to the culture or at least to some custodians of the culture. A Socrates, who challenges the prevailing tradition, is regarded as a corrupter of youth. Not all corrupters of youth have inherited the mantle of Socrates. Greed or destructive passion can be the motives for challenging traditional values. But those who undertake any radical exploration in values are perceived, by at least some interests, as subversive agents.

Nevertheless exploration in values, although dangerous in its more

---

3   Gunnar Myrdal, *An American Dilemma* (New York: Harper and Brothers, 1944), p. 1.

radical forms, is hard to avoid entirely. One reason is that tradition is rarely entirely consistent. Anthropologists have sometimes talked of the "cake of custom" that governs the lives of some tribes for many generations. But even in such cases there are likely to be conflicts of interest that imply conflicts of values. For example, the folklore of many tribes carries intimations of some difference of values between the young and the aged. Furthermore, any change in the conditions of life—whether introduced by weather, neighbors and enemies, or new techniques—requires decisions and modifications of behavior and the values assumed in behavior.

Educational institutions may quite intentionally and explicitly engage in the exploration of values and the questioning of some values. All public education in so heterogeneous a society as that of North America will lead students to question some of the values that they bring to school. That questioning provokes resentment of groups who have a stake in the maintenance of established values—of parents, politicians, patriotic organizations, religious communities, economic interests.

The fear of exploration, although often mindless or tyrannical in motivation, is not *entirely* groundless. Sociologist Louis Wirth has observed: "A society is possible in the last analysis because the individuals in it carry around in their heads some sort of picture of that society."[4] He goes on to point out that a society with no meaningful consensus will be threatened by the normlessness that Emile Durkheim called *anomie*. The social fabric—and individuals within it—may disintegrate.

We may conclude that the most complacent or fanatical supporters of acculturation must expect—at least in modern civilizations—that education will include some exploration of values. And the most venturesome explorers must assume some acculturation into a context of values. The relation between the two processes varies from culture to culture. It also varies in different age groups. Acculturation is most obvious with infants and children. Nobody expects kindergartners to challenge inherited values in the way that Ph.D. candidates may—but do not always—do.

EDUCATION AND CONFLICTS OF VALUES

People in the contemporary world are more impressed with conflicts of values than people in most past ages—or so, at least, it seems to us. We know, of course, that past generations have fought out their conflicts of values in wars or class struggles. We know that past civilizations have disintegrated, perhaps because of the loss of social cohesion and consen-

---

4 Louis Wirth, "Preface" to Karl Mannheim, *Ideology and Utopia*, trans. Louis Wirth and Edward Shils (New York: Harcourt, Brace and Co., Harvest Book edition, 1936), p. xxiii.

sus on values. But never before have mass communications saturated the home with such a cacophony of exhortation, enticement, and subliminal persuasion from so many clashing value systems. Family and school feel beleaguered as they try to maintain some values. And, more than in most pasts, family and school may fight each other.

A few examples will make the point. The first comes from East Germany. In the fall of 1976, pastors in the 4,300 Evangelical churches read statements calling for greater religious freedom and urging that the educational system allow children and youth to "live as Christians without being subjected to humiliation." In the summer of 1978 another statement, read in churches throughout the nation, objected to the compulsory military education being introduced into the public schools. The case illustrates the frequent conflicts of values that take form in conflicts of social institutions. Such a conflict is old and frequent in Western history.

A second example, closer to home, is sex education in the schools of the United States. The painful consequences of sexual ignorance are so obvious that the case for education about sex seems evident to many people. Of course, most past generations of children and youth—whether in our own society or in others—did not get their sexual knowledge primarily from formal instruction in schools. But the inaccuracies and gaps in the knowledge they got from parents or peers has had shattering effects upon many lives. So the prevalent "liberal" opinion in the United States favors sex education in the schools; it looks upon the opponents of such education as peculiarly benighted people.

Yet the conflicts of value in this area are more than most schools—especially when monitored by parents, school boards, and politicians—know how to handle. Few human activities and attitudes are so value laden as those related to sex. What values shall the school communicate—those of particular teachers, those of an official position, those of the "respectable" culture, or an amalgam of these and others? How shall high schools relate to pregnant girls in their midst? What language—that of textbooks, that of frequently embarrassed parents, or the surreptitious language of children and youth—shall it use? Shall avowed homosexuals be encouraged to teach about sex—or, to enter a stormy area—to teach at all in public schools? Shall any norms—of chastity, monogamy, marital fidelity—be taught? Shall children be made ashamed of parents living with partners to whom they are not married? Shall contraception be taught as though high school students are expected by the system to use it? Or shall a school, in despair over handling issues like these, simply communicate objective, "value-free" information—and risk the criticism of parents for whom the greatest offense of sex education is to assume that sex can be taught or practiced with indifference to values? Those most critical of the obscurantist objection of some parents to sex education in the schools can probably think, without using up much time, of some teachers whom they would not want teaching their children about sex.

Still another example is education about death. In the United States death is a subject that has come out of the closet, along with some other subjects, in recent years. It used to be said that the North American culture systematically tried to suppress thoughts of death to a degree quite unusual in most human societies. More recently, organizations and popular publications have given increased attention to death, and the schools have taken up the theme. A press report quotes a publication of the National Education Association: "The study of death is probably the last of the old taboos to fall in the schools."[5]

Of course, the subject could never be avoided completely. Even children die, whether from disease or from accident. No school can be so insensitive as to avoid notice of their deaths. Teachers die. More often, parents and grandparents die. Public figures die. The deaths of President Kennedy and Martin Luther King, Jr., were events shared, to a remarkable degree, by the whole nation. Television became the educator of the society in the public meanings of death.

As for formal instruction, the subject bristles with difficulties. The news report cited above says: "The strong possibility that the study of death might lead students into such prickly questions as religion, euthanasia and abortion has dissuaded some school systems from the subject." It goes on to note that "most teachers agree that death should be taught without many value judgments." If that is meant literally, it is about as incredible a statement as any educator could make. Obviously a teacher, without much evaluating, can quote statistics on death rates at various ages or explain something about the physiology of death. But to help a class relate to the death of one of its members is inescapably a matter of sensitivity, attitudes, and values. No one has yet proposed that electronic instruments take over that phase of education.

VALUES AND RELIGION

The examples just mentioned inevitably touch upon the relation of religion to education. For a great many people, values derive from a religious commitment. That commitment may throw people into conflict with the dominant values of a society or it may reinforce those values. It is hard to

5   Gene I. Maeroff, "Schools Take Up Study of Death," *New York Times,* March 6, 1978, pp. A1, 8.

imagine any serious religious commitment that does not shape the values of its adherents.

On the other hand, in an increasingly secularized world, it becomes obvious that many people maintain value-laden commitments without participation in formal religious organizations. The change from many past cultural situations is obvious. For example, John Locke's arguments for religious toleration, so refreshing and epochal in the aftermath of wars of religion, today seem strange in their exclusion of atheists, on the grounds that atheism dissolves "promises, covenants, and oaths."[6] Today, even though witnesses in courts usually take an oath that ends "so help me God," we know quite well that theists *may* be liars and atheists *may* be truth-tellers.

Surely it is a gain to realize that many widely shared values are, at least to some extent, separable from the religious beliefs and institutions that are not so widely shared. That awareness makes it possible to put some hope, however chastened, in the search for consensus in the United Nations, as in many a religiously diverse American city.

But that hope, which is shaky enough in our distraught world, has its limitations. Values that are more than superficial have some rootage in the loyalties and identities of persons and communities. And the deepest loyalties and identities of people constitute their overt or tacit religions. That is, religion almost by definition is the constellation of loyalties and the deepest recognition of identity that constitute selfhood and community. Sometimes that kind of religion is quite unrelated to the churches that people conventionally choose to participate in or avoid. But for most people, even in secularized cultures, profound loyalties and identities are related in some way to a concrete history and to cultic expression. That is as characteristic of military organizations and football teams (whenever these become formative of values) as it is of synagogues and churches.

The American experiment in separation of church and state has the purpose of maintaining religious liberty. As enshrined in the First Amendment to the Constitution, it provides that government may not "establish" or interfere with the "free exercise" of religion. Most American churches believe that they have a major stake in that freedom. Those who esteem and defend it must nevertheless recognize that it poses challenges to education. Public schools, which inevitably communicate values, must do so without imposing religious beliefs or practices.

Originally that was no great problem, because the First Amendment

6 John Locke, "The Spirit of Toleration," in *Locke: Selections,* ed. Sterling Lamprecht (New York: Charles Scribner's Sons, 1928), pp. 49-50.

limited only Congress, not states or local school boards. Even after the Fourteenth Amendment was construed to extend the First Amendment to all governmental agencies, there was little immediate impact, because most public school education went on in an ethos that was an amalgam of Protestant Christianity with the "civil religion" expressed in such historic American documents as the Preamble to the Declaration of Independence and Lincoln's Gettysburg Address. Many school children memorized these, sometimes in schools where they also heard daily readings from the Bible.

History offers little evidence that the old tactics were highly efficacious. And, as the religious pluralism of the American society has become more obvious, church leaders have frequently been in the forefront of the movement to insist that public schools avoid any imposition of the religion of some people upon other people. The questions remain as to how public education can (a) do something of its historical job of acculturation in values without imposing the values of some people upon dissenters and (b) do the work of exploration in values without alienating those who take offense at having their own values disturbed.

PLURALISM AND COMMITMENT

I have been building an argument. It states that education deals with values, both by acculturation and by exploration. Both processes are controversial, especially in a pluralistic society. It states further that both processes are inevitable and inescapable. It states also that both processes are difficult and controversial, especially within a self-consciously pluralistic society.

If this is the case, the outlook is for continued experimentation and controversy about the place of values in education, above all in public education. Experiments will center both on the techniques of moral education and on the more fundamental question of how to relate pluralism to public commitments in our society.

One recent discussion of the issue shows the intensity of the conflict. Carl Bereiter examines particularly (although not exclusively) the methods of Lawrence Kohlberg and of the Values Clarification movement as two quite different attempts to give respectability to moral education in the schools. Professor Bereiter quotes a poll of professional educators to show that 88 percent of the sample, though assigning primary responsibility for moral development to the family, advocate that the school engage in the enterprise. Then he states his own judgment that the advocates of moral education are covertly imposing doctrines on students and thereby intruding illegitimately into territories where they have no right.[7] The clash between Bereiter's opinion and the majority opinion is evidence of the persuasiveness of two quite different cases, each with a cogency that challenges but does not displace the cogency of the other.

I expect the conflict to continue because it is in the nature of education, especially in a pluralistic society, to communicate some values and to respect freedom by refraining from communicating others. On some issues the educational community can be a forum of competing values; on others it will take sides. From time to time the issues will change. In the past decade or two, for example, public education has made a commitment — more or less genuine and effective — to values of racial and sexual justice that are quite different from those of an earlier time. It has made some commitment to rights of students in relation to systems. It has tried to maintain, against increasing odds, a commitment to honesty on examinations. It is not a neutral forum on such issues. On the other hand it has relaxed or abandoned some commitments to dress codes, to traditional status patterns, to customs and beliefs about relations between the sexes. Here it has increased the zone of neutrality.

In a conformist society, an appreciation for pluralism can be a cleansing breeze. Conformists, of course, may find pluralism to be an amoral or immoral neutrality to values. Others may find it an affirmation of the value of human dignity and diversity. Yet in a society of rampant anomie and alienation, an evocation of shared purposes and values can be a creating and liberating act. Chaos as an educational device quickly exhausts its possibilities.

Michael Walzer has recently pointed to a fateful weakness in the "American liberal approach to moral life" as it affects education.[8] One typical posture is to relegate values to private life, excluding them from public conversation and education. The other is to reduce values to quantifiable cost/benefit analysis that spares people the difficult task of moral evaluation. The first approach leads to "intense subjectivity"; the second to "radical objectivity." Neither, says Walzer, "conforms to the realities of our common moral life." Neither can "be realized in any imaginable form of social life." An education in touch with reality must subject both "personal choice and utilitarian calculation" to "the discipline of a public philosophy." Although Walzer is writing primarily about education in universities, his theme has meanings for all the educational processes of a society.

7 Carl Bereiter, "Morality and Moral Education," *The Hastings Center Report* 8, no. 2 (April 1978): 20–25.

8 Michael Walzer, "Teaching Morality," *The New Republic* 178, no. 23 (June 10, 1978): 12–14.

THE SOCIAL IMPACT OF EDUCATION IN VALUES

I am advocating an attention to an education that both acculturates and explores, so far as values are concerned. I do so with an awareness that such education can never be reduced to a formula and can never avoid conflicts. It will be a messier, more awkward — but I hope more honest and exciting — process than much that passes for education.

The question remains as to whether education in values actually does any good. At least from the time of Socrates people have asked whether virtue can be taught. There is still much that we do not know about the answer.

What seems obvious is that all social institutions have some educational role and do, to some extent, communicate from generation to generation the values, doubts, and hypocrisies of the society. Whether they do so more effectively when they deliberately try or when they pretend to be value-indifferent, I do not know. But I think there is some gain in honesty, some loss in self-deception, when they recognize what they are doing. All this is what I have called the function of acculturation in education.

As for the exploratory function of education, the classical liberal faith is that exploration in values leads to improvement in values. The Socratic belief that the unexamined life is not worth living has had a strong influence in our culture. Its appeal is partly intrinsic — that examination of life is inherently a human value, leading to self-recognition, whether or not it results in "better" values. The appeal is also partly pragmatic — that examination discloses the fallacious and tawdry, thereby contributing to integrity and maturity.

Any simple faith in the benefits of exploration quickly runs into some negative evidence. Scholars in ethics can be as grasping, as prejudiced, as stubborn in controversy, as those who are quite innocent of ethical scholarship — just as psychiatrists can be as anxiety-ridden and self-deceived as those who never heard of Freud.

But there are probably some recognizable gains in the public, educational exploration of values. We can start from the observation that most people combine a mix of sensitivities, values, and beliefs that are not very well organized or coherent. Some elements in the mix reinforce other elements, but there are usually inconsistencies and conflicts. People live with the conflicts by forgetting or repressing what is inconvenient at a particular time or for a particular purpose. They can live with an immense amount of chaos within themselves.

What I am saying of individuals can also be said of cultures and subcultures. The same individual may experience different feelings, think different thoughts, and use different languages at home, in church, on the job, and in sports. In each case the individual is relating to the subculture most immediately present.

The term *cognitive dissonance* is sometimes used to designate the situation in which the person receives conflicting signals from outside or inside the self. Cognitive harmony is easier to handle than cognitive dissonance. But people have an infinite variety of ways of managing cognitive dissonance. Selective perception, the radical modification of perception, the segmenting of life—social/personal, body/soul, worship/work, ideal/real—these are a few characteristic ways.

The educational exploration of values, especially in the public arena, can raise to consciousness the disharmonies of value that are often quiescent. The experience may be painful. It may threaten satisfying self-images. It may also lead a person to confront conflicts and to recognize values more coherently. It may be a healing experience.

Gunnar Myrdal expresses the hopeful view of education when he says: "For the most part, people are subjectively honest and seek consistency; openly cynical people are rare if the whole society does not turn cynical."[9] Lest Myrdal seem naively optimistic, it should be noted that he is aware of the ability of people to rationalize inconsistencies and to resist the correction of beliefs that serve a convenient purpose. He is quite aware that both knowledge and ignorance, both attitudes and ideas, are largely "opportunistic." But he maintains a faith that people, when confronted with the inconsistency of their valuations or the errors of beliefs that support some evaluations, can change.

Myrdal brings another theme to bear on the subject of exploration of values: "In our civilization people ordinarily agree that, as an abstract proposition, the more general valuations—felt to be valid in relation to the whole nation or even to all human beings—are morally *'higher'* than those relating to particular individuals or groups. This is not an *a priori* assumption but a generalization founded on empirical observation. We all know that it is so."[10]

If Myrdal is correct, the educational exploration of values may confront people with their inconsistencies and lead them to modify their "lower" values to conform with their higher values. This process is probably most effective in a social situation where clashing values become highly visible and audible.

Evidence supporting Myrdal is found in the fact that the United States since the 1950s has gone through an educational process—in schools,

9 Gunnar Myrdal, *Objectivity in Social Research* (New York: Random House, Pantheon Books, 1969), p. 32.

10 Ibid., p. 16.

courts, factories, the armed forces, the streets—that has significantly changed values related to racial prejudice and discrimination. The same evidence shows also the ability of people and societies to resist changes in behavior and values.

The educator who intentionally explores values *has* to hope that such exploration will do some good—that it will contribute to the deepening, the clarifying, the harmonizing of values and even to some personal and social healing. That hope goes with the territory. The same educator will be the wiser to recognize the mysteries of human existence—its freedom, its sin, its intimations of grace—and not to expect too much of formal education.

Toward a Methodology of Teaching about the Holocaust

HENRY FRIEDLANDER

Brooklyn College of the City University of New York

The Holocaust — a term that has come to describe the Nazi extermination of the European Jews — had until recently a special meaning only for a small circle of experts. This has changed during the past decade of debate on torture, terrorism, and human rights. The increasing number of books, films, documentaries, and newspaper stories dealing with the Holocaust indicates that it has slowly begun to enter the mainstream of public discourse. It was inevitable that with instant popularity the Holocaust would also become a subject taught in schools and colleges.

Recently the *New York Times* editorialized that "the annihilation of European Jewry should be a mandatory subject" in our public schools. The editors refused to express an opinion on method and content; they asked the schools to make all curricular decisions.[1] But as colleges and school systems rush to implement the popular mandate, they have no clear idea about the nature, limits, and implications of the Holocaust as a subject. It is therefore essential that we discuss the methodological basis for instruction on the Holocaust. This essay attempts to do so. It does not present a lesson plan or course outline; it does not concern itself with the question of technique. Instead, it attempts, for purposes of discussion, to present arguments on why, how, and to whom the Holocaust ought to be taught.[2]

In the two decades that followed the end of the Second World War, the Jewish Catastrophe in Europe remained a hidden and buried subject.

1 "Teaching the Holocaust," *New York Times*, 11 September 1977.

2 This article is a revised version of a paper delivered at the First Western Regional Conference on the Holocaust, sponsored by the National Conference of Christians and Jews in San Jose, California, February 1977.

This repression was not total. There was much publicity concerning the camps, the Nuremberg trials, the rescue of the survivors, and the creation of Israel. This period also saw the publication of many memoirs, the collection of documents, and the appearance of the first substantial monographs. Nevertheless, the Holocaust remained a special case, a kind of curiosity. My study of university textbooks in the late 1960s clearly showed this.[3] The Holocaust did not become part of our historical consciousness.

The refusal to overcome and integrate the past (what the Germans have called the "Bewältigung der Vergangenheit") left psychological scars and, more important, made it impossible to view historical events accurately. The need to consider the Holocaust is of course obvious when we attempt to analyze historical trends closely connected with it. Thus any interpretation of modern German or modern Jewish history must deal with the problems posed by the Nazi murder of the Jews. But it is not as well understood that the Holocaust also has wider application. Nazi genocide forces us to reexamine our traditional interpretations of modern history and present-day society. Since the eighteenth century we have largely accepted the ideas of the Enlightenment, including the Idea of Progress. Even after two world wars we still tend to believe that the condition of modern man is improving, or at least moving in the direction predicted by the optimists of the nineteenth century. Historians and social scientists have made adjustments, but they have not abandoned this viewpoint.[4] But here a serious consideration of the Holocaust would necessitate a reevaluation.

Recently there has been a change. In the 1970s the Holocaust has become a subject of general interest. We have more research and more publications. We have also a growing number of conferences to explore the subject and to discuss its implications. Most important, we are also starting to teach about it.[5] This is an improvement. But at the same time there have also been two other, far more ambivalent, effects: proliferation and popularization.

The problem with too much being taught by too many without focus is that this poses the danger of destroying the subject through dilettantism. It is not enough for well-meaning teachers to feel a commitment to teach

3   Henry Friedlander, "Publications on the Holocaust," in *The German Church Struggle and the Holocaust*, ed. Franklin Littell and Hubert Locke (Detroit: Wayne State University Press, 1974), pp. 69-94 296-303. See also my *On the Holocaust* (New York: Anti-Defamation League, 1973).

4   George G. Iggers, "The Idea of Progress: A Critical Reassessment," *American Historical Review* 71 (October 1965): 1-17. For an optimistic view, see Peter Gay, *The Enlightenment: An Interpretation* (New York: Vintage, 1968), and for a pessimistic view, see Arthur Hertzberg, *The French Enlightenment and the Jews* (New York: Columbia University Press, 1968).

5   See *The Chronicle of Higher Education* 16, no. 10 (May 1, 1978).

about genocide; they must also know the subject. It is ludicrous for large school systems, like New York, to mandate teaching about the Holocaust without proper teacher training; even a curriculum guide and a few in-service hours will not be sufficient. For this reason small systems, like Brookline, Massachusetts, have been more successful.[6] But even in the universities dilettantism poses a problem. Because few departments in history, the social sciences, or the humanities have so far integrated the Holocaust into their curriculum, teaching it has remained a matter of chance. Unless someone already tenured in the department happens to know the subject and undertakes to teach it, the Holocaust has been offered only under pressure and without serious intent. The faculty used has tended to reflect this lack of departmental commitment: Often they are volunteers interested in experimentation and attracted by novel subjects; sometimes they are junior members drafted from vaguely related areas like Judaica or German literature; frequently they are local rabbis recruited as adjuncts.

Popularization poses a similar problem. Though distasteful to scholars and many others, there is nothing intrinsically wrong with the popularity of a subject. It shows that the subject has been accepted. But unfortunately it can also mean sensationalism and exploitation. The semipornographic film *The Night Porter* is a rather crass example of exploitation. The Holocaust demands treatment with taste and sensitivity; it is not likely to receive this if it becomes a media fad. A good example is Gerald Green's *Holocaust*, an NBC-TV extravaganza and a Bantam mass market paperback. This soap opera was poor history and bad drama.[7] It could be argued that this is simply poor taste, but not a pedagogical problem. However, this product has been peddled as history by NBC and various Jewish agencies. That can be dangerous, especially if this kitsch is seen by millions. Supporters have argued that because millions who had never heard of the Holocaust saw this production, it performed an educational function. But while all might agree that it is important for us to

6 Compare *The Holocaust: A Study of Genocide*, 2 vols., Curriculum Project Report No. 4042 by the Division of Educational Planning and Support, Board of Education of the City of New York, September 1977, and the Brookline, Massachusetts, guide: Margot Stern Strom and William S. Parsons, *Facing History and Ourselves: Holocaust and Human Behavior*, 1977. For a college guide, see *Thinking about the Unthinkable: An Encounter with the Holocaust*, Hampshire College, Amherst, Mass., 1972.

7 Gerald Green, *Holocaust* (New York: Bantam, 1978). For the controversy surrounding the television play and book, see the *New York Times*, drama section, 14, 16, and 23 April 1978; book review 16 April 1978, and letters 30 April and 4 May 1978. For the publicity blurb touting the television drama, see the glossy, five-part package entitled "Holocaust," an Educational Guide to the NBC Television Special, a National Jewish Interagency Project, coordinated by Barry Shrage and introduced by Rabbi Irving Greenberg, 1978.

understand the events of the Holocaust and their implications, no one has
yet explained why it is valuable for many millions simply to know that
genocide occurred. There is a difference between education and mass
culture; it is an error to confuse the two. Popularization is particularly
dangerous for complicated new subjects not yet fully understood or
academically accepted.

The problems of popularization and proliferation should make us careful about how we introduce the Holocaust into the curriculum; it does not
mean that we should stop teaching it. But we must try to define the subject of the Holocaust. Even if we do not agree about the content of the
subject, we must agree on its goals and on its limitations.

First we must ask why we should teach the Holocaust. There are a
number of reasons. One of them is our need to understand the past so
that we can explain the present. While this might be a truism that could
apply to all kinds of past events, it applies particularly to those of major
importance. The Holocaust is such a major historical event. It is not
simply an aberration or a footnote to the history of the twentieth century;
it is an event whose various aspects—political, ideological, administrative, technological, sociological, moral, and so forth—symbolize
the problems and dilemmas of the contemporary world. Like the fall of
Rome or the French Revolution, the Holocaust is one of those historical
events that represent an age.

But how does a study of the past illuminate the present? The obvious
lessons are often simplistic and cannot be applied; usually they are introduced for current political reasons. (In this way the lessons of the
Holocaust have been misused in the current debate about abortion and
affirmative action.)[8] One way to avoid such pitfalls is to see how scholars
have approached the subject. Thus in 1944 Paul Farmer analyzed the
historiography of the French Revolution, and discussed the French
historians who wrote about the Revolution in the late nineteenth and early
twentieth centuries. By doing this he not only illuminated the historical

8 Some of those opposed to abortion on religious grounds have argued that it compares to Nazi
genocide. They have pointed to the murder of the Jews as comparable to the prevention of birth after
conception. But the killing of the Jews was centrally directed, ideologically determined, and brutally
enforced; it cannot be compared to a medical procedure freely chosen by individual volunteers. It is
also interesting to note, though rarely mentioned, that the Nazis themselves prohibited abortion, imposing on its practitioners draconic punishments. The truth, if any, of the antiabortionist argument
must be determined on its own merits; the Holocaust cannot be used to validate political positions. In
the Bakke Case well-meaning people lined up on each side. Some saw in the creation of racial and
sexual quotas parallels to Nazi methods, but others argued that failure to assure sufficient representation for the underprivileged would perpetuate and increase the kind of exploitation practiced
by the Nazis in the occupied territories.

controversies about the Revolution, but also the political and social complexities of the troubled Third Republic.[9]

Tentatively, this method can already be applied to the Holocaust. Although there are numerous exceptions, we can place publications on the Holocaust into several large categories; each reflects different contemporary concerns. Thus Israelis write about the Holocaust from the vantage point of Israeli experiences and anxieties. Confronted with problems of security and survival, they tend to emphasize resistance; concerned with questions of national identity, they tend to focus on judeophobia.[10] East European and other Marxist authors tend to stress class structure and economic motives.[11] Theologians and moralists—both Jewish and Christian—emphasize heroism, compassion, and ethical dilemmas, as well as the Christian responsibility for anti-Semitism, when they deal with the Holocaust. For them these questions have been most applicable, particularly during the years of Vietnam and the Civil Rights struggle.[12] Sociologists, psychologists, and scholars from the humanities have tended to focus on the behavior of individuals. While the first two have usually emphasized the mechanical and passive behavior of victims in extreme situations, the third group has usually stressed their victory over adversity.[13] Historians, political scientists, and others concerned with public policy have concentrated on the bureaucratic and technological dimensions of

9   Paul Farmer, *France Reviews Its Revolutionary Origins* (New York: Columbia University Press, 1944).

10   See Henry Feingold, "Some Thoughts on the Resistance Question," *Reconstructionist*, May 1978, pp. 7-11, who has described this as the "Bauer-Suhl approach"; Yehuda Bauer, *They Chose Life* (New York and Jerusalem: American Jewish Committee and Institute of Contemporary Jewry of the Hebrew University, 1973); and Yuri Suhl, ed., *They Fought Back* (New York: Crown Publ., 1967). For a scholarly and exhaustive study of Jewish resistance, see Reuben Ainsztein, *Jewish Resistance in Nazi-Occupied Europe* (New York: Barnes and Noble, 1974). Some Israeli historians, like Leni Yahil, do not share this approach, and some non-Israeli historians do: A good example, combining resistance and identity, is Lucy Dawidowicz, *The War Against the Jews* (New York: Bantam, 1975), who however treats only the Polish Jews, consigning all others to an appendix.

11   One of the best such works is Tatiana Berenstein et al., eds., *Faschismus—Getto—Massenmord: Dokumentation über Ausrottung und Widerstand der Juden in Polen während des zweiten Weltkrieges*, issued by the Jewish Historical Institute, Warsaw, trans. from the Polish and Yiddish into German by Danuta Dabrowska (East Berlin: Rutten and Leoning, 1961). Also see below note 67.

12   See Philip Friedman, *Their Brothers' Keepers* (New York: Crown Publ., 1957); Franklin H. Littell, *The Crucifixion of the Jews* (New York: Harper & Row, 1975); A. Roy Eckardt, *Christianity and the Children of Israel* (New York: King's Crown Press, 1948); A. Roy Eckardt, *Elder and Younger Brother: The Encounter of Jews and Christians* (New York: Charles Scribner's Sons, 1967); and Alice and A. Roy Eckardt, "Studying the Holocaust's Impact Today," *Judaism*, Spring 1978, pp. 222-32.

13   Bruno Bettelheim, *The Informed Heart: Autonomy in a Mass Age* (New York: Avon Books, 1971); and Robert Jay Lifton, *History and Human Survival* (New York: Random House, 1970). For a book from the humanities, see Terence Des Pres, *The Survivor* (New York: Oxford University Press, 1976).

the Holocaust. There they seek answers to the problems of our mass society, where the individual seems powerless when confronted by the coercion of a faceless state.[14] It is not a question of the truth; all these approaches explain a portion of the truth. It is a question of different interpretations—different emphases—to shed light on different aspects, selected because of different present-day concerns.

But this attempt to use the Holocaust to illuminate the concerns of our age poses problems, because to do so means that the Holocaust must become a subject of legitimate public debate and scholarly controversy. For many this has been terribly difficult to accept. And there have been attempts to impose serious restrictions on discussions of the Holocaust by those who wish to elevate the subject to the level of sacred history and who denounce opponents for sacrilege. Thus at the very start of the study of the Holocaust, the legitimate intellectual and academic analyses by Hannah Arendt, Bruno Bettelheim, and Raul Hilberg were denounced in a mindless way. Podhoretz's "Study in the Perversity of Brilliance," Robinson's "Psychoanalysis in a Vacuum," and Eck's "Historical Research or Slander?" are particularly stark examples.[15]

And this attempt to stifle discussion continues. In 1970 Emil Fackenheim at a conference in Jerusalem lifted the discussion of the Holocaust unto a sacred level: "A Jew knows about memory and uniqueness. He knows that the unique crime of the Nazi Holocaust must never be forgotten—and, above all, that the rescuing for memory of even a single innocent tear is a *holy task*."[16] In 1977, at a conference in San Jose, he argued that those who disagree with him about the uniqueness of the Holocaust "insult" and "betray" the dead. At the same conference, and also in print, Bruno Bettelheim, once a victim of these arguments, denounced Terence Des Pres, accusing him by implication of spurious

14   Raul Hilberg, *The Destruction of the European Jews* (Chicago: Quadrangle, 1961); Uwe Dietrich Adam, *Judenpolitik im Dritten Reich*, Tübinger Schriften zur Sozial- und Zeitgeschichte (Düsseldorf: Droste Verlag, 1972); and H.G. Adler, *Der verwaltete Mensch: Studien zur Deportation der Juden aus Deutschland* (Tübingen: J.C.B. Mohr [Paul Siebeck], 1974).

15   Norman Podhoretz, "Hannah Arendt on Eichmann: A Study in the Perversity of Brilliance," *Commentary* 34 (November 1962): 201-08; Jacob Robinson, *Psychoanalysis in a Vacuum: Bruno Bettelheim and the Holocaust* (New York: Yivo, 1970); and Nathan Eck, "Historical Research or Slander?" *Yad Vashem Studies* 6 (Jerusalem, 1967): 385-430. For a detailed and bibliographically valuable attack on Arendt, see Jacob Robinson, *And the Crooked Shall Be Made Straight* (New York: Macmillan, 1965). For Hilberg's and Bettelheim's works, see above notes 13 and 14; for Hannah Arendt, see her *Eichmann in Jerusalem: A Report on the Banality of Evil* (New York: Viking, 1964).

16   Emil L. Fackenheim, *From Bergen-Belsen to Jerusalem* (Jerusalem: Institute of Contemporary History of the Hebrew University, 1975), p. 10. Italics mine.

scholarship and aid to fascism; as a psychoanalyst he compounded the attack by stating that Des Pres was doing it subconsciously.[17]

But the Holocaust is not sacred history; the Holocaust is a public event. Not only scholars in their histories, but also victims in their diaries and survivors in their memoirs have treated the Holocaust as a public event that deserves thorough analysis. The imposition of restrictions on the study of the Holocaust by those who wish to elevate it to sacred history limits serious discussion of the Holocaust as a historical topic and does so unjustly and to the disadvantage of knowledge. (Of course, there is room and need for commemoration. But this must not be confused with discussion and analysis; the tendency to mingle the two does damage to both. In addition, there are related theological concerns that deserve, and have received, attention.)[18]

As far as the study and teaching of the Holocaust are concerned, the problem is that one cannot have it both ways. One cannot treat the Holocaust as sacred history and also insist that it become a lesson and a warning for public discussion as well as an integrated part of our school curriculum. And throughout much of the debate about the Holocaust there is this attempt to have it both ways: to have it unique, and yet to have it as only the last example of two thousand years of persecution; to teach it as a moral lesson, and yet to make it so particular that no one else can use it. These are contradictions that must be resolved.

I must agree that it is difficult to accept a truly open discussion of the Holocaust, but there is no escape and we must welcome viewpoints different from our own. Of course, there are limits. Legitimate controversy excludes authors like Butz, who argue that the Nazis never killed the Jews. But like crackpots who maintain that the earth is flat or that man did not

17   Presented at the First Western Regional Conference on the Holocaust, San Jose, California, February 1977. See also Bruno Bettelheim, "Reflections (Concentration Camp Survival)," *New Yorker*, August 2, 1976, pp. 31-52.

18   Some theological works are: Richard Rubenstein, *After Auschwitz: Radical Theology and Contemporary Judaism* (Indianapolis: Bobbs-Merrill, 1966); Emil L. Fackenheim, *God's Presence in History: Jewish Affirmation and Philosophic Reflections* (New York: Harper Torchbook, 1972); Emil L. Fackenheim, *Encounters between Judaism and Modern Philosophy* (New York: Basic Books, 1973); and Irving Greenberg, "Cloud of Smoke, Pillar of Fire: Judaism, Christianity, and Modernity after the Holocaust," in *Auschwitz: Beginning of a New Era? Reflections on the Holocaust*, ed. Eva Fleischner (New York: Anti-Defamation League, 1974), pp. 7-55. For a critique of Fackenheim's and Greenberg's theology, see Michael Wyschogrod, "Faith and the Holocaust," *Judaism*, Summer 1971, pp. 268-94, and "Auschwitz: Beginning of a New Era?" *Tradition*, Fall 1977, pp. 63-78. For an extreme form of commemoration, see Irving Greenberg, "The Holocaust: The Need to Remember," Council of Jewish Federations, *General Assembly Papers*, 1977. For a solid treatment from the position of traditional Judaism, see Irving J. Rosenbaum, *The Holocaust and Halakha* (New York: KTAV, 1976).

evolve, one must simply disregard them. This is not possible when dealing with more respectable but politically tendentious authors like David Irving. They must be refuted thoroughly and dispassionately.[19]

One reason we study the Holocaust is to understand the present; another is to understand man and his society. Like few other subjects, the Holocaust permits us to glimpse human behavior in extreme situations. Much work has already been done in this area by psychiatrists and others: Bruno Bettelheim, Elie Cohen, Robert Jay Lifton, and now Terence Des Pres.[20] But the best way to study this is to consult the memoir literature as an original source—the best of the memoirs about life in the Nazi and Stalinist camps give us unusual insight into human behavior under extraordinary stress. Primo Levi's *If This Is a Man* is probably the best memoir of Auschwitz: Detached and clinical, it tells us something about daily existence and human perseverance. (I also recommend the sequel, *The Reawakening*, which tells with humor and pathos of his liberation and his sojourn in Poland and Russia prior to his return to Italy.)[21] Equally revealing are the short stories of Tadeusz Borowski. These terrible tales about Auschwitz haunt the reader with their stark simplicity.[22] (The best literature of the Holocaust has tended to imitate Borowski's style; but such stories transform simplicity into surrealism as authors like Jakov Lind apply the experiences of Auschwitz to the everyday world.)[23] Memoirs of life in the Stalinist camps provide insights similar to those about the Nazi camps. Here the literature is also vast. Susanne Leonhard's *Gestohlenes Leben* is the story of a highly educated Central European Communist; she spent years as a prisoner in the Vorkuta camp system of the Northern Polar region and as an exile in the Altai district of Central Asia, and her account, one of the best available, reflects the perceptions and sensibilities of a cultured and politically sophisticated European

19 David Irving, *Hitler's War* (New York: Viking Press, 1977). For a sober review that demolishes Irving's thesis, see Martin Broszat, "Hitler und die Genesis der 'Endlösung'; Aus Anlass der Thesen von David Irving," *Vierteljahrshefte für Zeitgeschichte* 25 (1977): 739-75.

20 For Bettelheim, Lifton, and Des Pres, see above note 13. For Elie Cohen, see his *Human Behavior in the Concentration Camp*, trans. from the Dutch (New York: Universal Library, n.d.).

21 Primo Levi, *If This Is a Man* (New York: Orion, 1969; paperback ed., *Survival in Auschwitz* [Collier-Macmillan, 1973]); idem, *The Reawakening* (Boston: Little, Brown, 1965; publ. in Great Britain as *The Truce*).

22 Tadeusz Borowski, *This Way for the Gas, Ladies and Gentlemen* (New York: Penguin, 1976). For two other important literary memoirs, see Elie Wiesel, *Night*, trans. from the French (New York: Avon Books, 1969) for a graphic account and religious response; and David Rousset, *The Other Kingdom*, trans. from the French (New York: Reynal and Hitchcock, 1947) for an impressionistic report.

23 Jakov Lind, *Soul of Wood and Other Stories*, trans. from the German by Ralph Manheim (New York: Fawcett Crest Books, 1966).

woman.[24] We even have memoirs that record experiences in both camp systems: Margarete Buber-Neumann recounts life in both Soviet and Nazi camps in vivid, journalistic language.[25]

To understand man and his society as revealed by the Holocaust, we must also study the intellectual milieu that made genocide possible. We must attempt to understand the totalitarian ideology. Much has been written about Hitler's ideological obsessions; the student can choose from a large number of interpretations.[26] But even more important, we want to know how leaders can motivate their followers to commit acts of inhumanity on a vast scale; how a world view can create a society where gas chambers for human beings are considered normal. We want to understand the psychology of the perpetrators, of the SS-men, bureaucrats and butchers, who did the deed. There is plenty of documentation: biographies and autobiographies, descriptions and interpretations, interrogations and rationalizations, and a vast number of documents.[27] But it is still difficult to understand the killers.

In this context we want to understand the causes, the limitations, and the dynamics of anti-Semitism.[28] Unfortunately, this subject is steeped in mythology. Popular understanding tends to link it to bigotry without differentiating sufficiently between ideological hatreds and everyday prej-

24 Susanne Leonhard, *Gestohlenes Leben* (Frankfort on the Main: Europäische Verlagsanstalt, 1956).

25 Margarete Buber-Neumann, *Als Gefangene bei Stalin und Hitler* (Stuttgart: Seewald, 1968).

26 For traditional historical biographies, see Konrad Heiden, *Der Fuehrer: Hitler's Rise to Power*, trans. Ralph Manheim (Boston: Houghton Mifflin, 1944); Alan Bullock, *Hitler: A Study in Tyranny* (New York: Harper Torchbooks, 1964); and Hugh R. Trevor-Roper, *The Last Days of Hitler* (New York: Collier Books, 1966). For psycho-historical biographies, see Rudolf Binion, *Hitler among the Germans* (New York: Oxford, Amsterdam: Elsevier, 1976); Walter C. Langer, *The Mind of Adolf Hitler* (New York: Basic Books, 1972); Robert G.L. Waite, *The Psychopathic God: Adolf Hitler* (New York: New American Library, 1977); and Erich Fromm, *The Anatomy of Human Destructiveness* (New York: Fawcett Crest, 1973).

27 Gerald Reitlinger, *The SS: Alibi of a Nation, 1922-1945* (New York: Viking, 1957); Heinz Hohne, *The Order of the Death's Head: The Story of Hitler's SS*, trans. Richard Barry (New York: Ballantine Books, 1971); and Helmut Krausnick et al., *Anatomy of the SS State*, trans. from the German (London: Collins, 1968). For biographies and autobiographies, see Hannah Arendt, *Eichmann in Jerusalem;* also *Commandant of Auschwitz: The Autobiography of Rudolf Hoess* (New York: Popular Library, 1961); Henry V. Dicks, *Licensed Mass Murder: A Socio-Psychological Study of Some SS Killers* (New York: Basic Books, 1972); and Gitta Sereny, *Into That Darkness* (New York: McGraw-Hill, 1974). For documents and interrogations, see *Reichsführer: Briefe an und von Himmler*, ed. Helmut Heiber (Munich: DTV, 1968); Robert M.W. Kempner, *SS im Kreuzverhör* (Munich: Rütten and Loening, 1964); and *The Stroop Report: "The Jewish Quarter of Warsaw No Longer Exists,"* trans. and ed. Sybil Milton (New York: Pantheon, forthcoming).

28 For one attempt to define terms and concepts, see Gavin I. Langmuir, "Prolegomena to Any Present Analysis of Hostility against Jews," *Social Science Information* 15 (1976): 689-727.

udice.[29] Traditional histories lump together judeophobia in various ages, from antiquity to modern times, treating anti-Semitism as a permanent and unvaried phenomenon. This analysis, which sees only quantitative differences between the anti-Semitism of medieval Christianity and that of modern anti-Christian ideologies, is not a very convincing explanation when applied to the Holocaust.[30] Studies of modern anti-Semitism are more useful. They analyze the social roots and political uses of modern anti-Semitism; they trace the birth of the anti-Semitic parties and of their transformation into totalitarian movements. They show how the new anti-Semitism based on race differed qualitatively from the preceding type based on religion. They thus delineate the radical nature of modern anti-Semitism.[31] But because they usually do not include the demonic, they fail to provide a fully satisfying explanation of how this ideology could lead to genocide.

A different approach, provocative and promising, is Norman Cohn's investigation of "how the impulse to persecute or exterminate is generated." In his first study he traced this impulse back to the Middle Ages and beyond. Analyzing the "apocalyptic fanaticism" directed against Jews as well as others by medieval millennial movements, he pointed out the similarity between their "militant, revolutionary chiliasm" and the totalitarian ideologies espoused by Nazis and Communists.[32] In his latest study he has continued this investigation of how genocide is possible. But this time he analyzed a "collective fantasy" directed not specifically against Jews, but against what medieval and early modern man, the educated as much as the ignorant, imagined as a society of witches. By investigating the background of the great witch-hunt, Cohn reveals the "inner demon"

29 This is most obvious in the publications of the defense agencies like the Anti-Defamation League, the American Jewish Committee, and the World Jewish Congress. See also Lucy Dawidowicz, *The Jewish Presence* (New York: Holt, Rinehart & Winston, 1977), chap. 13.

30 *Anti-Semitism*, Israel Pocket Library (Jerusalem: Keter, 1974); Malcolm Hay, *The Foot of Pride* (Boston: Beacon, 1950; paperback ed., *Europe and the Jews*); and E.H. Flannery, *The Anguish of the Jews* (New York: Macmillan, 1965). The best general history is Leon Poliakov, *The History of Anti-Semitism*, trans. from the French, 3 vols. (New York: Vanguard, 1964-75).

31 Eva Reichmann, *Hostages of Civilization* (Westport, Conn.: Greenwood Press, 1971); Peter Pulzer, *The Rise of Political Anti-Semitism in Germany and Austria* (New York: Wiley, 1964); Paul Massing, *Rehearsal for Destruction: A Study of Political Antisemitism in Imperial Germany* (New York: Howard Fertig, 1967); Robert Byrnes, *Anti-Semitism in Modern France* (New York: Howard Fertig, 1969); Andrew Whiteside, *The Socialism of Fools* (Berkeley: University of California Press, 1975); and Uriel Tal, *Christians and Jews in Germany*, trans. from the Hebrew (Ithaca, N.Y.: Cornell University Press, 1975).

32 Norman Cohn, *The Pursuit of the Millennium: Revolutionary Messianism in Medieval and Reformation Europe and Its Bearing on Modern Totalitarian Movements* (New York: Harper Torchbooks, 1961).

that can cause mass killings.[33] In a third study Cohn applied his investigation of historical psychopathology to the modern period. He analyzed a "fantasy at work in history" as exemplified by the modern forgery known as "The Protocols of the Elders of Zion"; he thus tried to show how the myth of the Jewish world conspiracy was a modern fantasy that provided the justification for the Holocaust.[34]

Complementing Cohn's studies are investigations into the social and psychological roots of twentieth-century unreason. The best of these is George Mosse's analysis of how nineteenth-century public festivals created the mythology and symbolism of a secular religion that culminated in the twentieth century in the mass pageantry of the Nazi revolution.[35] Related to this approach is the investigation of Nazi language. Here the best work, unfortunately not yet translated, is Viktor Klemperer's study of the *Lingua Tertii Imperii*. Klemperer was a Jewish professor who, though isolated and harassed, survived in Germany and evaded deportation. As a linguist he spent his years of inactivity observing the use and perversion of Nazi language. After the war he published his results in a fascinating book, part analysis and part personal memoir. He showed how Nazi language, devoid of reason, became a kind of exorcism, transforming clichés into realities. He dissected the exaggerations of this boastful language, indicating how words like "synchronize," "organize," "fanaticism," and "idealism" came to symbolize its poverty. His study remains the most successful attempt to analyze the political manipulation of culture and language under totalitarian rule.[36] In addition to the Nazi language analyzed by Klemperer, there is the specific language of the Holocaust. The former was the language of the propagandists, and it became the Nazis' linguistic milieu. The latter was the special bureaucratic language used by the technician who implemented the regime's terror. It contained those terrible euphemisms—*Aktion*, special treatment, *selekzya*, and so forth—used by both perpetrators and victims.[37]

Technology is as important as ideology if we want to understand man

33 Norman Cohn, *Europe's Inner Demons: An Enquiry Inspired by the Great Witch-Hunt* (New York: New American Library, 1975).

34 Norman Cohn, *Warrant for Genocide: The Myth of the Jewish World-Conspiracy and the "Protocols of the Elders of Zion"* (New York: Harper Torchbooks, 1969).

35 George L. Mosse, *The Nationalization of the Masses: Political Symbolism and Mass Movements in Germany from the Napoleonic Wars through the Third Reich* (New York: New American Library, 1975). See also his *Toward the Final Solution* (New York: Howard Fertig, 1978).

36 Viktor Klemperer, *LTI: Notizbuch eines Philologen* (East Berlin: Aufbau Verlag, 1946; West German ed., *Die unbewältigte Sprache* [Munich: DTV, 1969]).

37 See Henry Friedlander, "The Language of Nazi Totalitarianism," *Shoah* 1, no. 2 (Fall 1978): 16-19.

and his society. We want to know how technology as system and as tool fits into the Holocaust. The futurists have seen this most clearly. The prototype of many futuristic stories, including Orwell's, was the work of the Russian emigré Eugene Zamiatin. He wrote *We* in France during the 1920s, based on his experiences in Lenin's Russia. Unlike Orwell's *1984*, the futuristic society of *We* did not have to coerce its citizens; they coerced each other. They lived as numbers in cubicles whose sides, floor, and ceiling were composed of glass so that all could watch each other. For procreation couples could obtain tickets permitting them to lower the shades for a few minutes. Apart from that, privacy did not exist.[38]

As we have seen, mass murder is nothing new; but the technological dimensions of the Holocaust are sui generis. Technological efficiency made Nazi genocide possible. The Nazis rationalized the killings and built factories for mass murder. In their killing centers they processed human beings on the assembly line; they operated their installations on the basis of productivity, cost accounting, and space utilization. The technology of the Holocaust does not only mean that the Nazis had the ability to use modern wares — guns and gas — to kill large numbers of people rapidly. More important, they possessed the capability to organize genocide. This required a know-how unavailable to earlier generations. Like modern warfare, genocide required bureaucracy and logistics. Millions of Jews residing throughout Europe had to be identified, registered, isolated, and moved before they could be killed. Only modern technology could accomplish this. It required the collaboration of a large bureaucracy in government, the army, and industry. Civil servants far removed from the killing centers had to help. Technicians, not ideologues, were needed to make genocide work. Raul Hilberg has recently shown how the apolitical experts who ran the railroads participated; their technical knowledge was needed to move the victims to the death camps.[39]

A number of excellent studies have explored the technological dimensions of the Holocaust. They provide us with the best information we possess about what the Nazis called the "Final Solution." Of these Raul Hilberg's investigation of the "process of destruction" is still the classic work on the subject. This massive study describes in minute detail the conception and execution of the Nazi program of extermination.[40] In recent years two other works treating the technological dimensions have ap-

38 Eugene Zamiatin, *We* (New York: Dutton, 1952).

39 Raul Hilberg, "Confronting the Moral Implications of the Holocaust," *Social Education* 42 (April 1978): 272-77.

40 Hilberg, *The Destruction of the European Jews.* For an earlier attempt, see Gerald Reitlinger, *The Final Solution* (New York: Perpetua Books, 1961, first publ. in 1953).

peared. A Tübingen dissertation by Uwe Adam explains in great detail and with unusual sophistication the official German policy vis-à-vis the Jews during the period that preceded and led to the decision to kill them. Adam shows how the civil service, including the police bureaucracy, approached their collective task; like Hilberg, he describes how they identified, excluded, despoiled, and removed them. He describes the process of removal: first by forced emigration, then by deportation, and finally by extermination. His study ends with the decision to kill the Jews. Unlike others, who have maintained that this decision became final just before the war with Russia, he has placed it in the late fall of 1941 when the plan to dump Europe's Jews beyond the Urals in a defeated Russia proved no longer feasible.[41] H. G. Adler's exhaustive study fills the gaps in our knowledge of the ways used by the Nazis to accomplish mass murder. With infinite detail he treats the deportations of the German Jews and the bureaucracy that managed them. Mingling theoretical analysis, narrative descriptions, and case studies, he delineates the process that placed the Jews in Germany on the trains to the killing centers; using surviving Gestapo files, he traces specific decisions and the fate of individuals.[42]

As it is our aim to study man and society, we cannot escape searching for parallels. Those who argue for the uniqueness of the Holocaust find comparisons objectionable. But even if their position were correct, comparisons are essential if we are to learn the lessons posed by the Holocaust. However, we have seen that the impulse to exterminate is old and pervasive; we only have to read the newspapers to know that it still exists. In intent and performance Nazi genocide was not unique; in technological efficiency it was sui generis: For the first time a modern industrial state implemented a calculated policy of extermination. Of course, no single historical event duplicates the Nazi deed, but many share different aspects of the process that led to the death camps.

Norman Cohn has shown how mass murder was practiced in medieval Europe, and there are no doubt numerous other historical examples. In modern times the obvious comparison is the attempt to exterminate the Armenians. Without the capabilities of the German state, the Turks uprooted and killed a people that had long lived among them. Their process was an innovation later imitated and improved by the Germans.[43] Another comparison is the treatment of the American Indians by the U.S.

41 Adam, *Judenpolitik im Dritten Reich.*
42 Adler, *Der verwaltete Mensch.*
43 For an introduction, see Franz Werfel, *The Forty Days of Musa Dagh,* trans. Jeoffrey Dunlop (New York: Viking, 1935). Also Michael J. Arlen, *Passage to Ararat* (New York: Farrar, Straus, Giroux, 1975).

government during the nineteenth century. Although the massacres of
Indian men, women, and children occurred on a lawless frontier where
the victims dared to strike back, the intent and the execution were to uproot and kill an entire group.[44] Almost a century later, while waging a
war to liberate Europe from the Nazi yoke, the U.S. government applied
modern technological means to uproot native-born Japanese Americans;
it followed the process of destruction—registration, deportation, incar-
ceration—without the final step of extermination.[45]

In 1959 Stanley Elkins pointed out the parallels between the black
slaves in America and the inmates in the Nazi camps. Although the aims
of slavery were perpetual exploitation, not murder, many experiences
were similar. The fate of the African slaves in the ships transporting them
to the New World was not different from the tortures suffered by millions
on the trains that brought them to the Nazi camps. The dehumanization
of the black slaves compares with that of the inmates in the Nazi and
Stalinist camp systems.[46]

A very recent parallel was the war in Vietnam. Franklin Littell has
argued that "the death camps were built by Ph.D.'s," and the Holocaust
does shake our faith in formal education. Similarly, the barbarism of the
Vietnam war, including its body counts so reminiscent of SS statistics, was
directed by men and women highly educated in the sophisticated uses of
technology, from computer war games to the logistics of aerial combat.[47]

Comparisons, though essential, should not be used indiscriminately.
Unfortunately, there are those who dredge up a large number of apparent parallels to prove that Nazi genocide was not extraordinary; con-
tending that as a subject the Holocaust is "too narrow,"[48] they can avoid
dealing with the murder of the Jews. But comparisons are designed to
make us understand and learn from the Holocaust; they must not be used
to trivialize it.

A final reason why we should teach the Holocaust is that its lessons can

44 See Dee Brown, *Bury My Heart at Wounded Knee* (New York: Holt, Rinehart & Winston,
1970). For a good historical treatment, see Ronald Sander, *Lost Tribes and Promised Lands: The
Origins of American Racism* (Boston: Little, Brown, 1978).

45 See Michi Weglyn, *Years of Infamy: The Untold Story of America's Concentration Camps*
(New York: William Morrow, 1976); John Modell, ed., *The Kikuchi Diary: Chronicle from an
American Concentration Camp* (Urbana, Ill.: University of Illinois Press, 1973); and Miné Okubo,
Citizen 13660 (New York: Columbia University Press, 1946).

46 Stanley M. Elkins, *Slavery*, 2nd ed. (Chicago: University of Chicago Press, 1968).

47 Littell quote from conference in Phoenix, Arizona, 1978. See also Telford Taylor,
Nuremberg and Vietnam (Chicago: Quadrangle, 1970).

48 This was the phrase used by the editor, Albie Burke, of the journal *The History Teacher* (letter of February 23, 1978) rejecting an earlier version of this article.

help us teach civic virtue. Purists may frown on this practice, but to a
large degree this has always been part of education. Of course, I do not
mean that the Holocaust should simply be used to teach conventional patriotism and accepted moral values; instead, its lessons must be used to
demonstrate the need for what the Germans have called *Zivilcourage*. We
need to teach the importance of responsible citizenship and mature
iconoclasm. We must show how the only defense against persecution and
extermination is citizens prepared to oppose the power of the state and
to face the hostility of their neighbors to aid the intended victims.

But if we wish to teach the Holocaust in order to teach civic virtue, we
are forced to universalize it. A good example of this is Peter Weiss's *The
Investigation*, a play about the Auschwitz trial that does not mention
Jews.[49] I can understand why some consider such treatment offensive;
they remember the 1930s and 1940s when the democratic West refused to
recognize the existence of a Jewish people at a time the Nazis killed them
because they were Jews. But Weiss transforms Jews into mankind, not into
Poles or Czechs, to universalize the lessons and the meaning of the
Holocaust.

For some any attempt to universalize the lessons of the Holocaust is
anathema. As we have seen, they consider the Holocaust so unique that
they view all comparisons to parallel situations as a debasement, rejecting
all analogies to past and current racial conflicts as inappropriate. But
perhaps we can agree with the late Arthur Morse in his reply to
Fackenheim at the Jerusalem conference cited above: "It is not necessary
that the analogy be perfect for a young person to hurl himself into peace-
ful combat against what he regards as barbarism. For him that war in
Vietnam or that instance of racial injustice is his Holocaust of the
moment."[50] A few take an even more extreme position. Thus Lucy
Dawidowicz has argued that the Holocaust is a subject that only Jews can
understand and teach.[51] But only in a closed group—Jews teaching
Jews—can the Holocaust retain the particular alone. Certainly this ought
not to be our aim. For this reason it ought to be taught in the major
humanistic disciplines; exile to departments of Judaica spells ghettoiza-
tion for the Holocaust as a subject. The *New York Times* said it succinctly: "Just as the subject of slavery must not be consigned to black studies,
so the gas ovens ought not to be consigned to Jewish studies."[52]

We have seen why we should teach about the Holocaust; we now have

49 Peter Weiss, *The Investigation: Oratorio in 11 Cantos* (London: Calder and Bayars, 1965).
50 Arthur Morse in Fackenheim, *From Bergen-Belsen to Jerusalem*, p. 23.
51 At the meeting of the Modern Language Association, New York, 1976.
52 See note 1.

to decide what ought to be taught when dealing with it. Of course, the preceding discussion of "why" has already shown us the dimensions of "what." And teachers will construct their own curriculum to meet their particular goals. Here we simply need to delineate the essential topics and thus define the circumference of the Holocaust as a subject.

The first topic must be the German historical setting that produced Hitler and the Nazi movement.[53] German and Nazi history is well known and the literature is voluminous. Early interpretations went far back into the German past, to Arminius and Luther, to explain Nazism.[54] Most historians have rejected this sweeping indictment. Some have traced the roots of the Nazi phenomenon to the political, intellectual, and cultural trends in the nineteenth century; others have looked for answers in the political and economic turmoil of the Weimar Republic.[55] The events of 1918–1919 were crucial. The trauma of defeat, the failure of revolution, and the armed struggle between factions doomed the democratic experiment and made the triumph of fascism almost inevitable.[56] In this atmosphere the Nazi movement could grow, prosper, and seize the state. Once in power, Hitler and his cronies transformed Prussian authoritarianism into German totalitarianism.[57]

A second topic must be totalitarianism. There have been many theories to explain the totalitarian phenomenon. They cover the spectrum: from

53 Some textbooks: Marshall Dill, *Germany: A Modern History* (Ann Arbor: University of Michigan Press, 1970); Koppel Pinson, *Modern Germany* (New York: Macmillan, 1966); Golo Mann, *The History of Germany since 1789*, trans. from the German (New York: Praeger, 1968); and Hajo Holborn, *A History of Modern Germany*, 3 vols. (New York: Knopf, 1959-1969).

54 Rohan D'o Butler, *The Roots of National Socialism* (London: Faber and Faber, 1941).

55 For the nineteenth century, see Peter Viereck, *Metapolitics: The Roots of the Nazi Mind* (New York: Capricorn Books, 1961); Fritz Stern, *The Politics of Cultural Despair* (Garden City, N.Y.: Anchor, 1965); George L. Mosse, *The Crisis of German Ideology* (New York: Universal Library, 1964); and A.J.P. Taylor, *The Course of German History* (London: Methuen, 1961). For the Weimar Republic, see Arthur Rosenberg, *The Birth of the German Republic*, trans. Ian F.D. Morrow (London: Oxford University Press, 1931) and *A History of the German Republic*, trans. Ian F.D. Morrow and L. Marie Sieveking (London: Methuen, 1936); William Halperin, *Germany Tried Democracy* (New York: Norton, 1965); Erich Eyck, *A History of the Weimar Republic*, 2 vols. (Cambridge, Mass.: Harvard University Press, 1962-1964); Francis Carsten, *The Reichswehr in Politics* (Oxford: Oxford University Press, 1966); and Karl Dietrich Bracher, *Die Auflösung der Weimarer Republik* (Villingen: Ring Verlag, 1960).

56 See Henry Friedlander, *The German Revolution, 1918-1919* (Ann Arbor: University Microfilms, 1968); also Rudolf Schlesinger, *Central European Democracy and Its Background* (London: Routledge & Kegan Paul, 1953).

57 For the Third Reich, see Karl Dietrich Bracher, *The German Dictatorship*, trans. Jean Steinberg (New York: Praeger, 1970); Karl Dietrich Bracher, Wolfgang Sauer, and Gerhard Schulz, *Die nationalsozialistische Machtergreifung* (Cologne and Opladen: Westdeutscher Verlag, 1962); and Franz Neumann, *Behemoth* (New York: Harper Torchbooks, 1966); also Edward Peterson, *The Limits of Hitler's Power* (Princeton: Princeton University Press, 1969).

Hannah Arendt, who saw it as sui generis in our times, to Karl Wittfogel, who saw it as the last in a line of human despotisms.[58] To explain the origins we must understand the major trends in modern history that led to the triumph of a new kind of authoritarianism of both the right and the left. Nazism was only one manifestation. Like Communism, it was an international ideology. But while Communism, tied to the doctrine of international egalitarianism, became national only with difficulty, Nazism — and fascism in general — was tied to a racial and national doctrine, and thus found it difficult to be international. It attracted not only Germans; many different nationals marched under the swastika. The Nazi leaders considered themselves the vanguard of a European movement, but they usually assumed the roles of leaders of the German Reich. The soldiers and bureaucrats who fought and worked for them only paid lip-service to National Socialist doctrine; they continued to serve because they continued to equate Nazism with the Fatherland. Thus we can equate German and Nazi, something usually done in the study of the Holocaust, only with reservations.

Nazi ideology reflected this polarity. Their racial theory — what Hannah Arendt has called the biological interpretation of history — contained contradictions that were never resolved. Although less elegant and far less respectable than Marxism, racialism fulfilled the same function for the Nazis that Marxism did for the Communists (or that any religion, secular or not, has done for others). Anti-Semitism was only one aspect, though a central one, of this ideology (we must remember that gypsies were also killed in Auschwitz). The racial theory reflected the conflict between Nazi nationalism and internationalism. Ideology demanded that the Nazis prefer the nordic, but their world view required that they recruit others. Thus, while they tended to exclude non-Germans from policy decisions, they allied themselves with the Japanese and raised SS units in every European country. Similar contradictions existed in their views of the Jews. On one level they denounced them as "vermin," totally inferior, who were to be exterminated by gas. On another level they saw them as "devils," a group of extraordinary power, who if not exterminated would take terrible vengeance. Perhaps these contradictions did not matter; Nazism was not a rational ideological system that demanded consistency.

58   On totalitarianism, see Hannah Arendt, *The Origins of Totalitarianism*, 2nd. rev. ed. (New York: Meridian Books, 1958); Karl A. Wittfogel, *Oriental Despotism: A Comparative Study of Total Power* (New Haven: Yale University Press, 1957); and *Totalitarianism*, ed. Carl J. Friedrich (New York: Universal Library, 1964). On fascism, see Ernst Nolte, *Three Faces of Fascism*, trans. from the German (New York: Holt, Rinehart & Winston, 1966); Walter Laqueur and George L. Mosse, eds., *International Fascism* (New York: Harper Torchbooks, 1966); and Hans Rogger and Eugen Weber, eds., *The European Right: A Historical Profile* (Berkeley: University of California Press, 1965).

A third topic must be Jewish history, so that we can understand the victims and their response. Although it is probably not necessary to become familiar with the long course of Jewish history, some knowledge of the Jewish experience in post-Biblical times is desirable. However, to understand why the Jews became the target of Nazi hatred, we must examine the Jewish condition in the modern world.[59] This should not be confused with the investigation of anti-Semitism, which concentrates on the fantasies of the judeophobes; their vision of the Jewish situation had little to do with reality. But a study of Jewish post-Emancipation history will reveal the exposed position of the Jews in European society. To grasp this we must try to understand the struggle over Emancipation, the process of acculturation, and the Jewish participation in cultural and economic life.[60]

Modern Jewish history will also help us to understand Jewish response to Nazi persecution. The Jewish historical experience and the structure of Jewish communal life influenced that response; without knowing this we will never fully understand the life in the Jewish ghettos, the behavior of the Jewish councils, or the nature of Jewish resistance.[61] Of course, answers cannot be monolithic: Jewish experience and Jewish response differed from country to country. Here we can agree with Lucjan Dobroszycki's argument that the Jews in Nazi-dominated Europe could do nothing to alter events; conditions external to their control—the German

---

59   A good textbook is Howard M. Sachar, *The Course of Modern Jewish History* (New York: Delta Books, 1968). For a massive history from ancient times, see Salo Baron, *A Social and Religious History of the Jews*, vols. 1- (Philadelphia: Jewish Publication Society, 1937ff.). For an excellent study of how the Jews were perceived in Christian medieval Europe, see Joshua Trachtenberg, *The Devil and the Jews* (New York: Meridian Books, 1961); for the modern period, see George L. Mosse, *Germans and Jews* (New York: Universal Library, 1970).

60   Jacob Katz, *Out of the Ghetto* (Cambridge: Harvard University Press, 1973); Reinhard Rürup, "Kontinuität und Diskontinuität der 'Judenfrage' im 19. Jahrdundert," in *Sozialgeschichte Heute*, Festschrift für Hans Rosenberg, ed. Hans Ulrich Wehler (Göttingen: Vandenhoecke and Ruprecht, 1974), pp. 387-415; Michael R. Marrus, *The Politics of Assimilation* (New York: Oxford University Press, 1971); Monika Richarz, ed., *Judisches Leben in Deutschland* (Stuttgart: Deutsche Verlagsanstalt, 1976); Werner E. Mosse, ed., *Deutsches Judentum in Krieg und Revolution, 1916-1923* (Tübingen: J.C.B. Mohr [Paul Siebeck], 1971); Werner E. Mosse, ed., *Entscheidungsjahr 1932* (Tübingen: J.C.B. Mohr [Paul Siebeck], 1966); Ismar Schorsch, *Jewish Reactions to German Anti-Semitism* (Philadelphia: Jewish Publication Society, 1972); and Walter Laqueur, *A History of Zionism* (New York: Holt, Rinehart & Winston, 1972).

61   Isaiah Trunk, *Judenrat: The Jewish Councils in Eastern Europe under Nazi Occupation* (New York: Macmillan, 1972). For a specific ghetto, see the excellent study by H.G. Adler, *Theresienstadt 1941-1945: Das Antlitz einer Zwangsgemeinschaft* (Tübingen: J.C.B. Mohr [Paul Siebeck], 1955). For the history of one of the eastern ghettos, see Isaiah Trunk, *Lodzer geto* [Yiddish] (New York: Yivo, 1962); for the history in one specific country, see Jacob Presser, *The Destruction of the Dutch Jews*, trans. Arnold Pomerans (New York: Dutton, 1969).

timetable, the status of the territory, the attitudes of the local population, and the physical geography—determined their fate.[62]

A fourth topic must be the behavior of the bystanders, the reaction of the outside world to the fate of the Jews. Much has been written about this; works by Henry Feingold, Saul Friedländer, Arthur Morse, Alfred Häsler, and Leni Yahil are good examples.[63] Some studies record successful efforts to save Jewish lives; most however describe the failure to rescue Jews before and during the war. And there is evidence that some bystanders, particularly in Eastern Europe, applauded and aided the murder of the Jews. Even the Western democracies refused to intervene. Recently David Wyman analyzed "why the United States rejected requests to bomb the gas chambers and crematoria at Auschwitz, or the railroads leading to Auschwitz." He proved that in the summer of 1944 the Allies had the capability and the opportunity to disrupt the process of destruction; their refusal to do so, at a time when the flames in Birkenau were consuming the Jews from Hungary and the Lodz ghetto, was not based on valid military considerations. Wyman concluded: "That the terrible plight of the Jews did not merit any active response remains a source of wonder, and a lesson, even today."[64]

The fifth and last topic must deal with the Nazi concentration camps, the arena for the Holocaust. This is the "other kingdom" the memoirs describe. But while their names and their most gruesome secrets are now widely known, specific facts about them are still not common knowledge. Confusion about their origin, their history, and their function is widespread; students cannot distinguish between them and usually confuse the various types of camps. Most assume that all were killing centers, and that the methods used at Auschwitz and Treblinka applied also at Dachau and Buchenwald. Although the memoir literature is enormous, few analyses are available; there is still no satisfying history of the Nazi concentration camp system.[65]

62 Paper presented at the Second Western Regional Conference on the Holocaust, San Jose, California, 1978.

63 Henry Feingold, *The Politics of Rescue* (New Brunswick: Rutgers University Press, 1970); Saul Friedländer, *Pius XII and the Third Reich: A Documentation,* trans. from the French and German (New York: Knopf, 1966); Arthur Morse, *While Six Million Died* (New York: Random House, 1967); Alfred Häsler, *The Lifeboat Is Full,* trans. C.L. Markmann (New York: Funk and Wagnalls, 1969); and Leni Yahil, *The Rescue of Danish Jewry,* trans. from the Hebrew (Philadelphia: Jewish Publication Society, 1969).

64 David Wyman, "Why Auschwitz Was Never Bombed," *Commentary* 65 (May 1978): 37-46.

65 For a survey, see Martin Broszat, "Nationalsozialistische Konzentrationslager 1933-1945," in Helmut Krausnick et al., *Anatomy des SS-Staates,* vol. II (Munich: DTV, 1967) (for English translation, see above note 27). See also Henry Friedlander, "The Concentration Camps: History, Analysis,

142

The best general accounts are still the semi-memoirs by Kogon and Kautsky. Eugen Kogon was imprisoned in Buchenwald for six years as an Austrian anti-Nazi. He originally wrote his analysis for the U.S. Army after liberation; although Buchenwald-centered, it provides a good survey of the camp system. Benedikt Kautsky was the partly Jewish son of the famous Marxist theoretician; he was incarcerated as a Jew in Buchenwald for four years, but was "reclassified" as a non-Jew after his transfer to Auschwitz. His analysis of the camps treats the system, the SS, and the inmates.[66] In addition, there are scholarly studies of individual camps; reports and memoirs about almost all camps; analyses of camp economics; and investigations of the behavior of the inmates.[67]

Almost immediately after the seizure of power in January 1933, the Nazis created the concentration camps (*Konzentrationslager*, officially abbreviated as KL and unofficially as KZ). The earliest camps were *ad hoc* creations by the brown-shirted SA storm troopers. Located in jails, offices, factories, and other makeshift locations, they were places where the Nazis settled accounts with their political enemies. All were dissolved after several years. The first permanent camp, established by the SS in 1933, was KL Dachau near Munich. After the SS seized control of all camps and moved to regularize the system, Dachau became the model for all other camps, the training ground for generations of camp commanders. At first expansion was slow: KL Sachsenhausen was established near Berlin in 1936, KL Buchenwald near Weimar in 1937. During 1938-1939 more were added: KL Mauthausen in annexed Austria, KL Neuengamme near Hamburg, and the women's KL Ravensbrück near Berlin. Early in the war, more camps were established: in 1941-1942 KL

Sources," in *Third Philadelphia Conference on the Holocaust*, ed. Josephine Knopp (Philadelphia: Institute of the Holocaust, Temple University, 1978).

66 Eugen Kogon, *Der SS Staat: Das System der deutschen Konzentrationslager* (Munich: Verlag Karl Alber, 1964; English translation *The Theory and Practice of Hell* [New York: Berkley Publishing Corp., 1950]); and Benedikt Kautsky, *Teufel und Verdammte* (Zurich: Büchergilde Gutenberg, 1946; English translation *Devils and the Damned* [London: Brown and Watson, 1960]).

67 *Studien zur Geschichte der Konzentrationslager*, Schriftenreihe der Vierteljahrshefte für Zeitgeschichte, no. 21 (Stuttgart: Institut für Zeitgeschichte, 1970); Eberhard Kolb, *Bergen-Belsen: Geschichte des "Aufenthaltslagers" 1943-1945* (Hanover: Verlag für Literatur und Zeitgeschehen, 1962); Cohen, *Human Behavior in the Concentration Camps;* Joseph Billig, *L'Hitlerisme et le systeme concentrationaire* (Paris: Presses Universitaires de France, 1967); *De L'Université aux camps de concentration: Témoignages Strasbourgeois* (Paris: Societé d'Edition "Les Belles Lettres," 1947); Enno Georg, *Die wirtschaftlichen Unternehmungen der SS* (Stuttgart: Deutsche Verlagsanstalt, 1963); Joseph Billig, *Les camps de concentration dans l'economie du Reich Hitlerien* (Paris: Presses Universitaire de France, 1973); and Ota Kraus and Erich Kulka, *Massenmord und Profit: Die faschistische Ausrottungspolitik und ihre ökonomischen Hintergründe*, trans. Hanna Tichy (East Berlin: Dietz, 1963).

Gross-Rosen in Silesia, KL Stutthof in West Prussia, and KL Natzweiler in Alsace; in 1944 KL Dora-Mittelbau in Saxony. These were the main concentration camps, the so-called *Stammlager*.

At first the camps contained only the political enemies of the regime; to these were soon added nonpolitical groups: professional criminals, homosexuals, religious dissenters, and other so-called asocial elements. Jews were incarcerated only if they also belonged to one of these groups; as Jews they entered the camps in large numbers only after *Krystallnacht* in 1938, but most of these were eventually released and forced to leave Germany. The Gestapo and the criminal police (later part of the central office for national security, the RSHA) delivered the prisoners to the camps; the administration of the camps was under the KL Inspectorate, and the guards came from the SS death-head units. Theodor Eicke, the first Dachau commander, served as inspector and developed the system. Its aim was punishment and "reeducation"; labor was used as a form of torture. The system was based on extreme brutality, and a total disregard for human life. Each national camp system reflects its own traditions; unlike the Russian system, the German camps used military discipline as a form of control and torture. They were a caricature of a noncom's view of army life: the symmetry of barracks, flowers and trees, music and singing, marching and roll call, standing at attention. For punishment and torture the SS preferred physical activity: calisthenics, beatings, exhausting labor.

During the war this changed. Political opponents and resistance fighters from all European countries swelled the camp population; Jews who at first were confined to the ghettos, labor camps, and killing centers of the East later also flooded the camp system. While the size made the camps less manageable, the needs of the war economy made the labor of the inmates more valuable. The camps came to resemble the Soviet model where malnutrition, exposure, and death through labor took the place of capricious torture. Under Eicke's successor Richard Glücks, the KL Inspectorate became part of Oswald Pohl's economic empire, the SS central office for economy and administration or WVHA. Still, the old structure—roll calls, beatings—was always retained. Each *Stammlager* eventually headed numerous subsidiary camps; these covered Germany and a simple list fills a massive volume.[68] The camps became a world apart; the French called them *l'universe concentrationaire*.

68 Comité International de la Croix-Rouge, International Tracing Service, *Vorläufiges Verzeichnis der Konzentrationslager und deren Aussenkommandos, sowie anderer Haftstätten unter dem RF-SS in Deutschland und deutsch besetzten Gebieten, 1933-1945* (Arolsen, February 1969).

This system spawned the killing centers.[69] They were staffed by death-head units and commanded by Eicke's students. The three large camps in eastern Poland—Treblinka, Belzec, Sobibor—were operated by the local SS and Police chief Odilo Globocnik as part of Operation Reinhard; the one in western Poland—Chelmno (Kulmhof)—was run by a special *Einsatzkommando*. The techniques they used came from the experiences of the commandos that murdered the Jews in Russia and killed the ill in the so-called Euthanasia Program.[70] But the methods of running the camps came from the concentration camp system established in 1933. This helps to explain why the procedure of death by gas, introduced not only for efficiency and speed but also because it was considered more "humane" than shooting, was everywhere accompanied by dehumanization and brutality.

The death camps were surrounded by many smaller camps. These were *ad hoc* installations where conditions varied; some were forced-labor camps and some also smaller killing centers: The Janowska camp in Lemberg and camp Trawniki near Lublin are good examples.[71] No such camps existed in the west; but there the Nazis established transfer camps, antechambers for the killing centers: Westerbork in Holland; Malines in Belgium; Drancy and Pithiviers in occupied France. The worst conditions obtained in the camps operated by the French authorities in Vichy France at Les Milles, Rivesaltes, and Gurs.[72]

Two death camps—KL Auschwitz-Birkenau and KL Lublin-Maj-

69 Ino Arndt and Wolfgang Scheffler, "Organisierter Massenmord an Juden in nationalsozialistischen Vernichtungslagern," *Vierteljahrshefte für Zeitgeschichte* 24 (1976): 105-35; and Adalbert Rückerl, ed., *NS-Vernichtungslager im Spiegel deutscher Strafprozesse* (Munich: DTV, 1977). See also Central Commission for Investigation of German Crimes in Poland, *German Crimes in Poland*, vol. I (Warsaw, 1946); Leon Poliakov, *Auschwitz* (Paris: Julliard Collection Archives, 1964); Jean-Francois Steiner, *Treblinka*, documentary novel trans. from the French (New York: Simon and Schuster, 1967); Bernd Naumann, *Auschwitz: Bericht über die Strafsache gegen Mulka u.a. vor dem Schwurgericht Frankfurt* (Frankfort on the Main: Fischer Bücherei, 1968). "Killing Center" is Hilberg's term.

70 Rückerl, *NS-Vernichtungslager*; Hilberg, *The Destruction of the European Jews*, chap. 7; Joseph Tenenbaum, "The Einsatzgruppen," *Jewish Social Studies* 17 (1955): 43-64; Helmut Ehrhardt, *Euthanaisie und Vernichtung "lebensunwerten" Lebens* (Stuttgart: Euke, 1965); Klaus Dörner, "Nationalsozialismus und Lebensvernichtung," *Vierteljahrshefte für Zeitgeschichte* 15 (1967): 121-52; and Lothar Gruchmann, "Euthanasie und Justiz im Dritten Reich," ibid. 20 (1972): 235-79.

71 Arnold Hindls, *Einer kehrte zurück; Bericht eines Deportierten* (Stuttgart: Deutsche Verlagsanstalt, 1965; Publication of the Leo Baeck Institute); and Leon Weliczker Wells, *The Janowska Road* (New York: Macmillan, 1963).

72 Georges Wellers, *De Drancy à Auschwitz* (Paris: Edition du Centre, 1946); Joseph Weill, *Contribution à l'histoire des camps d'interment dans l'Anti-France* (Paris: Edition du Centre, 1946); and Hanna Schramm, *Menschen in Gurs: Erinnerungen an ein französisches Internierungslager, 1940-1941*, mit einem dokumentarischen Beitrag zur französischen Emigrantenpolitik, 1933-1944, von Barbara Vormeier (Worms: G. Heintz, 1977).

danek — were administered by WVHA and became an integrated part of the concentration camp system, combining in perfect balance the methods of total control with the procedures of mass murder. The most important of these, the largest of all extermination and concentration camps, was Auschwitz in Upper Silesia. Established as a concentration camp in 1940 with the function of killing center added in 1941, it eventually became a huge enterprise, the center of many subsidiary camps. Divided into three parts, it swallowed millions of victims. Camp I was the *Stammlager* at Auschwitz; camp II was the killing center at Birkenau; camp III was the BUNA industrial complex at Monowitz.

We have discussed the reasons why the Holocaust ought to be taught and have attempted to outline the topics any treatment ought to include. But while teachers must master the materials, not all students should or could profit from an intensive study of the Holocaust. A detailed investigation along the lines indicated above is obviously designed only for those who have a professional interest in the Holocaust or one of its facets. College students majoring in history or one of the social sciences ought to become familiar with the details; graduate and professional education should also include appropriate aspects of the Holocaust. Thus medical students can investigate it as part of their concern for questions of biomedical ethics; law students can study it to understand bureaucracy, administrative law, and the perversion of justice.

Most students are not professionally interested in the Holocaust. If they care about it at all, they come to it for various reasons: self-identity, moral commitment, concern with contemporary issues, and so forth. For them a specialized approach might not be appropriate. Here the problems and topics we have outlined could be covered in a less systematic fashion. Thus a study of the literature of the Holocaust could serve as a springboard for analysis.[73] Using various readings — memoirs, novels, plays, essays — students can engage in a semistructured discussion of the issues raised by the Holocaust. The growing number of books containing art from and about the Holocaust can serve as a visual supplement to the readings.[74] And as with literature and art, films about the Holocaust can become the focus for discussion and analysis. Films add immediacy for a generation born after 1945. Of course, one must be careful about the films one shows; too much visual horror can obscure understanding. A film like *Night and Fog* ought to be shown only after careful preparation

73   Lawrence Langer, *The Holocaust and the Literary Imagination* (New Haven: Yale University Press, 1975).
74   Sybil Milton, "Concentration Camp Art and Artists," *Shoah* 1, no. 2 (Fall 1978): 10-15.

to students who have already obtained some information; it must not be used as a shock treatment to arouse interest.[75] In addition to the excellent documentaries, like the BBC films *Genocide* and *The Warsaw Ghetto*, there is also a growing number of superior commercial films: De Sica's *Garden of the Finzi-Contini* is a sensitive study of human response, while Costa-Gravas's *Special Sections* is a penetrating study of bureaucracy and the process of destruction.

75   For an example of this unfortunate approach, see Roselle Chartock, "A Holocaust Unit for Classroom Teachers," *Social Education* 42 (April 1978): 278-85.

Hat and Cup in Hand: Political Pliancy and the Loss of Leisure in Universities

SEBASTIAN DE GRAZIA

Eagleton Institute of Politics, Rutgers University

At the onset of World War I the public grammar and high schools performed their task of instilling civic virtue and pride of country (teacher to class each morning: "We will now recite the Lord's Prayer and the Pledge of Allegiance"), and imparting more or less rudimentary skills of literacy and numbers (the 3-R's plus). The universities, supported by private gifts, choosing students by tuition, by family to some extent, and by contemporary signs of intelligence, illumined the panorama of man's past, presented the state of present knowledge in liberal studies, and extended the reach of man's intellect. And Thomas Edison wrote to the Navy Department suggesting it might be a good idea to hire a mathematician.

Today the government's scientific programs, mathematical and others, run into billions of dollars. The public grammar and high schools still perform their functions of instilling civic virtue and teaching elementary skills. But the universities, now supported more by governmental than by private grants and choosing students by contemporary signs of intelligence and by politically imposed aims of equality of opportunity and of postponement of labor-force entry, offer programs heavily weighted for the job market and in the applied sciences. Seemingly freer of outside pressure than in the so-called bourgeois universities preceding them, the curricula in the universities must pass under a yoke of vocational and government utilitarianism, the federal government pushing them on the military and political side, the state and local governments on political and current problems.

In 1957 the students of the University of Accra gave a performance of an ancient Greek play in the language of ancient Greece. An effort less related to the then needs and problems of Ghana would have been hard to imagine. The centuries-old universities of London, Oxford, and Cambridge out of which the University of Accra drew inspiration had put on Greek plays in ancient Greek many times, through efforts no less Herculean than that in Ghana, perhaps, and no more closely related to the problems and needs of Britain.

What is wrong with seeking and storing knowledge to apply or relate to problems? Nothing wrong, generally. It is one of the vital and vast enterprises of mankind, or of animal kind, or of all living things. You focus on a problem; you have before you a slice on a slide. You look on the world with intent: to solve that problem. Knowledge and its pursuit must pertain to that problem. In every land in the world the seeking and accumulating of such knowledge is a constant concern and endeavor. But if the university signifies objectivity in the pursuit of knowledge, application to problem solving is unwelcome; it brings on tunnel vision. Design on the world gives a fractionalized view.

All sciences talk of objectivity as desirable. Some say they have it, at least in comparison with others. Why it should be more possible in the sciences than in any other field of learning is not made clear. Awareness of bias is supposed to help, but the only painless way to objectivity seems to be teaching by bad examples, namely giving students historical cases of partiality and superstition. The idea of freedom from necessity or of knowledge for its own sake implies no purpose, exploitative or utilitarian or otherwise, on objects or persons in sight. J. H. Newman described it as "independent of sequel." Compared to this detachment, modern science seems not really serious about objectivity.

In the ideal of leisure the relation, if any, of knowledge to problems and needs is accidental; knowledge is to be sought for its own sake. This requirement the universities once satisfied with the classical or liberal arts or general curriculum, which has no utilitarian or vocational purpose. The state of leisure implies an assured wherewithal, full freedom from workaday necessity. This condition the universities provided with an American invention, the assurance to faculty of indefinite tenure: No professor need fear loss of provender for expression of his views or need work on practical problems in order to make a living.

Both requirements must be satisfied. The judges and justices of the courts of the United States have by the Constitution (Article III) been assured "during good Behavior" the lifelong wherewithal, "a Compensation, which shall not be diminished during their Continuance in Office," to provide them the conditions of objectivity and outspokenness. But they are bound by oath to consider the cases in law under the Constitution that come before them or that they ask to review. Clergymen often have a lifelong wherewithal but except under circumstances whereby churches may house scholars and scientists—unusual today but not uncommon in other times—their clerical duties leave them little room for knowledge for its own sake. A few rather ordinary persons—very different from you and me—have money enough themselves for a lifelong wherewithal: They may lack the love of knowledge for its own sake. Many, many other persons have what they call "leisure" but it fits neither requirement. They have free time, those daily hours salvaged from work time, that negative freedom, temporary release from work. The universities, though, through curriculum, tenure, and the classical literature that transmits the ideal, did help preserve leisure in a world about to exchange it for the chase after free time, in a world where the life free of workaday necessity was becoming harder and harder to achieve.

Writings on the life of leisure afford the wherewithal small notice. As the well-off and the noble were the main groups in which the leisure kind customarily found its fellows, the problem did not often appear. History reveals three or four main ways of keeping alive without work. Property in land or buildings is one. A system of tenant farming or of renting may call for little effort on the part of the owner. Tenant farming supported the Florentine villa as well as the *villula* in the Sabine countryside where Horace lived and ruled, and where so many leading colonial Americans from New England down to New Orleans set their dreams on location. Property in persons (slaves) or in human energy (workers) is another, somewhat more onerous, means of lightening the press of the everyday world. Property in quantity in stocks and bonds can also provide for an adequate income without work. The method proposed by Plato, that the state provide the necessities for a class of philosophers, draws upon a wider base. He secures room and board by having the government provide for it in taxes. This is the method governments favor today but in terms, as we shall see, that make the conditions of leisure impossible.

Lastly, there is the way of asceticism. Man in a friendly climate can keep alive on very little, pratically nothing but water and a few nuts or grains. Given a country sympathetic to both contemplation and asceticism, one can stay alive by eating wild plants or begging a bowl of cereal when hungry, as priests still do in Southeast Asia. Even for the Greeks, it was acceptable to reduce your desires and get along the best you could, perhaps with a handout from friends or strangers every now and then. Since they did not believe in the mortification of the flesh, the possession of what would today be called unearned income was almost essential. Agreed: The mortification of the flesh is unnatural and perverts the senses. Not many professors mortify the flesh, I should guess; yet on the average, faculty prebends rarely reach the salaries and fees of the professions of law and medicine. Remember the definition of a liberal education as that which enables you to despise the money it prevents you from earning? This fits the case. Moderation but not asceticism nor ecclesiastical poverty.

None of these methods are perfect. Their imperfection uncovers man's ties to the animal world. Man does not live by angel food alone. Like the animals, he must feed and take shelter. The methods above merely approximate the ideal of leisure by making a man's sources of support remote and reliable, difficult of being affected by anything but extraordinary disturbances, as it were, in trust. *Au fond*, the sources, no matter how secure, are dependent on the stability of a regime, and thus ever a possible threat — hopefully distant — to objectivity.

The university's tenure is nearly the last possibility left of being free of everyday necessity. In recent times it has still been able to keep this requirement of the leisure ideal only because teaching and research now fall in the category of work, and "We all must work, you know," as we truly do when teaching and research become problem-dictated. The university, insofar as it fulfilled both requirements, furthered the theoretical life, the *bios theoretikos*, a life exploiting the part of man that makes him distinctive in the animal world, the life of the mind.

Grosso modo, this was the situation when Edison made his suggestion to the Navy. How did the change come about? The oldest universities in the United States, true, had their roots in the vocations of theology and law; yet with time these schools began to conceive their program of studies as building upon a curriculum in the colleges of liberal arts or arts and letters or arts and sciences, however they were called or actually approximated. How then did we get the idea that the universities had to apply their mansions of knowledge to solutions of current problems? In the United States, and I take as my task principally the predicament of the United States, the reasons for the change can be grouped into two main factors: the intensification of a peculiar conception of work and a revolution in the nature of warfare, both mediated through the assumption of responsibility by government as prime mover.

The United States has developed an original political system whereby one's job confers one's primary status. Everyone is a citizen; not everyone has a job. If you have a job, it matters little that you are a citizen. To maintain the system, more and more activities have to be poured into the maw labeled "Work" so that by and by nothing one does falls outside. Whether work should be resegregated or not is a question with far-reaching implications. Should one try to save the existing system by carrying it to its logical conclusion of a Work Society, or should one try to find a way out of the obsession that work should be the country's ruling passion rather than the theater, love, God, family, war, or none or all of these? Today all literature on the general subject of work gets trapped in the rhetoric of the fray.

For contrast one may be allowed an example from outside the country. In a novel of some twenty-five years ago, *Paolo il Caldo*, by Vitaliano Brancati, the hero, a young man, is out one day walking with his uncle and hears himself being advised to leave off his advanced studies. "To devote myself to what?" he asks. "To leisure, my dear boy, to the most complete leisure." comes the answer.

> The most beautiful thing in life is to do nothing. And liberty signifies to be able to live doing nothing. This is true liberty. The rest is lies of the moralists. They've all reached an understanding, proprietors, priests, generals and communists, that it is necessary to tell people that work ennobles life, and to tell soldiers that to die is beautiful. And I am aware that it is useful to say this to the masses, because otherwise no one would wish to work and no one to get himself killed. But between us, let's speak the truth; beautiful is to live and not die, beautiful is to dispose at complete pleasure of one's own day and not to work. A dead man, for whatever reason he may be dead, is a stinking corpse, and a man that works is a slave. The communists want to free the farmers and the workers. How? Making them work for themselves. But the true liberation is to make them not work. I understand that this is not possible for everybody. Agreed . . . In this world we will amuse ourselves still for a few years; then an eternal service to work will begin. One will see files of slaves with a smile on their lips, because they have to bear witness that it is true that which the moralists, their bosses, have said, that is, that work is the joy of life. . . . Look at me carefully: I am perhaps the last free man that will die free. You . . . I don't know whether as an older man you will be forced to make yourself useful, which is to say, to live for others and to die for yourself. But as things stand today, you are master of your day.

Whether one considers this reflection of leisure honest or extreme, the tradition in the United States now appears weak and faint. Let us look at the ideal of work, education, and leisure in a recent report initiated by the federal government.

On December 19, 1971, the Secretary of Health, Education, and Welfare (HEW) charged a "task force" (why not "study group"?) with "examining health, education, and welfare problems from the perspective of one of our fundamental social institutions — work." The secretary in his foreword remarked that he asked for the report because he thought the subject was vitally important to much of what HEW does and because the president in his Labor Day address several months earlier said that "the most important part of the quality of life is the quality of work, and the new need for job satisfaction is the key to the quality of work."

The report, published as *Work in America* by the MIT Press in 1973, refers airily to the work ethic as though it were a superstition one should outgrow with one's second teeth. Yet you would have to return to Samuel Smiles, Poor Richard, Horatio Alger, and the monastic orders to find such a richly embroidered version of the Work Society. It even improves on the idea of competition: Workers now should compete not with others but "with themselves over time." The complete individuals can learn to covenant with their inner selves in schools. As a matter of fact, schools — the last remaining redoubt of nonwork activity — have to be captured. They should be looked on as workplaces like any other workplaces, "influenced by and influencing other workplaces." There should be universal manpower training. "Also, if we all could type . . . ."

It is hardly bearable to have to tell what the curriculum of the new lifelong schools is going to be. There will be "Information-rich Alternatives," for which the authors can cite only two examples: courses in "Institutional Management and Administration" and "Entrepreneurial Skills." The rich information is to be added as part of a "general education" for work, the rest consisting of what appears to be the three R's — "enhancing the young person's reading comprehension, arithmetical skills, and the ability to write and speak clearly," plus one: "the capacity for working closely with other people." The authors added, "We seem to have forgotten that these skills are the ones most sought after by employers."

After the general education for work, information-rich, the curriculum swings over into "Action-Rich Alternatives." Here one is to learn "a set of skills that the students can use while they are taking the course or ones they will need no matter what jobs they eventually take." The set of skills (and it must be admitted that they will prove useful) are first, for young women to learn how a car operates and how it is repaired; for a young man, how to cook. Then there is "learning to use tools," which would seem to be the old manual training courses. "Other skills, such as how to prepare one's income tax forms, how to go about buying a house, and how to be an effective consumer are practical skills that can be utilized in whatever career one chooses." To these should be added the universal typing courses alluded to before (which may make manufacturers of typewriters satisfied with *their* jobs). Also, "concepts" from such "academic" subjects as "mathematics and physics could be integrated with a work-related curriculum." So much for the Action-Rich Alternatives, except to add the part-school, part-job programs, which distinction will eventually disappear, since the programs will undoubtedly help speed up the school-places' transformation into workplaces.

But why, above, were quotation marks put around "academic"? Because everything is either work-related or academic. In the real world the hero is the Satisfied Worker (caps sic). Work in *Work in America* is the ultimate reality to which all shadows eventually must return for their *Urstoff*. "Every worker is a teacher and every workplace is a school, not because of the skills that one may impart, nor the organization or technology that is apparent in the other, but because they deal with the real world and man's mastery therein." So fierce is its focus on work, the report did not dream of considering alternative directions for America. The new cloud-cuckooland it depicts goes beyond the Work Society into the workhouse. Leisure, which offhand one might suspect to have some bearing on health, education, and welfare, not to mention on work, gets a single reference in the index. "Leisure, boredom in, 88."

After one reads this, the book quoted before it seems more prophetic than extreme. On receipt of such information- and action-rich products from the lower schools, what can the universities do to preserve the leisure ideal? They will have their hands full transforming themselves into workplaces. As of now, may luck be praised, the universities are *not* receiving the ten-o'clock scholars of that curriculum. Nevertheless the universities in the United States have long ago accepted vocational training as part of grateful service to the state. The Civil War period was a landmark. Senator Morrill's bill stipulated that the proceeds from "landscrip" were to be spent on the establishment and maintenance of one or more colleges in each state where instruction should be given in agriculture and the mechanical arts. As these schools developed (sometimes it took a hundred years) they became more liberal and scientific (for liberal studies had not been prohibited). Their initial practical and technical character was later strengthened by large congressional appropriations for experiment stations in the sciences related to agriculture.

Occupational courses and programs in universities proliferated mindlessly. In recent decades they have been used to lure youth, without noticeable bent for continued study, away from years of gainful employment. So necessary seemed going to university to get "a better job," and so important in the United States is a better job, that limited access to universities was soon viewed as a barrier to opportunity. The universities consequently became the targets of demands for equal access from groups who could claim that they had had an unfair history of inferior jobs and as a result inferior social mobility and status. In time persons of somewhat

greater means pressed the complaint with legislators that subsidy to anyone if it did not include them would begin to make *their* history unfair.
Age of college coinciding as it now does with age of voting, congressmen
paid heed to them, too.

In response the federal government applied the various temptations
and pressures at its disposal, in essence the offer of money or deprivation
thereof, and the universities with rare exceptions complied. The state
government, long experienced with the Morrill Act and constantly concerned with local employment, found it easy to follow the federal government's urging, and indeed to insist on its own needs' being taken care of.
The universities built hundreds of new campuses, hired thousands of new
professors, accommodated millions of new students, fattened staffs,
fooled with curricula, tacked on research programs, and opened up service stations not just for students but for neighborhoods, communities,
and local, state, and federal agencies.

What was there to marvel at when a few years ago the president of Harvard University reported that "the government has shown increasing signs
of acting in questionable ways to regulate the principal academic functions" of universities? A recent "seminar" of faculty (assembled by the
American Association of University Professors) and state legislators of
New Jersey arrived at this summation (in the *N.J. AAUP,* Fall 1978):

> The clearest concern of the educators present was the increasing state
> control of academic affairs. Among the legislators the concern was that
> the higher education community be able to justify their calls for fund-
> ing by providing demonstrable service to the state.

He who rides on my cart, counsels the Russian proverb, sings my song.

Related to this providing of demonstrable service to the state is the federal government's drawing on the universities for militarily oriented programs. Historically, the importance of university science to warfare has
not been ignored—in ballistics the trajectory arches from Archimedes the
sand-scribbler to Galileo the stargazer—but the connection was sporadic,
depending often on prevailing military technology. Not all states at war
have exploited the university's gathering of scientists. When they have,
they have typically reverted at war's end to antebellum practice. The
character of warfare inaugurated by nuclear weapons removed this possibility for the United States. After World War II demobilization and re-
conversion did occur, briefly. With the advent of the cold war the occasion disappeared.

We are no longer in a cold war; our plight now can best be described as
a state of seige. At one level there are the demands of readiness for so-

called conventional operations for Europe, Africa, and "the little wars in Asia" (Plautus). At the most strategic level lies the continuous readiness for all-out warfare. Just to avoid this warfare, we are fully mobilized and must stay fully mobilized. Readiness implicates the mobilization of research and development and trained technical personnel. Heavy support for nuclear research in the university went into full swing in 1940 (upon Albert Einstein's second letter to President F. D. Roosevelt), quickly achieving at the University of Chicago the first nuclear chain reaction. Today, forty years later, close to 90 percent of all federal research and development funds issues from three militarily based sources — the Atomic Energy Commission, the National Aeronautics and Space Agency, and the Department of Defense.

At the onset of World War II the United States decided to take advantage of colleges and universities for purposes of military research and the war training of technical personal in science, engineering, and management — rather than build new federal training and research facilities. It was a war decision that was to prove momentous for the postwar period. The universities were to become total institutions. They were to embody the growing national faith in the systematic application of aggregated brains to problems.

The portent of this is that the universities, already deeply penetrated by government, are caught in the state of seige, too. The federal government, in one way or another, will hold out money to them indefinitely. Whenever the question of "for how long?" was raised during wartime the reply used to be, "For the duration." There is no more a for-the-duration in ·the money that universities will be offered for research and development and programs of courses. A current sentiment echoed in a recent report of the Committee for Economic Development on nuclear policy (1976) is that the United States has "no choice" but to maintain technological leadership.

Money is hard to refuse. Today's universities are no exception to the rule. They let the government pull and squeeze them like an accordion, to be discarded when the bellows spring a leak, or to be patched with scotch tape. The support the government gives them is in the form of money earmarked (or restricted or categorized) for short-term research or teaching or for long-run buildings and equipment. The consequence: Universities are kept tilted over with masonry and faculty that they have committed themselves to maintain. They start up and phase out, as the winds of government priorities blow. In seducing them the government, in truth, made no promise of marriage.

The educational scene would be incomplete without the foundations.

To their credit they have one accomplishment: They have distributed money to centers other than campuses; perforce, else the original donor might have given it to universities himself, without the help of such elaborate middlemen. When the foundations go through universities, their attempts to solve social, nutritional, and health difficulties, both domestic and foreign, further burden the universities with problem-related research, courses, and faculty. Their support through short-run grants, often made conditional on matching grants or acquisition of new faculty, simply compounds the harm of government aid and deepens the entrapment in applied science.

So the universities come, month in, month out, hat and cap in hand, for the money to keep their curriculum lopsided with programs in applied science; to maintain the buildings they no longer need (now that the baby-boom is over, now that the bubble of "to get a better job" is pricked); to sustain the misplaced faculty and misguided students they are burdened with; to pick their way through the minefields of laws and regulations; and to hear themselves rebuked for keeping faculty on tenure and for dissipating public monies.

Is it any wonder that the vision of university presidents extends to their nose? Their function along with their "development offices" is to be ingratiating, to trek to Washington and state capitols, to importune legislators and government departments. The more successful they are, the stronger is their administration. The faculties' role is passive except to help in drawing up projects for getting money and to lay whatever weight they can, through their professional societies and lobbies, on the same legislators and government departments. Faculty in their meetings talk of servicing clienteles; they sound like stud farmers. Or else they devise curricula to corner job opportunities for graduate students; they sound like marketing analysts. If asked, why not forget the jobs and get down to framing a curriculum, they respond reasonably enough, "How can we then in good conscience go on recruiting students?" Faculty is now in the business of human capital formation.

The bourgeois university, for all the old grads' delight in winning football teams, was never like this. Though cluttered by grading and occasionally flicked by the reaction of trustees to anticapitalist ideas, the curriculum remained comparatively free of outside interference. The private patron, it will be noted, is out of the scene. As income and inheritance taxes channel his money to government or constrain him to give it to foundations, his amateur standing is supplanted by the best and brightest specialists, the foundation executives. These kings of the knowledge heaps sit in their rich halls and daily review the procession of petitioners.

They are not kings, though; they are powerful vassals whose lord is the government.

Out of this appears a bleak future for the leisure ideal. The universities will shrink. Private patrons dwindling, high school graduates dropping, price per barrel of oil rising—there seems little alternative. The easy way out will be to eliminate faculty tenure, put those who work on political, military, or work-related grants or contracts in padded problem-boxes with wall-to-wall carpeting, and continue to call them universities. A department of education or other government agency can coordinate their activities and manipulate the purse strings according to fluctuating priorities.

Government, like labor and industry, is interested in education as a means to other ends. It is fitting that a government bureau supervise this "education." On its executive board or interagency council should sit representatives of those other government agencies implicated in what passes for the higher learning. Just to list some of them is instructive of the ends that universities serve for the government: the National Aeronautics and Space Agency, the Atomic Energy Commission, the National Science Foundation, the Veteran's Administration, the Office for Civil Rights, the Equal Employment Opportunity Commission, the National Institutes of Health, the Social Security Administration, the Departments of Defense, Labor, Energy, Agriculture, and so on. The list is far from complete. (And representatives are not included of the professional societies, of labor, industry, telecommunications, microprocessing, and so on into the private sphere.) Were all these special interests and aims taken away, the residue might be a university.

Understandably enough, scholars and scientists want to stay in universities. They know by instinct that leisure lurks there and if there is a chance anywhere of doing what they love to do, there they will be able to find it. Government and industry have taken notice of this scientific penchant for leisure. Strewn about the country are intellectual hot-houses, centers and institutes for "research" (not to be confused with "study") where there are no teaching duties or money worries or housing worries, no noise or ugly surroundings, no obligations to write or produce. Sprinkling with dollar bills makes the plants grow.

There may be an institute or two that is more of a university than most universities. Were its span of studies greater, the Institute of Advanced Studies (as of 1978) would be one. I know of no other example. These other thoughteries typically offer a sham leisure. Scholars and scientists have to stay put in one place; in film parlance, they are on set, confined to the premises, until the project is canned. They used to be dubbed "shangri-la's"; their current nickname is "think-tanks," which nicely expresses their constraint. The denizens swim around, not in the sea, but in a tank. Whatever these fish do is called "work," to be sure, "research work." So they do feel under pressure "to produce" even though it is not required in writing in their limited contract, and to produce something with which their patron is intensely concerned to extract, most often to provide something of "demonstrable service to the state," something improving our military posture or contributing to our "technological leadership."

But if the shrinkage is taken with courage, it may be a boon. Holding as their guide the restoration of the leisure ideal, the universities should defend the liberal arts as the heartland. Separate the institutes and professional training schools from graduate schools. Set them free to win their own status. Universities need not and should not be the only centers of intellectual endeavor. John Marshall spent six weeks in Judge Reeves's law school. Let business apprentice businessmen: Chase-Manhattan does it. Let government apprentice bureaucrats: the Civil Service Commission will be glad to take on more in-service training; so will government departments like Agriculture. The Plumbers' Union has been apprenticing plumbers for years. Hospitals take in interns. Let applied scientists apprentice their aspirants.

Francis Bacon wrote that knowledge is power. He omitted an adjective. *Applied* knowledge is power. Let it stay with the applied scientists. The applied-scientist-as-hero seems better designed for American literature than the professor-as-hero. Let government and problem-related money flow to institutes, academies, seminaries, centers, and professional training schools of their own or industrial sponsorship. They can do the job better. Keep graduate schools for advanced theoretical studies in all fields of knowledge — biology, jurisprudence, mathematics, history, physics, theology, music, philosophy, languages and letters, and others covered by the curriculum of liberal arts. If certain graduate studies (or "basic researches") turn out to have applied value, the technological institutes will pick them up, never fear. The instrumentation chaps will drop in for tea with the basic guys, and vice versa. ("Which'll it be, your pad or mine?")

C. P. Snow deplored the separation of science and the humanities as two cultures. He might have divided them differently. There do exist the applied and the theoretical, never necessarily distinct, but two distinct cultures nevertheless. Keep graduate schools theoretical by selling all heavy scholarly and scientific machinery and laboratory equipment. Machines cost time and money, focus attention and quickly obsolesce. The great theoretical advances (which will obsolesce slowly) in nuclear physics prior to World War II could have been achieved, without huge laboratories or budgets, by scientists thinking about billiard balls or playing with orange peels, matchsticks, and tinfoil. One does not need machinery to be an empiricist, an experimentalist, or a pragmatist. If professors want a typewriter or computer, let them acquire it themselves. Galileo and Newton built their own telescopes, though the scientific good they got out of them was less than the enthusiam they put into them. John Dewey typed his own letters, badly to be sure, on his own typewriter.

Sell all excess masonry, too. Reject all gifts — from government, foundations, corporations, individuals — unless they can be converted freely into forms of long-term investment. Reject earmarked gifts — even for trees and gardens — absolutely. Nothing should be called a university that requests or accepts earmarked grants. Pitch tuition low and standards high. Do not lure students. The university is not a utopian microcosm. The city is as good as the country. Reduce board and room to a minimum. Rid the place of motel accommodations, infirmaries, country clubs, counseling, chapels, job placement, and entertainment. What is this, grand opera? Rely on private, religious, and student initiative for rooming houses, doctors, restaurants, sports, psychiatrists, places of worship, employment agencies, movies and concerts. Make the head of the university a rector, even rector magnificus. Transform administrators into beadles. Enlarge commons. And then faculty offices — what can be less conducive to study than these open doors to colleagues, students, administrators, research assistants, telephones, memos, politicking, committee meetings, project-team huddles, faculty and staff meetings? Away with faculty offices. Professors can study at home, at clubs, or in libraries, and can see students after class, while out walking, or in commons. Let faculty renew faculty. But first get a good faculty. (Ay, there's the rub.) Steady the university at a moderate size in a contiguous walking area. A university is a society of faculties pursuing knowledge independent of sequel, and teaching students who wish to do much the same. It should be the one place in a madly changing, regressive world, where history almost stands still.

The only question is, wage slaves, where do we find courage?

Three-Dimensional Education

JOHN E. SMITH

The National Humanities Institute, Yale University

Education, like religion and party politics, is an explosive topic about which many people have strong opinions, leading in turn to equally strong differences of opinion. I believe that this is just as it should be, for these topics concern what an ancient Greek philosopher called "the things that matter most," the ideals determining the course and worth of life itself. A genuine cause for alarm would exist if the vigor of the discussion about education should cease and be replaced by apathy or indifference. In this regard even the one who expresses views in a dogmatic way is superior to the one who is indifferent; the dogmatist at least cares.

It should not be difficult to understand why education or, more properly, teaching and learning, should engage so much of our attention. What happens in our educational institutions at all levels determines, for the most part, the make-up of the new generation and with it the future of national life and even of civilization itself. The case of Socrates forcefully underscores the point, even if the outcome was tragic in itself. He antagonized those who opposed him not primarily because of his alleged disrespect for the gods of popular religion, but because he exhorted the young to seek self-knowledge, and to think for themselves, to learn how to discern what is and what is true as against what is deceptive and false, and, most important, to seek as guides for human conduct those virtues which mark out the "good of the soul," and make it possible for people to live together in *civil* society. Socrates, in short, was a teacher, par excellence, but he was a gadfly to his contemporaries because, instead of focusing on the acquisition of information about the world and the development of skills and crafts, he insisted on the absolute importance of the ethical quality of human life. Without, he argued, the power of wisdom, of courage, of temperance, and, above all, justice, there can be no civilized life, individual or social.

In my title, I refer to "three-dimensional" education and I mean to set that off from an education of but two dimensions and to do so with the help of the Socratic insight. Time and again the aims of education have been stated as the stocking of the mind with knowledge, including the development of the ability to think clearly, and the preparing of a person to engage in some vocation or profession as a means of livelihood. But important as these two dimensions undoubtedly are, the third and far most important dimension is missing—the aim and task of developing *civilized* persons, or those who have the self-knowledge, the self-control, the sense of responsibility and the ideals and concerns that make it possible for them to live in a civilized society committed to the realization of freedom and justice. Without this third dimension, all of our knowledge is vain and our vocations and professions fall to the level of mere competitive struggles for money and power.

Civilization depends on the existence of civilized persons; that is the fact. The loss of the third dimension in our educational thought and practice is at the root of our modern difficulties in every region of life. The urgent question is, Can this lost dimension of education be recovered? I believe that the answer is yes, but that answer has to be prefaced by an if—if we can succeed in making the humanities come alive and fulfill their essential role, which is, and has always been, contributing to the development of civilized persons. Man is both a knower and a maker, but it takes little historical knowledge to become aware of the fact that all knowledge and all activity can be put to evil and destructive ends. Unless human beings come to see themselves as responsible beings—man is the only animal capable of *answering* for himself and his deeds—the question of *worthwhile* ends and goals will not arise. But if it does, we are lost if we have no knowledge of or insight into the ideals that make civilization possible. The vast resources of the humanistic studies can provide this insight and thus form the missing third dimension in our educational venture.

Too often it has been supposed that before we can make plain the role of the humanities in liberal education, we must first *define* them. Nothing could be further from the truth. As Kant pointed out long ago, the only study that can *begin* with definitions is mathematics; all other inquiries may aim at definitions only as a possible *outcome* of having plumbed the field. There is no dispute about what constitutes the humanities—literature, the languages, art, philosophy, history, religion, and I would include science as a human achievement—the task is to express their significance in terms that highlight their contribution to human development. To this end, I propose the thesis that the humanities are "the mirror of man," the glass in which we see reflected both what man *has been* and visions of what he *may become*. The mirror reflects the actual works of man, the persistent expression of human concerns, experiences, desires, needs, and aspirations across a great variety of cultures and civilizations. But more than that; the mirror also reflects an ideal dimension in the form of visions of the good life, the values to be pursued and the evils to be avoided. Every theory of "human nature" embraces both poles in that every grasp of what man *is* is intertwined with some image of what human life ideally *should be*. The mirror, in short, reflects both the actual and the ideal so that when we look into it we achieve not only self-understanding, but some conception of what we should strive for if we are to conduct our lives as *human* beings.

I set for myself two tasks — first, to speak generally about what I shall call the "three lessons" to be learned from the mirror, and, second, I shall attempt to illustrate from my experience in the program of the National Humanities Institute at Yale and in summer seminars sponsored by the National Endowment for the Humanities for people in the professions the vital contributions of the humanities in liberal education to the resolution of some of the most perplexing problems we face in the areas of law, medicine, education, mass media, civil rights, and social and economic priorities. We cannot, in the nature of the case, speak of having in hand ready-made solutions, but we can help to develop *persons* who will view these problems from the perspective of humane visions and the values involved and who will not forget that regardless of the size and remoteness of modern organizations and institutions, the focus has always to be on *people* and their welfare.

Stated briefly, the three lessons taught by the mirror of man are, first, the *discovery* and the *recovery* of the complex of ideals and norms upon which our Western civilization has actually been founded and which at least until the erosions brought about by skepticism and nihilism have made life worth living; second, since we see *ourselves* in the mirror, what it reflects provides an essential opportunity for *self-criticism* and the candid perception that being human embraces a considerable capacity for inhumanity and irresponsibility; third, and in some ways most important, the reflection of man in the great imaginative literature of the ages provides an inexhaustible storehouse of *vicarious experience*, overcoming parochialism and extending our horizons. Before explaining these lessons in some detail, I believe one qualifying word is in order. I do not say that the three contributions singled out exhaust the role of the humanities, nor do I believe that the school, college, or university can or should be the only institutions responsible for the development of civilized persons. Many more obligations have been thrust upon our educational systems than they can legitimately bear, but I would still insist on the need for education at every level to recover what I have called the third dimension, which is in fact a matter of moral education in the broadest sense.

Many young people remain largely ignorant of the ideals that have guided and shaped the civilization of which they are a part. We have so exaggerated what is true, namely, that values cannot be "taught" after the fashion of mathematics or chemistry, that we fail even to teach students *about* the values that have in fact sustained our civilization. Through the teaching of history, philosophy, and religious studies, each new generation needs to be made aware of both our debt to and the contemporary importance of the moral and religious sources upon which our lives have depended — the norms of justice, mercy, righteousness, and love derived from the Judeo-Christian tradition; the ideals of truth and of virtue bequeathed by the Graeco-Roman traditions; the convictions of the Enlightenment concerning inalienable rights, human equality, and the need for representative forms of government; the experience of democracy and free institutions. Even more important, we have failed, largely because of a fear of bias and partisanship in a pluralistic society, to focus on the reality of the moral situations that constantly confront us so that the ethical dimension is obscured and moral sensitivity erodes. A recent book by Milton Konvitz, *Judaism and the American Idea*, furnishes an excellent example of the manner in which the faith of an ancient tradition can be revivified and brought to bear on such problems as the rule of law, democracy, religious freedom, and human rights. I choose one telling example from this book. The ancient belief that man is a creature of God, says Konvitz, stands as a bulwark against any creed, political or otherwise, that would envisage man as basically a creation or merely an organ of the state. That ancient belief belongs to our Western heritage and should be known to every educated and civilized person. Why is such a piece of knowledge less important than the great storehouse of knowledge imparted in the study of nations, parliaments, physical systems, industrial corporations, primitive tribes, and social orders? The answer is surely that it is of equal if not greater importance in the end than all the factual knowledge we have because it concerns the *humanity* of man in opposition to those who see man as no more than a thing among other things. The moral and religious roots of our civilization should receive no less attention in our education than the study of galaxies, genetics, or constitutions. The sad fact is that study of those roots is often neglected entirely.

The second lesson to be learned by looking into the mirror of the humanities — that it provides us with an essential opportunity for self-criticism and honest appraisal of our inhumanity—is likely to come as a surprise to all who associate the "humanities" with the idealized universal man of the Renaissance. The truth is that the very reason why we need to be concerned with the development of civilized persons is the presence in all human beings of tendencies and motives that work against the preservation of civilization. Our capacities for irresponsibility, prejudice, self-deception, personal and social immorality, are manifest on every page of written history. To ignore this dark side of man or to attempt to explain it away by placing the responsibility for it *everywhere else but in man himself* is basically dishonest and beneath the dignity of the one being who is answerable for himself and his deeds. Examples from the literature of the humanities are as numerous as the stars and, fortunately, much closer. Where shall we find a more candid portrait of man the political animal than in Machiavelli's *The Prince*, and who can equal his ruthless realism of insight into the wiles, the machinations, and the dissembling necessary to gain and hold political power? Machiavelli has often been attacked for seeming, at least, to condone both the methods and the cynicism of *Realpolitik*, but surely he is to be commended for holding up the mirror in which can be seen the stark realities of politics and the human will to power.

At an even more fundamental level, consider the consummate skill with which Dostoevsky portrayed the tragic dialectic of human freedom in his sketch of the "Grand Inquisitor." Seeing himself as vastly different from a stone or a star, man strives for freedom and self-determination both in the beliefs he holds and the deeds he performs. The cherished freedom, however, is burdened with care, responsibility, and risk; too often the burden of it becomes so onerous that we stand ready to abrogate our freedom or to delegate it to another, and there are always those who are eager to usurp all the freedom we seek to escape, thus turning us into bondsmen entirely given unto the hands of an alien authority. No merely conceptual, philosophical analysis of the ambiguity of human freedom could possibly match in vividness and persuasiveness Dostoevsky's dramatic presentation of human frailty in the face of the awesome demands of being free. One need not spell out the lesson in didactic fashion; it is enough to insist that a civilized person needs to be confronted with these humbling truths about mankind. As Pascal pointed out, there is a glory in man's reaching for infinity through the power of his mind, but there is also the bitter truth that man is the being who can dissemble, who tries to hide and escape the responsibility of his freedom. Nietzsche was right in saying that there is something hypocritical in man's claim to be in pursuit of truth when he is not honest about himself and his own situation.

The third lesson from the mirror has to do with the almost limitless range of *vicarious* experience opened up to us in imaginative literature, history, and the arts. We are all greatly limited in what we can directly live through and experience for ourselves. But our horizons can be vastly extended to an understanding of, a sympathy for, and participation in other cultures and civilizations through the humanistic studies. Consider the vicarious experience of the grandeur and the terror of human life as portrayed by Tolstoy in *War and Peace*; the depths of human folly and human aspiration depicted by Dante in the *Divine Comedy*; the quest for integral selfhood so brilliantly set forth by Goethe in his treatment of the Faust legend. Or, closer to home, consider the doors and windows opened by such writers as Faulkner and Eudora Welty on American southern culture. Reading them gives a vivid sense of "being there without being there," which is what vicarious experience essentially is.

How are future generations of Americans to understand and participate in the many foreign cultures that a shrinking world demands that we encounter when our experience and horizons remain parochial? Not the least of the tragic aspects of the massive tragedy that was Vietnam is to be found in our equally massive ignorance of the culture, the religion, and the *ethos* of the people involved. The fact is that not everyone in the world thinks of human life exclusively as we do in economic and military terms. But unless our educational system can recover what I have called the third dimension, matters of this sort will not be considered and the horizon of the next generation will turn out to be as limited as our own.

I come now to some practical considerations—the humanities at work, as it were—that point the way to what can be done in the way of revitalizing the humanistic studies. As I pointed out earlier, I am relying here on experience gained at the National Humanities Institute in New Haven and in summer seminars sponsored by the National Endowment for the Humanities. The essential first step is that of overcoming the isolation of the various fields of study from each other through a cooperative approach aimed at restoring the integrity of experience and of the world, which in themselves are innocent of the selectivity and abstraction upon which all specialized inquiry is based. Scientists long ago discovered that problems that might prove insoluble for a single investigator may ultimately be resolved by many individuals attacking the problem from several sides. Students and teachers of the humanities can profit from the practice of the natural scientists. By focusing attention on specific problems, historical periods, value conflicts, social, political, and economic issues, interdisciplinary courses can be developed that require the combined knowledge and teaching skills of those in several different fields of study. Consider an art historian who comes to the realization that Western perceptions of Oriental peoples, their appearances, customs, values, and so forth, have been to a large extent determined by the sketches, drawings, and paintings made by the artists who participated in the great voyages of discovery that first brought us into contact with Eastern peoples. The study and interpretation of these artifacts will obviously require the efforts not only of an art historian, but of a geographer, an anthropologist, and perhaps a philosopher and a historian of religion. A course developed to focus on the central theme — the initial perception of new and unfamiliar people and cultures — will not appear to be a course "in" one subject or one "department," because the emphasis will not be on subjects or departments at all but rather on the unifying theme itself, which all participants are attempting to illuminate through the facet of the topic assigned to them. From the standpoint of the teachers involved, an enterprise of this sort is most exciting because one is relating what one knows to something that transcends all the participants and this is very different from routine and often stultifying discussion with "professionals" in the same field. From the standpoint of students, what could be more important than their witnessing cooperative scholarship at work and, in the case of this particular example, discovering the existence of prejudice, sterotype, and misconception in their own images of people from other cultures?

Examples could be multiplied, but the point will remain the same. All the important landmarks, artifacts, events, and so forth, of civilization are too rich and complex to be treated from the vantage point of a single field of inquiry. The proper study of the works of Shakespeare, for example, is not to be accomplished from the field of "English" alone. Needed as well will be the insights of historians, philosophers, sociologists; and, since students cannot be expected to work out the necessary syntheses themselves, scholars will have to work together among themselves to provide them.

I wish now to call attention to another vital role to be played by the humanities in connection with perplexing issues facing professional people in the course of carrying on their work. On two occasions in recent years I have conducted a seminar for those in the professions of law, medicine, journalism, education, and public administration on the topic of "The Ethical Dimension in Contemporary Society." I choose two incidents to illustrate my point. A doctor in charge of a sophisticated neonatal clinic in the Midwest indicated that more than once a week, in consultation with parents, guardians, clergyman and other physicians, he is called upon to decide whether to remove infants with various birth defects from life-sustaining apparatus. He confessed that although this is his responsibility, he often finds himself at a loss to set forth the rationale for his decisions, and needs an opportunity to talk with philosophers, students of ethics and religion in order to gain insight and perspective on his own activity. And the striking fact is that at this point he lamented his failure during the period of his own liberal, as distinct from professional, education to pay more attention to the entire spectrum of the humanities and those concerns about the bases of civilized life that I have called the third dimension in education.

A second example involves the legal profession. A member of the seminar not a lawyer opened the discussion by asking whether lawyers are ever determined in their work by a concern for the "truth" or "justice" of the case at hand, or whether they see their task as simply that of representing an "interest" in opposition to another interest regardless of such ideal considerations. A young lawyer responded by saying that he entered the profession with a strong sense of obligation to justice, but soon discovered that the tide was against him and that more often than not the chief concern is to represent an interest well and "win" in court. A seasoned jurist countered by saying that it is the task of the lawyer to present the case and not to judge it and still less to prejudge it and consequently he cannot determine the "truth" or the "right" of the case in advance. The full depth of the ethical dimension of the legal profession opened up before us. To whom and to what is the lawyer responsible, and what is he to do when his responsibility to the client comes in conflict with his responsibilities both to himself and to his society? We soon found ourselves back to where the seminar had started—a discussion of the trial of Socrates and his condemnation, among other things, of the rhetoricians who aimed at making the worse case *seem* the better. The striking fact was that all participants agreed that the underlying questions of values, priorities, responsibilities, and obligations are inescapable and once again there was the lament that overemphasis on "practical" subjects thought to be essential for professional training had crowded out those "impractical" courses in the humanistic studies.

The plain truth is that the matters with which the humanities deal are inescapable because they concern us as *human beings*. If we are to remain civilized and succeed in preserving civilization, our liberal education must recover that third dimension which requires us to come to terms with "the things that matter most."

The Three Faces of Humanism and Their Relation to Problems of Science and Education

CATHERINE ROBERTS
Berkeley, California

Plato understood that all attempts to form a nobler type of man—i.e., all paideia and all culture—merge into the problem of the nature of the divine.
—Werner Jaeger

Although the perennial problem of the nature and ultimate purpose of education has never been more acute, everyone would agree that all education has to do with the improvement of human beings and is thus an essential part of every system of humanistic thought. Whether education involves the acquisition of scientific truths, the mastery of special skills and techniques, or the assimilation of cultural traditions, it confers upon the individual knowledge of certain aspects of reality he did not previously possess — and it has always been a fundamental educational assumption that he is thereby, in varying degrees, bettered.

But, as recent editorials in this journal clearly show,[1] in its striving for educational betterment the twentieth century has a concept of knowledge quite different from that of its predecessors. Wholly antipathetic to the more subjective educational attitudes of the past, which invariably regarded the development of moral character and an understanding of the good life as the most essential components of the knowledge of the edu-

Versions of this article have appearaed in Tract, No. 14, March 1975 (Ggryphon Press, Llanon, Wales), and in Occasional Papers *(The Farmington Institute, Oxford, England, n.d.).*

1 Douglas Sloan, "The Higher Learning and Social Vision," *Teachers College Record* 79, no. 2 (December 1977): 163-69; and idem, "On the Possibilities of Newness," *Teachers College Record* 79, no. 3 (February 1978): 329-38.

cated, contemporary education is largely based upon the supposition that scientific rationality, objectivity, and amorality are the prime conditions of knowing. Truth, it is said, is "correct apprehension [of] and assertion"[2] about physical reality and is best revealed when such knowledge can be scientifically verified by anyone, regardless of his moral character. Knowledge pertaining to aesthetics or to values, meaning, and ethics, being other kinds of apprehension of and assertion about other kinds of reality, is scarcely looked upon as valid revelation of truth at all but rather as dispensable subjective expression of opinions and feelings about beauty, goodness, and other irrelevancies.

This generally accepted view that subjects that do not lend themselves to objective scientific investigation are by their very nature of minor significance in educational improvement is being vigorously challenged by a number of educators. They see quite rightly that it is a view based upon the disastrous epistemological error made by our rational age in assuming that only knowledge acquired scientifically is correct apprehension and truthful revelation of that which is most humanly significant. That this is a false assumption is becoming increasingly obvious. Educational dissemination of scientific-technological knowledge is not creating a better world of wiser, nobler, happier men; on the contrary, mankind, more fully educated in scientific fact, theory, and method than ever before, stands largely helpless and confused before unprecedented misery for which it is itself mainly responsible. Demands for inclusion of art, literature, music, ethics, religion, and the humanities in all curricula arise out of a growing conviction that since scientific knowledge has no claim to supreme validity and indispensability, those who are to be improved desperately need to learn in nonscientific ways about other truths. Yet increasing educational emphasis directed by opponents of the scientific *Weltbild* toward the expressive disciplines and the liberal arts tradition, although a giant step in the right direction, will not suffice evolutionally without the still more embracing conviction that we really do know what educational improvement is and what it is for.

In what follows I will attempt to show that the nature and ultimate purpose of education becomes most comprehensible when educational improvement is seen as an aid to man's spiritual evolution. Education of this kind, based on the realization of ethical potentiality by subjective knowledge of objective truths, is an indispensable part of one particular system of humanistic thought—here designated theocentric human-

2 A phrase of Martin Heidegger's discussed by Paul Friedländer in his thought-provoking chapter on Truth in his *Plato: An Introduction* (London: Routledge & Kegan Paul, 1958).

ism — that envisages the progressive advance of the human race toward divine goodness through knowledge that spiritually improves the knower. Other kinds of humanism rely upon the scientific concept of knowledge and educational improvement to attain their specific ends. If, then, contemporary education presents grave problems to educators and society at large, attempts to solve them must to a large extent depend upon how well we understand the origin and development of the different forms of contemporary humanism and what each intends to do for man.

THE EMERGENCE OF TRIPARTITE HUMANISM

Humanism has ever been concerned with the progressive realization of the human potential. It did not arise *de novo* in the Renaissance. A deep concern for what man can do to better himself cannot be dissociated from any stage of man's evolution, and certainly not from his civilized state. Anyone who has devoted even a portion of his life and thoughts to the amelioration of the human condition is worthy of the name "humanist," and that includes very nearly all of us. But what *kind* of humanists are we?

In its primal form humanism, indissolubly bound to religion, was theocentric in nature. However great the conceptual divergences inherent in their monotheistic and polytheistic predilections, men everywhere believed in the existence of divine reality as the supreme Good of the universe and realized that this indisputable objective truth necessitated a human-divine relation. World religions and religious philosophies have thus ever been united in a humanistic *Weltbild* that sees the divine Good as the central fact of human existence. Everywhere the most enlightened theocentric humanists have been religious thinkers who have helped men to establish, in accordance with the divine ethic, just, harmonious, and gentle relationships with other living beings. While such humanists have played an enormous role in man's spiritual ascent by exhorting him to acts of righteousness and love and compassion, their pure forms of theocentric humanism have not always been influential in guiding religious development. Religions, particularly when institutionalized, have often been dominated by those who speak in the name of the human-divine relation for less worthy ends. Seeking secular power rather than ethical enlightenment for themselves and their followers, such lesser humanists have temporarily retarded the spiritual development of their religions.

Christianity, for example, whose ecclesiastical leaders included many who preached a humanism that sharply deviated from the theocentricity of its founder, succeeded in the first fifteen hundred years of its existence in tightening its authoritative hold on the Western world partly through political intrigue, war, terror, violence, torture, and many other equally unchristian acts. However sincere some of these Christians may have been in their desire to strengthen Christianity, they succeeded only in weakening it and impeding its progress. Yet it must not be forgotten that throughout its whole history the Christian world has also been held together by another kind of religious authority — by those Christians, known and unknown, who spent their lives ministering to the spiritual needs of their fellowmen. By giving to them out of their own inner light an abiding sense of faith, hope, and love and a desire to participate in the human-divine relation by following the dictates of the divine ethic, these Christians were helping men to realize their potentials. It was this pure theocentric humanism, coexisting with the more degenerate forms, that established harmonious bonds among men and between human and non-human life and helped to keep true Christianity alive. As a latent spiritual-ethical force, it still remains the innermost essence and authority of all religions and religious philosophies.

Some twenty-five hundred years ago, when humanism was still universally theocentric, there arose in the Mediterranean area a deviant form that was anthropocentric in nature. This new form of humanism, arising among the Greeks, was a natural outcome of the Homeric heritage. This is not to say that it arose out of Homer's anthropomorphic theogony but rather out of his view that since only the gods are immortal and divine, man himself, lacking both an immortal soul and a divine spark, has a strictly limited potential. The traditional Olympian view placed an impenetrable barrier between the human and the divine, regarding one of the greatest sins to be hubris, in which a man aspired higher than befitted a mortal. Although man must thus forever remain a mortal, unable to partake of divinity, his own humanness, the Greeks reasoned, must be such a great and wonderful thing that he could do no better than to keep his thoughts centered upon himself rather than upon the divine that transcends him. The Greeks thus came to believe that man's inner greatness, purely human in nature, was capable of expressing itself without divine aid. They looked upon ethical standards as man-made, having become supremely confident that the human potential can come nearest to realization when men are physically, intellectually, and spiritually free to realize it in their own way. In their adoption of anthropocentric humanism as the most rational and therefore truest *Weltbild,* the Greeks were led into the terrible error of supposing that the human potential concerns man alone. The truth of the matter is that this view of the human potential is a Western delusion — perhaps the greatest delusion that evolving man has ever experienced.

Recognizing this truth full well, Plato ran counter to the mainstream of Greek humanism. Unable to accept the narrow Homeric limits of the human potential, Plato saw evolving man as destined to approach divine reality and to become progressively godlike in the process. In challenging the excessive anthropocentricity and unbridled individualism of the society in which he lived, and in correcting Protagoras's dictum that "man is the measure" to read "God is the measure," Plato proclaimed the religious truth that if the human potential is to become progressively realized, humanism must be theocentric. Man's divine spark, he knew, can glow only in seeking its transcendent source. Borrowing the best from the spiritual heritage of his world, and adding enormously to it through his own genius, Plato never founded a religion but created a theocentric *Weltbild* based upon the choice between good and evil that many since have called sublime. Some of his humanism found its way into Christian theology. Some of it was rediscovered with boundless admiration by Renaissance scholars.

That great upsurge of human vitality known as the European Renaissance was as intensely preoccupied with the human potential as classical Greece had been. Although the men of the Renaissance questioned religious authority, religion continued to play a dominant role in their lives, and there was no definitive break with Christianity. The most enlightened Renaissance humanists were, in fact, deeply religious men who, as Plato, knew that the human potential is indissolubly related to divine reality and the problem of good and evil. Other Renaissance humanists found that by questioning the divine ethic, they were able to sever some of their ecclesiastical bonds. Proud of their newly found strength and excited by the prospect of ever greater individual freedom, they thought the human potential could best be realized by turning away from the divine toward the natural world, including man. In seeking truth by the exploration, observation, and investigation of physical reality, they acquired a better understanding of the natural world, and in studying the intellectual greatness of man down through the ages, they became more confident in the mighty reasoning powers of the unaided human mind. Thus the mainstream of European humanism gradually became more closely aligned with Greek anthropocentricity than with Platonic theocentricity. This is not to say that anthropocentric humanism as we know it today emerged fully formed in the Renaissance. There was no complete and final liberation from religious tradition or authority. It was too early for the flowering of modern agnosticism and atheism. The European transition from theocentric to anthropocentric humanism was a gradual one, requiring both the rise of science and the decline of Christianity.

These developments were interdependent and simultaneous. Western science began to emerge during the Renaissance as a part of the rebirth of learning, and the new objective truths attained through scientific observation, experiment, and theoretical abstraction compelled Europeans from the sixteenth century onward to look at themselves, their world, and their God in a new light. As science kept revealing fascinating truths about the reality of the physical world, and as Christianity, weakened by a long history of deflections from the theocentric exhortations of Jesus, no longer had the vitality to keep men's interest centered upon the higher realities of the spiritual world, it was only natural that Western thought became progressively materialistic and secularized. Forgetful of its theocentric authority, Christianity was gradually swept along with the anthropocentric tide, becoming at last, in our day, a humble and silent witness to a scientific humanism proudly proclaiming that man is the central fact of human existence. And because the scientific *Weltbild* dominates world thought, the concept of a divine ethic is today wholly neglected by anthropocentric humanists and by a surprisingly large number of theocentric humanists of all religious affiliations. For some time there has been in nearly all religious societies a flight away from the human-divine relation toward various degrees of anthropocentricity. This is a natural expression of the general spiritual decline of world religions, which seem to be increasingly content with degenerate forms of theocentric humanism. The decline is perhaps most clearly revealed in the widespread religious resignation before the material benefits of scientific and technological progress. Contemporary religions, unsure of their role in human evolution, are expending much thought and energy in attempting to live as amicably as possible with those who, in the name of science, are determined to help realize the human potential atheistically. In being thus spiritually intimidated, world religions have become enormously weakened ethically. They have forgotten that the divine ethic is objective, absolute, and unchanging. In accepting "situation ethics" as the best norm for a scientific age in rapid development, contemporary religions have often become unprotesting observers of ruthless ethical depravity within the scientific community. The picture is not, however, completely black. There are, in fact, good grounds for optimism.

For we are witnessing signs of an incipient spiritual awakening among some of the peoples of the world. Based on a deeply felt revulsion against the inadequacy of the materialism, rationalism, and atheism of the scientific world view and the anthropocentricity that is associated with it, the awakening is reaching out to the spiritual, the irrational, the suprarational, and the transcendent. Everywhere personal experience of the human-divine relation is being sought. Spiritually, these religious strivings are sometimes misguided and immature, as, for example, in the use of drugs to expand consciousness and in the creation and enjoyment of the superstars of a commercialized, degraded form of religion. It is to be expected that the spiritual awakening, when more fully underway, will become purer: a genuine religious striving for a better world by means that do not tarnish the goal. So far, contemporary religions have generally failed to grasp that because the true spiritual awakening, as yet in its infancy, has arisen in a morally outrageous world, it is primarily an ethical awakening concerned with the improvement of human conduct. They need to recognize that their own theocentricity, based upon man's relation to the divine Good, is in itself a source of great ethical strength and power. It seems inevitable that religious thought will turn in this direction and that its now latent energy will be able, when needed, to reveal itself ecumenically to a world that is already spiritually alerted. Another great upsurge of human vitality can thus be expected, but in contrast to that of the Renaissance, this rebirth will be ethical in nature. And we can be equally sure that anthropocentric humanism will not have the slightest chance of withstanding the force of this pure theocentric thrust.

Until then life goes on—which is to say that a world in spiritual awakening still allows scientific authority to place first priority upon the endless acquisition by all amoral or immoral means of new scientific knowledge in the hope of increasing man's understanding of physical reality and of increasing his mastery over it. What else has an atheistic world to hope for? It believes this is the only way to the true realization of the human potential, to the unfolding of man's inner greatness. In neglecting the divine even more completely than did the Greeks, the scientific age has so far been eminently successful in carrying out its intention: Twentieth-century advances in science and technology have been staggering.

Now, however, the scientific age stands deeply alarmed at the fruits of its labors. For scientific and technological progress, when unrestrained by the divine ethic, promotes overindustrialization, depletes resources, pollutes air, land, and water, eradicates wild animals and plants, and inflicts suffering and death upon other sentient organisms that are propagated in enormous numbers for unnecessary food, clothing, amusement, and experiment. Physically, intellectually, and spiritually, the globe is becoming increasingly unfit for habitation. Some think it already too late to make amends to nature and that man, and the whole biosphere with him, is doomed to a premature death. Others, less extreme, foresee a time of trouble more terrible in its austerity than anything evolving man has yet experienced.

The effect of these dire prospects upon humanistic concern for the further realization of the human potential has been startling. First of all, it is focusing global interest as never before upon nature. All over the world anthropocentric and theocentric humanists are pondering our plight from the opposing perspectives of Man-Nature and Man-Nature-God. What is perhaps even more startling is that a new form of humanism is also emerging. Neglecting the human-divine relation, it is, in essence, but a variant of atheistic anthropocentricity but differs from it in its concern for nonhuman as well as human life. Actually, the new form of humanism refuses to distinguish between them. Seeing the human as nothing but a part of nature and the divine as nonexistent, it considers the duality Man-Nature and the triad Man-Nature-God as equally spurious. Having eyes only for Life—life upon this earth as one unified whole—it can best be called biocentric humanism. Should its adherents object to being called humanists at all, preferring to be regarded as the bearers of a new ideology based upon a view of the essential Oneness of life that refuses to harbor thoughts of human superiority, let them remember that in stressing the kinship between human and nonhuman life, it is not to the plants or the animals they are turning to save the world. They are turning to man, and to man alone, to persuade *him* to better *his* ways so that evolving life will not perish. They are, of course, humanists too.

Contemporary humanism has thus three faces, all of which are profoundly concerned with the future evolution of man:

1. the theocentric face, which looks first to Divine Reality

2. the anthropocentric face, which looks first to Man

3. the biocentric face, which looks first to Life

Which of the three visions is closest to the truth? The answer, I am convinced, depends upon which vision has the greatest ethical sweep. Let us compare them.

ANTHROPOCENTRIC ETHICS

Although anthropocentric humanism, being atheistic or agnostic in essence, cannot expect evolving man to become more godlike, it does expect him to realize more completely his biological potentialities for intelligence and rational behavior. But in denying him a divine spark, soul, or spirit to ensure his immortality, its evolutionary goals are limited to the earthly survival and well-being of the individual and the species. This face of humanism predominates in our scientific age.

Its chief exponents are found in contemporary biology and medicine.

Unrestrained by thoughts of the divine ethic, many of them are seeking knowledge that will enable them to transform human beings into increasingly artificial individuals who can look forward to a longer life based upon scientific directives for the use of drugs, surgery, genetic engineering, or manipulation of the breeding process. Regarding death as the supreme evil, the ethical code of biologists and medical scientists provides first of all for the prolongation of human lives at any cost. An enormous amount of time and energy is spent in experimental work to enable individuals to live longer upon the earth. But why should men live longer here? No anthropocentric humanist has a satisfying answer to this question. Sometimes it evokes vague hopes that evolving man can thus become more human but most often it remains unanswered. And without a specifically spiritual answer, the ethical code of anthropocentric humanism remains *wholly* anthropocentric and therefore incompatible with man's ascent toward the divine. Man-centered and earthbound, it is a dreary utilitarian ethic that obstructs the flight of the human soul toward the spiritual radiance that is its destiny.

Anthropocentric humanism has also its special code of ethics for nonhuman life. Shameful and degrading to mankind, it has been accepted by anthropocentric humanists within and without scientific circles as the only ethical code possible for a scientific age in rapid development. Briefly, it is based upon the delusion that regardless of the pain, fear, and prolonged misery they may endure, laboratory animals in unlimited numbers must be utilized and sacrificed in unlimited ways for the physical wellbeing and survival of the human species. The end, the anthropocentric humanist asserts, justifies every conceivable means. By any ethical standard, this is a monstrous lie in his soul.

The anthropocentric face of humanism, looking first to man, is blinded by egoism and self-love to that which lies above and below the human. Narrow and distorted, it is a grossly imperfect ethical vision that can never truly serve the spiritual needs of evolving life.

BIOCENTRIC ETHICS

Seeing life on earth as an expression of the evolutionary facts and theories of modern science, biocentric humanism, just as its anthropocentric counterpart, denies life a divine origin and purpose. Exclusively concerned with the continued existence of the physical reality of earthly life, both forms of humanism neglect the existence of divine reality and thus see life's evolution as an autonomous process leading nowhere in particular. The biocentric vision differs from the anthropocentric in purporting to help not only man but all other creatures to live, propagate, and realize their biological potentials on earth; seeing life as a unified whole, it desires harmony among the component parts and exhorts man to divest himself of his arrogance, brutality, and greed to ensure the maximum well-being and survival of all. In its respect for all life, biocentric humanism is already on a higher ethical plane than the anthropocentric goal of all good to man alone.

Yet any vision that shuns as though it were the plague the human-divine relation of religion eliminates the fundament of human existence. Although sincerely desiring the realization of the biological potentials of the whole of existing life, the biocentric face of humanism, also agnostic or atheistic, is blind to the unique nature of man. By overemphasizing the oneness of physical life and man's undeniable kinship with the animals, it may even impede the further realization of human potentiality. For evolving man, however imperfect, has already attained a spiritual vision of the divine ethic that evolving nonhuman lives, devoid of conscience, cannot share—and it is upon this unique vision that not only ecological betterment but the future course of evolution depends. As a philosopher-friend once remarked about humanitarian efforts to help animals that spring only from a sense of kinship with them:

. . . there has to be some glimpse or vision of the numinous appearing in such a labour if it is to light candles that don't go out.[3]

Biocentric candles will be ephemeral because biocentric humanists see such a minute part of the truth of human evolution. They paint a picture of an autonomous development devoid of spiritual purpose or progress, where the human-divine relation is a figment of the imagination, where physical death is personal extinction, where the possibilities of realizing individual potentials through immortality and reincarnation are as emphatically denied as the spiritual hierarchy of nature, and where most emphasis is laid upon biological development of matter and form and the accompanying increase in mental functioning of the brain. When *Homo sapiens* is viewed in this way as a product of primate development rather than a species in spiritual ascent toward virtue, the unique nature of man must remain hidden.

Recognition of his uniqueness is nevertheless mandatory in our present circumstances. With whatever intuitive knowledge of good and evil each of us has within, we need to seek, find, and emulate the ethical purity man has so far attained during his evolution. However great contempt we may harbor for a Hitler, a Nixon, or for moral imperfection in general, it

3   Harold Wakeford Cox, Personal correspondence, December 13, 1973.

is the already realized potentials of righteousness, compassion, and love that properly define human uniqueness. What the saints did is what man can do. And despite the enormity of evil that other men have done, it is not true, as some biocentric humanists believe, that the higher limits of man are no compensation for the depths to which some members of the human race have sunk.[4] Evil, after all, is finite, and good infinite. The depths have a limit. The heights are limitless.

It is being said that the Judaeo-Christian statement in Genesis referring to man's dominion over nature is a religious doctrine that unwarrantably gives man absolute authority over the nonhuman. If the majority of Jews and Christians, still evolutionarily imperfect as all other men, have mis-used their power over nature in this way, this is, however, not so much the fault of Genesis as their faulty reading of it. They have interpreted its message incorrectly because they have failed to heed the spiritual wisdom inherent in all religions and expressible in the two words *noblesse oblige*. This means that the more spiritually enlightened individuals are morally bound to help in all possible ways those who are less enlightened. Biocentric humanists have not yet recognized this great religious truth that the essential uniqueness of *Homo sapiens* is intended to be used for the good of other species.

This is understandable in an irreligious age of science. Neglecting human uniqueness, biologists all over the world are now inflicting monstrous suffering and death upon millions of sentient, nonhuman lives; while within science there is only sporadic, ineffectual opposition to these acts that so flagrantly flout the divine ethic and impose extreme disharmony and injustice upon the natural order of things. And most educators, assuming that what science does must be right, see no ethical problem here.

Earthly harmony and justice can best be realized through the religious perspective. Looking first away from transient, impermanent earthly life to the reality of the divine and the divine ethic that knows not change, man participates in the human-divine relation, glimpses cosmic hierarchy and purpose, and then falls naturally into proper ethical balance with other human and nonhuman beings.

The biocentric face of humanism, looking *only* to mortal life, mistakes the physical reality of its fleeting earthly existence for the Whole. Denying the validity of human knowledge of the divine ethic, it is a one-sided ethical vision that can bestow upon evolving life only a limited amount of good.

---

4 · J.A. Livingston, *One Cosmic Instant: A Natural History of Human Arrogance* (Toronto: McClelland and Stewart, 1973).

Submitting only to the teachings of biology, contemporary anthropocentric and biocentric humanists sharply limit their intuitive ethical visions in refusing even to consider the possibility of a higher reality than evolving man or evolving life. For divinity and the divine ethic, they say, is not. Let us know turn to those who say it is.

THEOCENTRIC ETHICS

Since the essence of religion is man's relation to the divine, it follows that theocentric — or divine-centered — humanism necessarily encompasses the progressive, and in some cases temporarily regressive, development of all religions, all religious philosophies, all religious attitudes and states of mind. At this stage in evolution the existence of worldwide religious diversity rather than one unified religion is, in part, a consequence of the disagreement prevailing among theocentric humanists about the nature of the human-divine relation. Men differ in their intellectual, emotional, and spiritual powers and conceive the divine in different ways.

The Christian question, "In what sense can God be outside the world, and in what sense in it?" becomes, however, a question of universal religious applicability when the word "God" is replaced by "divinity" or "the divine." Hindus, Buddhists, Jainists, Zoroastrians, Taoists, Orphics, Platonists, Gnostics, Jews, Christians, Mohammedans, theosophists, anthroposophists, and others have attempted to answer it and in doing so have disclosed their own theocentric inclinations toward theism, deism, pantheism, and mysticism.

Theism, in its broadest sense, simply signifies recognition of the existence of the divine, but in a narrower sense it is also used in opposition to deism and pantheism to denote a transcendent divinity whose immanence is restricted to what has been called the indwelling and immortal spirit, soul, or spark of things. Deism is based on the concept of a transcendent divinity wholly distinct and apart from the world. Pantheists see the divine everywhere, holding that the universe is the phenomenal manifestation of the divine or even that no other divinity exists than the existing world. The mystical tradition asserts that the divine, whatever it is and wherever it may be, is knowable — and that in varying degrees — through a special kind of experience inaccessible to the ordinary perceptive powers of the mind and senses.

While these conceptual and empirical differences hold religious groups apart, they do not prevent them from working in spiritual unison to set the theocentric position in bold relief against the other faces of humanism. Theists, deists, pantheists, and mystics all seek fuller knowledge of that transcendent spiritual perfection or divine First Cause from which the world of matter arose. Since they see the source of life in this divinity, they also see that all forms of life must be in some way divinely related. The Oneness of life is also a part of the theocentric position, but in contrast to the biocentric, it is based on spiritual rather than physical unity. Theocentric humanists see all forms of life, higher and lower, bound by a divine principle that ensures their spiritual evolution toward a common goal: Oneness is thus a becoming, a potential that is being realized in varying degrees by all living beings regardless of whether they possess profound spiritual enlightenment or only the rudiments of spiritual consciousness. Theocentric humanism thus sees life's spiritual Oneness in terms of potentiality and hierarchy. Biocentric humanism, on the contrary, sees the Oneness of life as physical rather than spiritual, and already realized. All living forms having descended from the same primordial slime, they are bound by a vital principle that ensures the further propagation of evolving species, whose essential Oneness cannot be augmented. Biocentrically, the fact of the physical kinship of all forms of life is adduced by science, not by recourse to a false belief in its divine origin. Denying that life arose from anything but matter, biocentric humanists see its evolution wholly in terms of autonomous physical, and concomitant mental, development that lacks both goal and direction. Theocentric humanists, recognizing that the physical originated from the spiritual, see evolution as life's spiritual return, guided from without, to the divine source of its being. Regardless of their religious affinities, theocentric humanists are thus obliged to work together because of the common knowledge they share: They all know that the divine is.

And ever since man was, he appears to have known that the divine reality is the light that leads him out of the mists and shadows.

And the light shineth in darkness; and the darkness comprehended it not.

The human mind associates darkness with evil to be avoided and light with good to be absorbed. The divine light, infinitely more radiant than the light of the physical universe, becomes the supreme desideratum for men in spiritual evolution.

Some have held that the divine is wholly unknowable and that any attributes it may possess must lie beyond human perception. Evolving man has, however, always reached out toward the divine *as though* it were the highest good to which he could aspire. In equating the divine with the supreme cosmic Good, he intuitively recognizes that its goodness is more than an attribute. Conceptually, if not empirically, the two become an indissoluble one, the divine Good, which cannot be dissociated in his mind from the human problem of good and evil.

The true theocentric position points to a conclusion that seems inescapable: Ethics is not a man-made creation but man's superhuman link with the divine. In this vision the sweep of theocentric ethics bursts the limits of purely human thought and imagination to become a spiritual reality of seemingly infinite magnitude and promise for evolving life.

PURPOSELESS EVOLUTION OR SELF-TRANSCENDENCE?

The life sciences tell us that from its obscure beginning some three billion years ago, life has evolved autonomously into a thriving biosphere of enormous richness and variety, in which plant and animal species are ever striving for ecological balance. Evolutionary development of life from the primitive to the complex has reached its highest point in the human species, whose intellectual, emotional, religious, and ethical attributes are dependent upon the human nervous system, which in its development has far surpassed that of any nonhuman species. Science further asserts that evolution can have no final purpose, since, in some remote future, life on this planet is doomed to destruction by increasingly unfavorable solar developments. Denying the religious teachings of the immortality of the individual soul, and its existence in the spiritual world apart from the terrestrial body, biologists and medical scientists can envisage no higher goal for any individual or species than the scientifically contrived prolongation of its physical existence as long as possible. If, in the case of *Homo sapiens*, this artificially extended physical survival be accompanied by progressive development of intelligence and rational behavior, so much the better; if not, at least the scientific mind must be given credit for its brilliant attainment and application of objective knowledge about physical reality in order to postpone the inevitable. And since the whole gigantic expansion and differentiation of terrestrial life is purposeless, what more, they ask, can be expected of us? A great deal, the theocentric humanist would answer.

Biologists must correct this fundamental misconception that evolutionary purpose is nonexistent because valid knowledge of it cannot be acquired with the rational objectivity of science. They must see that evolutionary purpose has to do with life's spiritual ascent toward the Good, and that this is a suprarational, intuitive truth needing neither proof nor reason but being self-evident and of unquestioned validity for those who seek truth in the light of the human-divine relation.

All kinds of valid knowledge make known truth, but let us free ourselves from scientific authority and try to place them in their proper hierarchical order. In ascending the hierarchy, knowledge becomes more subjective and intuitive. The hierarchy is thus based upon the spiritual transformation effected in the knower, with supremely valid knowledge bringing about the greatest change. This is just what the scientist tries to avoid. He seeks truth only where he can be most completely detached from it. In the search he ignores his feelings and, apart from a moral compulsion about accuracy in observation and assertion, he dispenses with his intuitive sense of right and wrong. Even when his imaginative, intuitive, or aesthetic insight enables him to discover natural laws, he attempts to be wholly objective about his discoveries for the sake of fuller comprehension. Truth, for him, is only correctness of apprehension, valid knowledge as thought or speech, and it concerns a world of physical reality wholly separated from himself.

But if, as Plato believed, objective reality ascends to the higher spiritual truths, the knowledge of which profoundly influences the knower and makes more correct his apprehension, then the hierarchy of truth, and the increasingly valid human knowledge accompanying it, constitute a spiritual force as yet unrecognized in evolution. Awareness of a force that causes life to transcend its own reality would give scientists a more subjective approach to knowledge in harmony with what Michael Polanyi called "ultra-biology," or its ultimate extrapolation: the abandonment of detached scientific objectivity (which is itself often a delusion) in favor of personal commitment to seek superior knowledge for the purpose of self-transcendence.[5] An ultra-biology bringing biologists closer to virtue is a concept that brightly illumines evolutionary purpose. For evolving man has within him divine reality that seeks its source, and supremely valid human knowledge brings about the fullest realization of the human potential for self-transcendence. The highest knowledge thus appears as self-knowledge. Know Thyself! Recollect! Thou art in truth more real than thou now knowest.

If science be the attempt to discover truths exhibiting objective reality as an ordered and interrelated system, then biological science, in which evolving life studies itself, should include cognizance of all the humanly significant truths that life is able to comprehend. Yet the life sciences today exclude justice, beauty, virtue, and other Platonic absolutes from their domain in the delusion that they have no real existence but are merely epiphenomena or fleeting ideas in the human mind. Science thus denies man's age-old intuition that there are, in fact, the higher truths, the things that really are, possessing far more permanence and reality and significance than natural phenomena. Students of life need to recognize

5 Michael Polanyi, *Personal Knowledge: Towards a Post-Critical Philosophy* (London: Routledge & Kegan Paul, 1958).

that objective spiritual truths in which the knower can subjectively participate are the most completely knowable truths of life, where, in agreement with Platonic thought, correct apprehension cannot be separated from reality of being.

There is no doubt that most biologists would profit by closer acquaintance with the subjectivity of art, literature, poetry, and music. Although the true relation between beauty and goodness remains obscure and mysterious, when the pursuit of beauty is most successful it may well rest upon some intuitive sense of ethical self-transcendence. Since, however, artists, writers, poets, and musicians are seldom as saintly as religious teachers, the subjectivity of these creative, imaginative fields of endeavor may not yet be fully developed. Perhaps only when the seeker of subjective knowledge is consciously aware of the human-divine relation is there correct apprehension of evolutionary purpose as an ascent toward the Good and an ethical compulsion to participate in it. Although philosophers have certainly experienced in varying degrees both the apprehension and the compulsion, it is religion that fires man's deepest spiritual intuitions and draws him upward to still higher levels of goodness. Pursuit of all knowledge will one day be undertaken theocentrically.

> As a scientist who has studied philosophy, I maintain that religion is the only possible completion of scientific inquiry, unless one is content in such inquiry to be bound within the narrow limits of space and time and material things.[6]

The theocentric humanist believes that evolutionary purpose will be greatly served when science becomes spiritualized and when the ethical truths of religion again become one of the fundamental insights of the educated.

It has been claimed that the concept of evolution is of fairly recent European origin, but this contention is not everywhere accepted. The theosophists, for example, assert that in very ancient times there was one universal religion that was scientifically, philosophically, and ethically concerned with evolutionary progress of life and the universe, but that for certain reasons it long since became an esoteric doctrine. They further claim to have recovered from Eastern religious teachers a small fragment of this spiritual wisdom, partly by occult or recondite means that emphasize the scientific necessity of an extensive psychic exploration of the supersensible world. Anthroposophists and others, who see in Christianity

---

6 W. Brown, *Psychological Methods of Healing* (London: University of London Press, 1938); quoted in *The Aryan Path* 47, no. 5 (September/October, 1976): 222.

and their own novel interpretations of it a higher spiritual wisdom than in the Eastern religions, also assert that knowledge of cosmogony and the evolution of life has been spiritually revealed in our time to certain individuals possessing highly developed powers of extrasensory perception. That such evolutionary visions, originating from apparently different sources, are often in essential agreement is a surprising fact.

Although such assertions about the past, present, and future course of cosmic evolution, often made dogmatically down to the minutest detail with respect to the physical reality of the universe, cannot be accepted as intuitive knowledge of unquestioned validity, they remain thought-provoking hypotheses that provide alternatives for those religionists who find the evolutionary theory of modern science difficult to reconcile with theocentricity and for those scientists who find Darwinism and neo-Darwinism an inadequate basis for the scientific *Weltbild*. More important, the impressive spiritual vistas these hypotheses open up are superbly relevant to any discussion of evolutionary purpose, and an age in spiritual awakening will be intuitively certain that they must rest upon some kind of valid knowledge of the human potential, the interrelation of spirit and matter, karma and reincarnation, cyclic development, and life without beginning or end.

A century ago this statement could be found in theosophical literature:

> *We are at the bottom of a cycle and evidently in a transitory state.* . . . We are in a barren period; the eighteenth century, during which the malignant fever of scepticism broke out so irrepressibly, has entailed unbelief as an hereditary disease upon the nineteenth. The divine intellect is veiled in man; his animal brain alone *philosophizes*.[7]

Since then these ideas have shown increasing correspondence with the facts. Abetted by the gross materialism and ethical chaos of the atheistic *Weltbild* of science, Western man now seems to have reached a level of unprecedented spiritual darkness while sensing all about him that some great religious awakening is in the air. Whether this collective turning of the human spirit toward the light is the first of its kind or only one in an endless chain of similar cosmic events in which evolving life participates is a question far beyond the scope of this brief discussion on the three faces of humanism. Here our prime concern, perhaps comprising but an evolutionary instant on the cosmic time scale, is with man's more immediate prospects and how they are linked to the problem of good and evil.

---

7   H.P. Blavatsky, *Isis Unveiled: A Master Key to the Mysteries of Ancient and Modern Science and Theology* I, *Science* (Los Angeles: The Theosophy Co., 1968; first published 1877).

It is unfortunate that evolutionary visions, whether orthodox or unorthodox from the scientific point of view, often understate the problem of ethics. At this particular moment in human evolution, when men are committing one atrocity after another in complete disregard of the cosmic law of justice, harmony, and goodwill that is inherent in the divine ethic, nothing can be of greater evolutionary significance than ethical enlightenment. How can mankind now emerge into the light without first learning how to distinguish and choose between good and evil? Socrates and Plato, both theocentric humanists, asked this question more than two thousand years ago. Mankind has not yet fully understood its import. Perhaps it needed first to reach the turning point at the bottom.

For theocentric humanism, in all its various expressions, is essentially a doctrine of self-transcendence. Evolving man is, and always has been, on his way to becoming something more than human. He is approaching the divine Good and in doing so can only become ethically better. To conceive divinity on an infinitely higher plane than the opposing forces of good and evil and thus beyond ethics may represent a high order of spiritual enlightenment but one that, I believe, neglects that important part of the ascent immediately before us. In a world of injustice, deceit, and suffering, any theocentric assertion about the need for ethical enlightenment cannot be in vain. About cosmogony and the origin and development of terrestrial life, the theocentric humanist cannot say dogmatically: It was thus. But he does know intuitively that the evolving human race is spiritually embarked upon its apotheosis for the sake of the cosmic Good, and that this immense journey has now reached a point where ethics must overshadow all other human concerns for as long a period of evolutionary time as is spiritually necessary.

Let us now turn to a problem of current interest to illustrate that theocentric humanism, proclaiming that evolution is purposeful, is better able than the other faces of humanism to provide ethical solutions to problems of our scientific age. Biologists have found that hybrid DNA molecules produced by the isolation and rejoining of gene segments taken from various bacterial, animal, and viral sources are able to replicate in the cells of *Escherichia coli*, a harmless bacterium commonly present in the human intestinal tract. At the same time they were aware that the manipulated bacterial cultures, possessing unknown biological properties, might prove highly pathogenic and infectious. The further possibility existed that the bacteria, if not handled with adequate precaution, might inadvertently "escape" from the laboratories to sweep through the human population. Since further research in this field might thus endanger public health, a group of leading American biomedical scientists, exercising a self-restraint unprecedented in the history of experimental science, voluntarily put into effect some years ago a temporary moratorium on their experiments in this field and exhorted their colleagues everywhere to do the same.[8] It was stated at the time that a committee was expected to be set up to sponsor large-scale experiments on animals to determine just how dangerous the new microorganisms were, and that effective precautionary measures could then be recommended. The matter has been widely discussed since then. After more than two years of controversy, the National Institute of Health issued in 1976 its guidelines, whose voluntary restrictions were to keep the recombinants from escaping from the laboratories. A few days later, however, the City Council of Cambridge, Massachusetts, voted a ban on recombinant DNA research at Harvard University. The debate became more intense. Nobel laureates were found on both sides, with George Wald, in particular, expressing especially clear and forceful objections to continuing such research.[9] Yet as far as I am aware, no scientist taking part in the controversy has given any thought to the fact that the use of laboratory animals in genetic engineering, as in any other field of biomedicine, is flagrantly unethical.

On the contrary, biologists chose to try to solve the problem by an intensification of animal experimentation. From the standpoint of theocentric humanism this was the worst possible choice, clearly revealing the ethical chaos prevailing in the scientific community. After having admitted that bacteria artificially transformed into types hitherto unknown in nature may be an immense hazard to the health of the world, scientists believed that this entitled them to sacrifice as many nonhuman lives as needed—and that this procedure, apparently unanimously approved by anthropocentric and biocentric humanists, was the only rational approach to the problem and therefore the right one.

Regardless of what leading biologists may think, it is not right by any ethical standard. Despite mankind's growing desire to enlighten and purify a world dominated by the scientific *Weltbild*, biologists still prefer to walk in the fog and mire of ethical confusion. To attempt to solve an alarming problem of scientific ethics for which they alone are responsible by rapacious demands for more and more laboratory animals to be subjected to mutilation or disease or death is a flagrant denial of the divine ethic. Evolving man, now at the turning point, cannot allow science to continue its coarse and brutal practice of regarding dogs, cats, monkeys,

8 *Nature* 250 (July 19, 1974): 175; and *Nature* 250 (July 26, 1974): 279.
9 G. Wald, "The Cast against Genetic Engineering," *The Sciences*, September/October 1976, pp. 6-12.

and other highly developed animals merely as tools to be employed and destroyed at will. Biologists need to learn respect for the natural rights of nonhuman forms of life and the justice, gentleness, kindness, and compassion that go with it. Respect for life is a prerequisite of any real advance that is now open to biological science.

No true theocentric humanist can tolerate that ethical problems of contemporary science be "solved" by the further mistreatment of nonhuman life. The present dilemma of biologists requires the exercise of much more self-restraint and self-sacrifice than is called for in setting up a temporary moratorium on their research.

Biologists could first of all commit their potentially dangerous cultures of genetically transformed bacteria to the autoclaves for destruction by sterilization — an act that would at the same time help to clear the fog and mire of genetic engineering laboratories, replacing purely scientific intent with a cleaner atmosphere of ethical and evolutionary thought. Secondly, biologists could refuse to produce further microbial chimeras for which the evolving universe has no use whatever. And they could at the same time renounce the use of experimental animals in all scientific research. If these suggestions have a wholly unrealistic ring to scientific ears, it can only be repeated that biomedicine cannot carry on indefinitely in its present direction, intent upon prolonging human life by outrageous means. The future of biology and medicine does not lie in scientific tampering with life, be it the creation of viable microorganisms artificially assembled from various living sources or by the ruthless exploitation of highly developed animals. True biological and biomedical advance will one day be measured by its contribution to the establishment of harmonious and just relations among living things. For no field of science can avoid the spiritualization that is to come.

Evolution is not purposeless. Man is to transcend himself, and this he cannot do by regarding subhuman species as existing for his sake alone. As he is yet ignorant of the final destiny of the plant and animal kingdoms, he must accept as a theoretical possibility that matter is to become spiritualized and that all life is destined to self-transcendence. His evolutionary duty toward nature then becomes one of offering the living creatures with whom he comes in contact his physical, intellectual, and spiritual help in the hope of assisting in the realization of their earthly potentials. It is said[10] that when his camel is about to foal, the Bedouin of the Arabian desert takes his prayer rug and kneels beside the animal and

10   J.A. Boone, *Venskab med Dyr*, Danish translation of *Kinship with All Life* (New York: Harper & Row, 1968; Copenhagen: Strubes Forlag, 1968).

its unborn offspring, speaking eternal truths, reading oriental literature, reciting the Koran, and praying. Sheer nonsense? Far from it. Although it cannot be expected that the camel understand what the kneeling Bedouin at its side is trying to communicate, his words and thoughts constitute a form of spiritual energy, creating a better spiritual environment and thus helping to realize the potentials of both the man and the beast. This is one of the highest forms of spiritual help a man can give others in a time of crisis. It is a theocentric act, directed by, and toward, and for the sake of, the divine Good.

The life sciences, still embedded in anthropocentricity and biocentricity, have not yet seen the theocentric face of humanism and its vision of evolution toward virtue. Events are, however, moving with extraordinary rapidity, and many signs of the times are indubitably theocentric. The latest report to the influential Club of Rome, for example, devotes many pages to the great spiritual-ethical resources of world religions and how they could be better utilized to enhance world solidarity.[11] Established science, as all other human endeavors, may be ethically regenerated sooner than we think. A spiritualized biology and medicine, everywhere more esteemed than at present, is an inevitable development of the forces of theocentric humanism that are now gathering spiritual momentum.

Nor will contemporary education be able to withstand these forces. Still dominated by the anthropocentric and biocentric humanism of our scientific age, it tends largely to neglect virtue and thereby impoverish rather than improve those who are being educated. Only when education regains its lost sense of the divine can it exert its optimal influence upon evolving man.

Contemporary education has not yet directly considered the idea that its ultimate purpose is a religious one. But those educators who are actively contesting the supremacy of scientific-technological knowledge in education are creating an avant-garde for the spiritual regeneration of their profession. When, for example, Douglas Sloan asserts the primacy of the intuitive imagination and points to a new epistemological radicalism beginning "to argue persuasively that the arts and religion and the humanities are not expressions of feeling or fancy or folk preference, but real sources of knowledge about the world in which we live,"[12] and

---

11 Ervin Laszlo, ed., *Goals for Mankind: A Report to the Club of Rome* (London: Hutchinson, 1977).

12 Sloan, "The Higher Learning and Social Vision"; and idem, "On the Possibilities of Newness."

when Peter Abbs asserts that many educators no longer even speculate "as to whether education *might* consist of more than learning, might, for example, involve the development of the whole person,"[13] they are pointing, albeit somewhat indirectly, toward the religious insight that has sustained education in the past.

Of considerable interest in this connection is the work of Edith Simon, an Edinburgh writer and artist who is attempting to "reassert fundamental religious values through the medium of art."[14] One of her projects is a chapel for multidenominational meditation designed as a pair of sheltering hands to be constructed of modern materials such as laminated timber and glass-fiber-reinforced plastic. She believes that for the sake of ethics and human brotherhood, art and religion should work together to oppose the omnipotent cynicism of our times:

. . . as always in periods of spiritual vacuum, a search for fresh values is generated, which is bound to fail unless accompanied by an access of energy, passionate conviction, and exhilaration, such as only participation in creative endeavour can instill.

Science . . . progressively explained away so many mysteries as to foster the assumption that it had explained them all away, but the unprovable is with us forever, and it is there that dynamics and communication reside, with Art as a perpetual attempt to bring order into chaos, and to establish communication.

It is becoming increasingly obvious that the noblest expressions of art and other subjective, imaginative, and creative endeavors can spiritually transform us more than a science believing itself to be a wholly objective search for the truth. Were education to lean more in their direction, it would be in a far better position to grasp the intuitive truth that human ethical potentiality is there to be realized because the universal goal of all our striving is the divine Good.

In an important essay, E. F. Schumacher asserted that the essence of education is the transmission of ideas about values to live by,[15] and it is now clear that his vision of what contemporary education ought to be arose out of religious convictions that he elaborated shortly before his

---

13   Peter Abbs, *Root and Blossom: The Philosophy, Practice, and Politics of English Teaching* (London: Heinemann, 1976).

14   B.G. Cooper, "The Art of Edith Simon: A Multi-Faith Chapel Project," *The Aryan Path* 47, no. 5 (September/October 1976): 219–20.

15   E.F. Schumacher, *Small Is Beautiful: A Study of Economics as if People Mattered* (London: Blond & Briggs, 1973).

death.[16] Insisting that "education which fails to clarify our central convictions is mere training or indulgence," Schumacher's essay offers tacit support for Arnold Toynbee's conviction that "we will have to revive religion as the major human concern that it has been in the past and that it ought always to be."[17] Both men were aware that the supreme fact of earthly life is the human-divine relation, and Toynbee went so far as to state unequivocally that the goal of education must be a religious one. In the natural order of things all genuine education, regardless of the kind of knowledge it imparts, is but an aid to religion. And since the common intent of all religions is to teach men how to be good, is it not obvious that contemporary education would recover its identity, integrity, and fire were it to direct its main efforts to developing spiritual consciousness that is always able to distinguish good from evil and act accordingly? Can virtue, then, really be taught?

This great Platonic question has been answered by one contemporary classical scholar as follows:

> It can be taught if teaching is understood to be what Socrates describes in the *Theaetetus* as assisting in bringing to birth truths with which another is pregnant, but not in the Sophistic sense of handing over ready-made packets of knowledge.[18]

To this I would only add the qualification that the teacher himself be ever seeking virtue through self-knowledge.

To the reader who cannot help pondering the spiritual mystery of evolving life and seeking the truth about it, I would like briefly to sum up what has been said about the three faces of humanism by offering, in a spirit of humility and goodwill, these thoughts for his consideration:

> *The purposeful evolutionary vision of theocentric humanism is an intuitive truth possessing an ethical sweep that anthropocentric and biocentric humanism lack. Theocentric humanism is destined to become, as it may have been in the past, a universal humanism of religion, science, philosophy, art, and education to facilitate life's further self-transcendence. May we have the strength and wisdom and joy to help one another on the way by means that are in ethical harmony with the divine Good we are approaching.*

16   E.F. Schumacher, *A Guide for the Perplexed* (London: Jonathan Cape, 1977).

17   A. Toynbee and D. Ikeda, *Choose Life: A Dialogue* (London: Oxford University Press, 1976).

18   W.K.C. Guthrie, *A History of Greek Philosophy, IV: Plato, The Man and His Dialogues: Earlier Period* (Cambridge: Cambridge University Press, 1975).

The Teaching of Ethics in the American Undergraduate Curriculum, 1876-1976

DOUGLAS SLOAN
Teachers College, Columbia University

This article is an attempt to look at main developments and issues in the teaching of ethics to undergraduates during the past century. Although I had suspected as much, it was not until I was well under way in working on the piece that I began to realize the extent to which a look at the teaching of ethics provides, as it were, a central window on the whole of American higher education. The teaching of ethics has been uniquely and inseparably connected with the most important issues of modern higher education, issues involving the curriculum, institutionalization, professionalization, epistemology, the "two-cultures" split, the community, indeed, the very purposes of higher education. It is with this larger perspective in view that I have sought to understand the place and problems of the teaching of ethics, not only with respect to ethics courses as such, but also in the larger curriculum. Even as concern with the teaching of ethics has time and again flagged or even disappeared at one point in American higher education, it has without fail and almost immediately reappeared at another, for the issues with which it deals have been those integral to the entire enterprise.

Two disclaimers are, perhaps, called for at the outset. The study does not presume to offer a systematic account of the development of ethical

I wish to thank the Hastings Center for whom this study was prepared and whose support made possible the research on which it is based. I am also indebted to Philip H. Phenix, Lawrence A. Cremin, and Trygve R. Tholfsen, and to the members of The Hastings Center and the participants in The Hastings Center project on the teaching of ethics for their helpful criticisms of earlier drafts. Any errors of fact and of interpretation remain my sole responsibility. This article also appears in Daniel Callahan and Sissela Bok, editors, *The Teaching of Ethics* (New York: Plenum Press, 1980).

theory. Nor does it attempt to deal exhaustively with all influences on the teaching of ethics that have originated in the wider society and its institutions. I have endeavored, however, to take the theoretical and social-institutional contexts seriously and to bring out those aspects of both that have borne directly on the problems of the teaching of ethics, or that in my judgment help to illuminate those problems most clearly.

MORAL PHILOSOPHY IN
THE NINETEENTH-CENTURY COLLEGE

Throughout most of the nineteenth century the most important course in the college curriculum was moral philosophy, taught usually by the college president and required of all senior students. The moral philosophy course was regarded as the capstone of the curriculum. It aimed to pull together, to integrate, and to give meaning and purpose to the students' entire college experience and course of study. In so doing it even more importantly also sought to equip the graduating seniors with the ethical sensitivity and insight needed if they were to put their newly acquired knowledge to use in ways that would benefit not only themselves and their own personal advancement, but the larger society as well.[1]

Moral philosophy was not a new-comer to the college curriculum but had a long and respected tradition behind it. Moral philosophy had been part of the arts course of the medieval university. Under the influence of the English and Scottish universities, the early American colleges—Harvard, William and Mary, Yale—continued to accord moral philosophy a prominent place in their teaching. It was not until about the time of the Revolution, however, that moral philosophy began to assume the importance in the college curriculum that it was to enjoy throughout most of the following century. It was then that the colleges began to face entirely new tasks and problems. The expansion of knowledge was beginning to demand that colleges introduce new professional emphases as well as a wide range of new subject matter in science, philosophy, and literature alongside the core of the classics and mathematics. The need, moreover, to reconcile many of the philosophic and scientific influences of the Enlightenment with traditional religious and

---

1 For two general discussions of nineteenth-century moral philosophy, see D.H. Meyer, *The Instructed Conscience: The Shaping of the American National Ethic* (Philadelphia: University of Pennsylvania Press, 1972) and Wilson Smith, *Professors and Public Ethics: Studies of Northern Moral Philosophers before the Civil War* (Ithaca: Cornell University Press, 1956). Also see George P. Schmidt, *The Old-Time College President* (New York: Columbia University Press, 1930) and Gladys Bryson, *Man and Society: The Scottish Inquiry of the Eighteenth Century* (Princeton: Princeton University Press, 1945). For early American moral philosophy, see Norman S. Fiering, "Moral Philosophy in America, 1650-1750, and Its British Context" (Ph.D. diss., Columbia University, 1969).

ethical concerns was becoming ever more pressing. Finally, as colleges increased in number after the Revolution, they continued to carry a major responsibility for preparing leaders for the newly developing society.[2] By the early 1800s moral philosophy had begun to appear to be the central point in the college curriculum where these many new concerns could be pulled together and addressed as a whole.

The full significance and centrality of moral philosophy in the nineteenth-century college curriculum can only be understood, however, in light of the assumption held by American leaders and most ordinary citizens that no nation could survive, let alone prosper, without some essential common social and moral values shared by all. For the creation of these common social values Americans looked primarily to education. The faith in the power of education to build a sense of national community and purpose has been deeply ingrained in the thought of Americans from the beginning. We see it in Jefferson's conviction that an enlightened citizenry is essential to a democratic society—and by enlightened he did not mean merely being able to read and write in order to get ahead but the capacity to understand important social issues that confront all citizens and to contribute to their solution. We see the same faith in the unifying purposes of education in Horace Mann's idea that the common school would be "the balance-wheel of the social machinery." This faith in education was certainly one reason, among others, for the explosion in the founding of educational institutions of nearly every kind during the years before the Civil War. Schools, colleges, churches, utopian communities, newspapers, literary and historical societies, academies, lecture series, and other educational agencies spread rapidly during the nineteenth century. In addition to serving more limited purposes, each of these was seen as contributing in its own way to what Perry Miller once described as a great search for national identity—for common social values in a culture that seemed in so many ways torn and fragmented.[3]

Within this larger educational expansion the college was considered

2   On the role of the colleges in preparing national leaders, see James McLachlan, "The American College in the Nineteenth Century: Toward a Reappraisal," *Teachers College Record* 80, no. 2 (December 1978): 287-306. I have dealt with the response of the college to the intellectual and social challenges of the Enlightenment in Douglas Sloan, *The Scottish Enlightenment and the American College Ideal* (New York: Teachers College Press, 1971).

3   Perry Miller, *The Life of the Mind in America from the Revolution to the Civil War* (New York: Harcourt, Brace & World, 1965). Also see Lawrence A. Cremin, *Traditions of American Education* (New York: Basic Books, 1977) and Douglas Sloan, "Harmony, Chaos, and Consensus: The American College Curriculum," *Teachers College Record* 73, no. 2 (December 1971): 221-51.

to have a special and leading role to perform. It was once fashionable to describe the early college as an institution much inferior to the modern university. Thanks to recent research, however, we are beginning to realize that the nineteenth-century college probably deserves far more respect than it has often received. We are beginning to realize that the colleges before the Civil War were not educationally backward, but that their curricular offerings were often relatively quite substantial, up-to-date, and useful. We are becoming aware of the extent to which the colleges were open to more than a privileged upper-class elite and were drawing fairly large numbers of poor and middle-class students. We are also beginning to recognize that the colleges were not usually narrow, sectarian institutions, but were more often community projects. Although they may have borne the name of one religious body, it is becoming increasingly apparent that they were probably more often than not supported by the entire community, were responsive to community needs, and were essentially community colleges.[4]

At the same time, the early colleges had a national orientation. They were seen as part of a larger movement to shape the wider society and to provide common national goals and values. It was widely assumed that the man of learning, as such, exerts an uplifting and unifying influence on society. Jefferson had often spoken of the importance of having men of learning in positions of leadership. Higher education was to produce, in Jefferson's own phrase, just such an "aristocracy of talent and virtue." Underlying this view of higher education was the further assumption that the higher learning constituted a single unified culture in itself. The different branches of knowledge—literature, the arts, and science—were regarded as equals in a single culture of learning. Only if there existed such an intellectual unity among the different branches of knowledge could learned men provide effective cultural leadership for the wider society. Intellectual unity was thus regarded as an essential safeguard against cultural and moral chaos. It is against the background of these assumptions that moral philosophy acquired its central impor-tance in the college curriculum.

The foremost task of the moral philosopher was to demonstrate to his students that humans are fundamentally moral creatures and that man's ethical striving is undergirded and sustained by a moral universe. The

4 See David B. Potts, "American Colleges in the Nineteenth Century: From Localism to Denominationism," *History of Education Quarterly* 11 (1971) : 363-80; David B. Potts, " 'College Enthusiasm!' As Public Response, 1800-1860," *Harvard Educational Review* 47 (February 1977) : 28-42; McLachlan, "The American College"; Stanley M. Guralnick, *Science and the Ante-Bellum American College* (Philadelphia: American Philosophical Society, 1978) ; and Sloan, "Harmony, Chaos, and Consensus."

task was nothing less than to show that religion, science, and the human, mind all, if rightly understood, revealed and contributed to the highest values of the individual and of society. Thus the philosophers took on the task of establishing a firm ground for the unifying moral principles considered so necessary for the health of the nation. In so doing they were responding to the needs of a society that believed in progress but feared the rapid changes the nineteenth century was daily thrusting upon it. The values to which moral philosophy pointed provided an anchor of stability for a nation in change, while at the same time promising continued progress to a people who strove for the realization of the highest ethical ideals. The effort of the moral philosophers was, as D.H. Meyer has written, "to shape and instruct an American public conscience, to create an ethical frame of mind that would direct a new nation seeking a moral as well as a political identity in a changing world."[5] Many of the leading academic philosophers—Francis Wayland, Mark Hopkins, Noah Porter, and others—became through their public lectures and textbooks teachers to the nation at large, giving instruction in the values and attitudes they thought necessary for the nation as a whole to share. Moral philosophy owed its importance in the nineteenth century not only to being part of the college course of study but to being essential as well to the national curriculum.

Within the college itself moral philosophy was important as more than merely another single course. Moral philosophy carried the task of preserving unity in the college curriculum and, thereby, of ensuring the existence of a unified and intelligible universe of discourse. Again moral philosophy represented a response to the needs of the times. Al-. though it was assumed that all branches of learning constituted a single, unified culture, strains were already appearing early in the nineteenth century among the different fields as science, literature, philosophy, the arts each threatened to go its own way.[6] At the same time new subject matter continued to make claims for inclusion in the college curriculum. Intellectual and curricular fragmentation threatened to destroy the very basis of reasoned, ethical discourse and to lead directly to moral and ethical chaos.

Attempting to meet the challenge head-on moral philosophers worked to preserve the unity of learning in two ways. First of all, they sought

5 Meyer, *The Instructed Conscience*, pp. viii-ix.

6 For early conflicts between men of science and men of letters, see Howard S. Miller, *Dollars for Research: Science and its Patrons in Nineteenth-Century America* (Seattle: University of Washington Press, 1970), pp. 22, *passim;* also Frederick Rudolph, *Curriculum: A History of the American Undergraduate Course of Study Since 1836* (San Francisco: Jossey-Bass Publishers, 1977), pp. 107-109.

to provide a means of bringing together all the subject areas studied by the student and by relating these to higher laws, to furnish an integrating principle for the entire curriculum. Mental philosophy and moral philosophy, for example, had always been closely connected, and the nineteenth-century philosophers stressed more than ever the role of the mind as a prime source of moral truth, whether through intuition and introspection, conscience and the "moral sense," or the use of ordinary reason. This emphasis on the mind also enabled the philosophers to draw connections between knowledge of moral laws and what it discovered about the laws of nature through science. Some moral philosophers, from John Witherspoon in the eighteenth century on, harbored the hope that moral philosophy could approach the same exactness as a mode of knowing as was enjoyed by science.[7] Just as science was thought to reveal the divine handiwork in nature, so moral philosophy demonstrated moral purpose and design in human affairs. The moral law was considered to be as real and as inexorable as the law of gravity and both pointed to a divine governor of the world. By emphasizing ethics and the moral law as also the common element of all religion, the moral philosophers represented a secularizing and moralizing of the religious impulses—an influence that was to become increasingly pronounced. At the same time, however, putting the emphasis on ethics rather than theology also made it possible for them to assert the underlying unity of religion at a time of mounting sectarianism and religious disagreement. They could argue that there was no fundamental conflict among religion, science, and morality and that all working together made possible the moral and material progress of society.

Moral philosophy also served to promote intellectual harmony by introducing into the curriculum a wide range of new subject matter and attempting to exhibit for the student its ethical dimensions. Much of what we now recognize as the social sciences first appeared in the college curriculum in the moral philosophy course.[8] The attention given in

7 John Witherspoon, President of Princeton, for example, told his senior class in moral philosophy, "Yet perhaps a time may come when men, treating moral philosophy as Newton and his successors have done natural, may arrive at greater precision." John Witherspoon, *Lectures on Moral Philosophy* (Princeton: Princeton University Press, 1912), p. 4.

8 In his moral philosophy lectures Witherspoon touched on such topics as epistemology, political science, economics, jurisprudence, family and marriage, primitive customs, religion, personal and social morality, aesthetics, and others. Ibid. For discussions of the relations between moral philosophy and the later social sciences, see: Gladys Bryson, "The Emergence of The Social Sciences from Moral Philosophy," *International Journal of Ethics* XLII (April 1932); idem., "The Comparable Interests of the Old Moral Philosophy and the Modern Social Sciences," *Social Forces II* (October 1932); and idem., "Sociology Considered as Moral Philosophy," *Sociological Review* 24 (January 1932). Also see Bryson, *Man and Society*.

moral philosophy to mental philosophy and social institutions as necessary to the construction of sound ethical theory also demanded the study
of an increasing number of related fields. Moreover, the high value
placed on scientific method—an introduction to scientific method, usually of a simplified Baconian type, was usually the first topic of the
moral philosophy course—required increased precision and delineation
of related fields of study.

The results were three-fold. First, moral philosophy became an important source for the origin and development of what later developed
as political science, economics, philosophical ethics, psychology, anthropology, and sociology. Second, as these subjects split out of moral
philosophy, they based much of their claims for autonomy on the very
scientific status moral philosophy accorded them. Finally, as these subjects became fields of study in their own right, they often carried with
them the moral and ethical imperatives of moral philosophy. The later
conflict within the social sciences as to whether they could remain both
scientific and ethical was to become, as we shall see, one of the major
questions in American higher education.

The final, and in some ways the most crucial and difficult, use of
moral philosophy was to help form the moral character and disposition
of the individual student. This required that students' own ethical concerns be awakened and that they be inspired to pursue their own
continuing moral development. It also demanded that the theoretical
underpinnings of ethics, which were a main component of the course,
be presented so as to confirm students in their own ethical striving.
Furthermore, it meant providing concrete examples of ethical concern
and conduct in the person of the moral philosopher himself. The scientific claims of moral philosophy were not taken to mean that the personal example of the teacher was unrelated to the content of instruction.
It was the teacher's task to exhort, admonish, and inspire students to
recognize that the demands of morality were real and all-encompassing.
Although such things are difficult to measure, evidence in students' tes-
timonials suggests that many moral philosophers may very well have
made their greatest impact through the influence of their own personalities.[9] Others, by the same token, suffered their most important failure

9 See Meyer, *The Instructed Conscience*, p. 126. "There is no part of the University
work from which the student derives more real mental strength than from the course in
Philosophy under President Bascom," wrote one University of Wisconsin alumnus in
1885. "It is especially fortunate," he said, "that Dr. Bascom is so thoroughly master of the
subject; and along with a perfectly clear and adequate explanation of all obscure points,
he imparts to the students a share of his own healthy enthusiasm." Quoted in Merle Curti
and Vernon Carstensens, *The University of Wisconsin, A History, 1848-1929*, vol. I (Madison: University of Wisconsin Press, 1949), p. 280.

in their inability to bring their course to life or to inspire through personal example.

It is important to point out, however, that moral philosophy was not expected to carry the whole burden of forming the students' characters and guiding their conduct. The entire college curriculum and environment had the same purpose. The classics themselves had long maintained their place in the curriculum, in part, because they were considered essential for understanding perennial ethical issues. Sermons in college chapel and, not infrequently, evidences of religion drawn in a science class by a devout professor, were intended to give further witness to the moral law. The mental discipline that study of the classics and mathematics was thought to impart was viewed as indispensable to the development and exercise of moral discipline. This discipline was further reinforced by the strict *in loco parentis* regimen of the college schedule. The entire college experience was meant above all to be an experience in character development and the moral life, as epitomized, secured, and brought to a focus in the moral philosophy course.[10]

This preeminence of moral philosophy in the undergraduate curriculum did not survive the nineteenth century, and the reasons for its decline were the result partly, though not entirely, of internal weaknesses. In retrospect we have become aware of many of the inherent problems of the moral philosophy course. For one thing, the desire for social unity and harmony was so consuming that the philosophers often studiously avoided issues that involved conflict. Consequently, they were sometimes blind to or silent on some of the most critical ethical problems of the times. Wilson Smith, for example, has pointed out that ante-bellum moral philosophers, with the exception of a few like Francis Wayland, almost to a man entirely neglected the question of slavery.[11] The desire to seek harmony and to avoid conflict also meant that their pronouncements often rose little above the level of truisms—a tendency further encouraged by the exhortative, presumptuous, rhetorical style of the moralists.[12] The stress on harmony, the avoidance of conflict, the desire to promote progress—all gave to moral philosophy built-in conservative tendencies that lent themselves to the support of the status quo and the dominant interests of the society. It was no accident that the virtues and moral qualities cherished by the philosophers

10 See Sloan, "Harmony, Chaos, and Consensus."
11 Smith, *Professors and Public Ethics*, pp. 67-70.
12 Meyer, *The Instructed Conscience*, pp. 74-75, 114.

were also highly congenial to the solid citizen, the banker, the merchant, the respectable church-goer.[13]

Perhaps the greatest weakness of moral philosophy was that the unity of the curriculum it strove to maintain was becoming illusory even by mid-century. It is ironic that the main proliferation of new subject areas in the college curriculum, besides those in natural science, came from precisely those areas that moral philosophy itself had first nourished. Moral philosophy had cast a false patina of unity over the curriculum, which it was powerless to maintain. The increasing fragmentation of knowledge signalled the rapid decline of moral philosophy. Intellectual disintegration also meant, however, as the philosophers had predicted it would, increasing neglect within American higher education of the ethical foundations of the pursuit of knowledge and of its moral uses.

Still, the nineteenth-century conception of moral philosophy did not simply disappear, for its influence and the concerns it had generated continued to be felt in American higher education. The old moral philosophy had emphasized the relation between society and morality, economics and ethics, science and value. This was a perspective that would resurface repeatedly among at least a few in twentieth-century American higher education, each time, its critics to the contrary notwithstanding, as the reassertion of a long and venerable American tradition. For all its conservatism and weaknesses, the old moral philosophy had a radical potential as D.H. Meyer has clearly demonstrated.[14] In their understanding of the moral law as ultimately transcending politics, personalities, and conventional wisdom, the nineteenth-century moral philosophers established a tradition and provided resources for those who would continue to argue that social criticism and ethical deliberation lie at the heart of what it truly means to be an institution of higher education. Furthermore, the philosophers' view of the intimate relation between the unity of knowledge and the possibility of meaningful moral discourse appeared to receive continued confirmation. Finally, the nineteenth-century moral philosophers saw the essential unity of the three dimensions of the teaching of ethics: the cultural—the search for common values—the intellectual—the investigation of the philosophic ground of values and moral action—and the individual—the formation of character and conduct. The fracturing of this three-fold task was to remain a perplexing problem for higher education. If they fell far short in their undertaking, the nineteenth-century college moral philoso-

---

13 Ibid., pp. 104-107; and Smith, *Professors and Public Ethics*, pp. 3-4.
14 Meyer, *The Instructed Conscience*, pp. 85-86, 119-20.

phers, nevertheless, knew where many of the main problems lay. They had a clearer sense of the important issues in the relations between knowledge and values than they have often been given credit for.

ETHICS AND SOCIAL SCIENCE IN THE NEW UNIVERSITY

The decline of moral philosophy in American higher education was already well under way as early as the 1880s.[15] Yet many colleges continued for some time to hold out. In 1895 the Amherst College Catalogue devoted the entire first page of the section on "The Course of Study" to a description of the course of Ethics taught by the President of the College to the senior class.[16] But by 1905 ethics had disappeared from its front page billing in the catalogue and was to be found as merely one among several courses offered in Amherst's Philosophy Department as an elective for sophomores.[17] The loss of ethics' exalted place in the Amherst curriculum indicated by these catalogue entries is emblematic of a major sea-change that had overtaken the whole of American higher education. So deep and thorough were the transformations taking place in American higher education that even those institutions, such as Amherst, that would continue to regard themselves as the nation's major bulwarks of defense for traditional philosophies of higher education found themselves profoundly and permanently affected.

The passing of the older conception of moral philosophy did not mean the immediate disappearance of a pervasive ethical perspective in American higher education. In many respects, in fact, the late nineteenth and early twentieth centuries witnessed an efflorescence of moral reform activity, and with it an explosion outward into the whole society of the kind of moral enthusiasm and exertion the earlier moral philosophers had taken it upon themselves to inculcate. In the face of mounting social problems in the late nineteenth century the strong traditions of social-cultural reform established in America before the Civil War began to reassert themselves with renewed vigor. A myriad of social-

15 According to D.H. Meyer, the last American textbook in moral philosophy of the traditional type was *Our Moral Nature*, written by James McCosh, President of Princeton, and published in 1892. Ibid., p. 130.

16 "The aim of the course," read the catalogue, "is, by the philosophic study of the social and political relations of the individual to his fellow citizens and to the State, to promote that moral thoughtfulness . . . which is the strongest element in true patriotism." Amherst College, *Catalogue*, 1895, p. 32.

17 Amherst College, *Catalogue*, 1905.

cultural reform movements and activities began to appear in response to the increasingly complex problems of urban-industrial America.[18] The splintering of moral philosophy into many separate new subjects was in part a result of what today is sometimes called an explosion in knowledge; it also represented an extension outward of the reform spirit and moral concern that moral philosophy itself had helped to nourish. It was in this climate of social reform, moral uplift, and educational enthusiasm that the university movement of the latter nineteenth century was born.

The so-called rise of the university is too complex an affair to be captured and explained in a single phrase or formula. Much of the initial impetus for the university came from educational reformers who wanted an institution to do better what they felt the college and moral philosophy course had failed to do—to train a generation of leaders imbued with a sense of responsibility and commitment to the nation. Daniel Coit Gilman, President of Johns Hopkins, the model of the research university, spoke for most of his fellow university reformers when he said, "The object of the university is to develop character—to make men."[19] The university also took upon itself the task of providing training for the burgeoning career opportunities in an expanding industrial-managerial society. It coupled these functions with a commitment to support and lead scientific research, both in the faith that scientific expansion of itself promoted social progress and that scientific methods of analysis were the tools most needed by a new generation of national leaders.

Soon a new social theory of higher education began to emerge to give direction to the university's diverse functions and to justify the leading role in society that was being claimed for it. The paramount need of American society, university spokesmen began to argue, was for guided social change under the direction of trained experts. The man of learn-

18 This social reform activity included the establishment and support of schools, universities, university extension, manual training and technical institutes, parks and playgrounds, settlement houses, institutional churches, women's study and social science groups, civic improvement organizations, public museums and art institutes, libraries, and concert orchestras. In accounts of the time these activities were often lumped together and described variously as moral uplift, social reform, civic improvement, cultural uplift, and, in a popular phrase of the day, working for "the higher life." See Jane Allen Shikoh "The 'Higher Life' in the American City of the 1890s" (Ph.D. diss., New York University, 1972). Also, Helen Lefkowitz Horowitz, *Culture and the City: Cultural Philanthropy in Chicago from the 1880s to 1917* (Lexington: The University Press of Kentucky, 1976).

19 Quoted in Richard J. Storr, "Academic Culture and the History of American Higher Education," *Journal of General Education* 5 (October 1950): 13.

ing was still important, but he was now redefined not so much as a man of culture and an exemplar of a unified single culture of learning, but rather as the specialized expert. This educated elite of experts, imbued with the ideals of social service and equipped with specialized knowledge, would apply its intelligence to the management of a society that had become too complex to be left to the direction of ordinary men. Central to the institutionalization of this vision was the elective principle that under the leadership of Charles W. Eliot at Harvard became the main concept for organizing—or, as its critics claimed, for dismantling—the academic curriculum. The elective principle encouraged the expansion of knowledge and, with the growth of university departments around the new disciplines, early undergraduate specialization, the proliferation of vocationalism and professional and graduate education, and an increasing emphasis on research.[20]

Equally important in institutionalizing the new theory of education was the formation during the 1880s and 90s of learned societies based on specific fields of inquiry and supported institutionally by the growing departmental organization of the university. Increasingly research specialization and scholarly approval by professional colleagues in the same field became the main criteria of academic appointment and promotion.[21] Professionally organized itself and assuming the role of standardizing and certifying entry into all professions, academic and otherwise, the prestige of the university was firmly secured by the end of the century.[22] Although the university was numerically a minority in comparison with the college, which the majority of students continued to attend, it was the university that increasingly set standards and determined the goals of all of higher education.[23]

With the benefits of an enormous increase in knowledge and improvement of scholarly methods and standards, the specialization and

20 See Hugh Hawkins, *Between Harvard and America: The Educational Leadership of Charles W. Eliot* (New York: Oxford University Press, 1972).

21 On the growing importance of university research and specialization see, Robert A. McCaughey, "The Transformation of American Academic Life: Harvard University, 1821-1892," *Perspectives in American History* 8 (1974) : 237-332.

22 On the role of the universities as certifiers and entries for the professions, see Burton J. Bledstein, *The Culture of Professionalism: The Middle Class and the Development of Higher Education in America* (New York: W.W. Norton, 1976). Also, Robert H. Wiebe, *The Search for Order, 1877-1920* (New York: Hill and Wang, 1967), p. 121.

23 The impact of the university on the college curriculum and teaching is dealt with in George E. Peterson, *The New England College in the Age of the University* (Amherst, Mass.: Amherst College Press, 1964) ; and Willis Rudy, *The Evolving Liberal Arts Curriculum: A Historical Review of Basic Themes* (New York: Teachers College, Columbia University, 1960).

professionalization of the faculty also brought problems. The vision of a unified curriculum and culture of learning was being abandoned, and the ethical, social, and character concerns once central to higher education were giving way to an emphasis on research and specialized training as the primary purpose of the university. With the new status and scholarly achievements of the faculties came an academic style that was becoming, in the words of Frederick Rudolph, "indifferent to undergraduates," "removed from moral judgment," and to an increasing degree "unrelated to the traditional social purposes of higher education."[24] The emphasis on the subject rather than the student and on specialization rather than synthesis were to be sources of strength, but also of large unresolved, often unaddressed problems.

At first the new social sciences and the learned societies that supported them carried both the ethical and scientific orientation of moral philosophy in which they had been nourished and which they hoped to replace. Many of the new subjects and their corresponding professional bodies were founded expressly to apply the latest social science methods and findings to the solution of pressing social problems. However, active social reform proved increasingly incompatible with the new canons of scientific objectivity and with an academic career built on scholarly productivity. As a consequence, during their first years, the professional societies were wracked by fierce disagreement over the place of ethics in a proper social science. The central question in the controversies, it should be stressed, was at first not so much whether social science had an ethical dimension but more what that dimension was and how it should be expressed.

Many of the young social scientists—men such as economists Richard T. Ely, Henry Carter Adams, Simon Nelson Patten, and Edmund J. James—brought a strong ethical concern to their subject. Ely himself had been deeply influenced by his own college moral philosophy course, and he combined a commitment to Christian Socialism and an appreciation for the rights of labor with a stress on scientific method.[25] Most, like Ely, held to a conception of science shaped by evolutionary thought and the German historical school, which emphasized the uniqueness of each historical situation and hence the possibility of social change guided by inductive empirical science. Their conception of an ethical

24 Rudolph, *Curriculum*, p. 157.
25 Mary O. Furner, *Advocacy and Objectivity: A Crisis in the Professionalization of American Social Science, 1865-1905* (Lexington: University of Kentucky Press, 1975), pp. 49-54; and Benjamin G. Rader, *The Academic Mind and Reform: The Influence of Richard T. Ely in American Life* (Lexington: University of Kentucky Press, 1966).

social science committed most of them to actual social reform activity outside the walls of the university and to popularizing their science through books and lectures for the public. They also took the lead in organizing professional societies as part of their larger effort to give effective institutional force to their ethical science, and to combat older views, which they considered both socially conservative and unscientific. The American Economics Association, for example, was founded in 1885, primarily under the leadership of Ely, then a young professor at Johns Hopkins, to make the ethical ideal in economic life a reality and to challenge the dominant position in academia of the classical laissez faire political economists.

By the mid-1890s, interestingly, nearly all of the originally more activist academics had begun to dissociate themselves from reform causes and to emphasize instead their devotion to scientific research and their professional ties. They had discovered, for one thing, that their activities as popularizers and reform advocates—as ethics teachers to the nation at large—required precious time from their scholarly and scientific research. Because of their espousal of unpopular social causes they found themselves embroiled in disputes with their university presidents and boards of trustees in ways that threatened the very existence of their still precarious academic careers. And probably most important, they found themselves being criticized by social scientists of their own generation who charged that their popularizing activities and their image as agitators and radicals called into question their standing as responsible, objective-minded scientists. During the latter 1890s Ely severed almost all his connections with reform activity as did most of the others.[26] As they retreated from reform, the professional organizations to which they belonged also ceased raising ethical questions and began to concentrate almost entirely on detailed, carefully defined empirical research.[27]

The shift from advocacy and activism to an emphasis on "value-free inquiry" and professional organization was only partly the result of fears for the loss of newly won and very prestigious academic careers. It was also a rejection of sentimental "do-gooder" attitudes prevalent at the end of the nineteenth century. More important, it also reflected, as Robert L. Church has clearly shown, a growing consensus on the part of the social scientists as to how they might best, to use his phrase, "make a difference in the real world."[28] The shift represented a widen-

26 Rader, *The Academic Mind and Reform*, p. 153.
27 Ibid., pp. 130-158; and Furner, *Advocacy and Objectivity*, pp. 290-92 and *passim*.
28 Robert L. Church, "Economists as Experts: The Rise of an Academic Profession in America, 1870-1917," in *The University in Society*, vol. II, ed. Lawrence Stone (Princeton: Princeton University Press, 1974), see esp. pp. 573, 596.

ing conviction among all the social scientists that they could make this "difference" and establish their authority most effectively by fully embracing the role of the indispensable expert who provided needed knowledge to those leaders in government and business who were in positions actually to shape public policy. Their unquestioning faith in the progressive nature of science enabled most of them to accept in good conscience the simplifications their emphasis brought to their personal and organizational lives, assuming that as scientific problems were solved the ethical issues would take care of themselves. The shift also was necessary for the internal unity and harmony required for the establishment of an authoritative professional community. Controversy threatened the credibility of the professionals in the eyes of the public, for if the experts quarrelled among themselves, who was to take their pronouncements seriously. Controversy also diminished the respect among peers so essential to the maintenance of professional standards. By dispensing with ethical questions, the academics also eliminated a major source of potential controversy.[29]

The withdrawal of social scientists from active social reform did not mean their immediate abandonment of a concern for the ethical dimensions of their subjects. The majority still assumed that there was no fundamental conflict between ethical idealism and scientific objectivity. Indeed, as has been indicated, they had become convinced that it was as scientific experts that they could have their most effective influence on the world of affairs. Many of the most important figures in establishing the social sciences as university disciplines conceived of themselves as equally ethicists and scientists. They had entered their field in the conviction that the scientific study of society could give ethics a concreteness and a reality that neither the abstractions of their moral philosophy mentors nor the exhortations of contemporary social reformers could achieve.

The first two decades of the century witnessed a vigorous discussion in the social science literature regarding the relationship between ethics, on the one hand, and, on the other, scientific research, technology, and social organization. In the writings of such leading figures in the new social sciences as George Herbert Mead, Albion W. Small, James Mark Baldwin, James H. Tufts, John Dewey, and others, the theme was developed that ethics is not fixed once and for all, but, like man, is

---

29 The importance of internal harmony for the development and maintenance of modern professional communities is developed with respect to the study of early social sciences by Thomas L. Haskell, *The Emergence of Professional Social Science: The American Social Science Association and the Nineteenth-Century Crisis of Authority* (Urbana: University of Illinois Press, 1977) , see esp. pp. 162-63.

evolving and that social science reveals the conditions and possibilities under which new ethical ideas can be created and realized.[30] The discussion was picked up and carried on also by lesser lights in the field.[31] Underlying this essentially evolutionary understanding of ethics and science was usually the assumption that man is basically an ethical being, or in the words of James H. Tufts, "a progressive being" whose science is itself a creative projection of man's creative potentialities.[32] This outlook portrayed the social sciences almost by definition as being integrating and ethical in nature.

Another outlook was also becoming more and more pronounced. This view stressed the notion of value-free objective research and the need to draw ever tighter the lines demarcating disciplinary boundaries. The evolutionary, ethical view of the social sciences, largely because of its uncritical, often utopian faith in science, was vulnerable to encroachments by the harder professional, objective notion of science, and, in fact, helped smooth the way for the latter's acceptance. By the time of World War I social scientists had not only disengaged themselves from direct social action, but their fields were becoming increasingly dominated by a stress on scientific method as ethically neutral, on a scientific, objective, and quantitative understanding of social science research, and on tighter professional, organizational control. A conviction that ethics and social science were inseparable not only was yielding to confusion about the exact nature of the relationship, but this in turn was giving way to spreading embarrassment among professionals over colleagues who persisted in writing and speaking of the possibility of an ethically oriented science. This continuing shift is clearly apparent

---

30 See, for example, James H. Tufts, "The Present Task of Ethical Theory," *International Journal of Ethics* 20 (1910) : 141-52; George H. Mead, "The Philosophical Basis of Ethics," *International Journal of Ethics* 18 (1908) : 311-23; Thorstein Veblen, "Christian Morals and the Competitive System," *International Journal of Ethics* 20 (1910) : 118-85; Albion W. Small, "The Significance of Sociology for Ethics," *The Dicennial Publication of the University of Chicago*, vol. IV (Chicago: The University of Chicago Press, 1903) , pp. 111-50; Charles H. Henderson, "Practical Sociology in the Service of Social Ethics," *The Dicennial Publication of the University of Chicago*, vol. III (Chicago: The University of Chicago Press, 1903) , pp. 25-50; John Dewey, "The Evolutionary Method as Applied to Morality," *Philosophical Review* 11 (1902) : 107-24, 353-71; and Charles A. Elwood, "The Sociological Basis of Ethics," *International Journal of Ethics* 20 (1910) : 314-28.

31 For example, Charles W. Super, "Ethics as a Science," *International Journal of Ethics* 24 (1913/14) : 265-81; G. Gore, "The Coming Scientific Morality," *Monist* 14 (1904) : 355-77; J.W. Garner, "Political Science and Ethics," *International Journal of Ethics* 17 (1907) : 194-204; and E.C. Hayes, "Sociology as Ethics," *American Journal of Sociology* 24 (1918) : 289-302.

32 Tufts, "The Present Task of Sociology," pp. 148-49.

in psychology and sociology, two subjects closely connected originally with the teaching of ethics.

Long after moral philosophy and psychology had separated, the study of motives as the springs of human action had continued to furnish topics within the study of psychology and ethics alike. Mind, consciousness, and purposive striving continued for some time to be important concerns of psychology. The trend, however, was to eliminate ethics and value theory as integral parts of psychology.[33] By 1920 psychology as a field of study and as an organized discipline had been thoroughly transformed.

The desire to imitate the exactitude of the natural sciences led psychologists to want to eliminate the imprecision of research methods based on introspection and the generality of such nonempirical notions as purpose and consciousness, and to seek instead complete objectivity and quantitative certainty. The behaviorist position in psychology, presented with great force by John Watson in his major writings between 1913 and 1919, tossed out all talk about self and purpose that had been so much a part of the older psychology and of ethics as well.[34] The oft-quoted statement made by E.L. Thorndike in 1918 that, "Whatever exists at all, exists in some amount," symbolized the wholly physical, empirical, quantitative character of the new psychology.[35] Ethics was no longer a constituent part of psychology.

33 This trend can be illustrated by a glance at the subject headings of *The Psychological Index*. Begun in 1894 as a bimonthly and edited for fifteen years thereafter by James Mark Baldwin of Princeton and James McKeen Cattell of Columbia, *The Psychological Index* was an extensive bibliography of the literature of psychology and its related subjects and for years was a major research and reference guide in the field. J. Mark Baldwin and J. McKeen Cattell, eds., *The Psychological Review* and *The Psychological Index*, published bimonthly by Macmillan and Company. In the 1894 edition of the *Index* "Ethics" held its traditionally high position within psychology as a subheading under the major topic of "Higher Manifestations of the Mind," along with such other subheadings as "Logic and Science," "Ideals and Values," "Theory of Knowledge," "Aesthetics," and "Feelings." Ethics maintained this position until 1906 when confusion seems to have begun to set in about the proper place of such topics in a psychological index. That year, although the subheading remained the same, the major heading was changed to "Philosophical Implications of Psychology," and within a few years the major heading was changed once again to simply "Attitudes and Intellectual Activities" and the subheading from "Ethics" to "Psychology of Behavior and Morals." In 1915 the major topic heading changed once more, this time to "Social Functions of the Individual." The index listings and the reinterpretations of ethics within psychology that they represented were, however, only mildly indicative of the profound changes that had been occurring within psychology.

34 For an interesting discussion of the significance of behaviorism, see Edward A. Purcell, Jr., *The Crisis of Democratic Theory, Scientific Naturalism and the Problem of Value* (Lexington: University of Kentucky Press, 1973), pp. 34-38.

35 See, for example, Lawrence A. Cremin, *The Transformation of the School* (New York: Alfred A. Knopf, 1962), p. 185.

For a time sociology presented something of a special case among the social sciences. Sociology preserved the connection between ethics and science longer than did such other fields as economics and political science. Sociology, however, was also burdened with its own peculiar difficulty, for, far more than the other fields, it lacked a clearly defined scientific focus and methodology. The place sociology was to occupy in the curriculum and the task it was to perform remained during the first decade of the century open questions and potential sources of creative debate about the place of ethics in the university. For that reason it deserves a bit of special attention.

By 1900 sociology was being increasingly taught in American colleges and universities, usually in connection with economics and political science departments, but it had yet to achieve autonomy as a discipline in its own right.[36] Probably the single person most responsible for the establishment of sociology as a university discipline was Albion W. Small. In 1890 as the newly appointed president of Colby College in Maine, Small altered the topics of the moral philosophy course he taught, replacing the "history of metaphysical philosophy" with "modern sociological philosophy." Small soon left Colby for the new University of Chicago where, in 1892, he formed the first graduate department of sociology anywhere and shortly thereafter launched the *American Journal of Sociology*, the first sociological journal in the United States.[37]

Small, like Comte, Spencer, and Lester Frank Ward before him, conceived of sociology as the unifying science of the study of man and as a preeminently ethical science. He viewed sociology as a holistic science, one that would synthesize all the fields of knowledge and bring them to bear in the service of man. "Sociology, in its largest scope, and on its methodological side," he wrote, "is merely a moral philosophy conscious of its task, and systematically pursuing knowledge of cause and effect within this process of moral evolution."[38] The whole point of science, Small argued, was to contribute to the enhancement of man's capacity to realize his highest values. "Science is sterile," he wrote, "unless it

36 For a discussion of the development of sociology within Harvard's Department of Economics, see Robert L. Church, "The Economists Study Society: Sociology at Harvard, 1891-1902," in *Social Sciences at Harvard, 1860-1920*, ed. Paul Buck (Cambridge: Harvard University Press, 1965), pp. 18-90.

37 Vernon K. Dibble, *The Legacy of Albion Small* (Chicago: The University of Chicago Press, 1975), pp. 2-3.

38 Albion W. Small, *Adam Smith and Modern Sociology* (Chicago: University of Chicago Press, 1907), p. 22.

contributes at last to knowledge of what is worth doing. . . . Sociology
would have no sufficient reason for existence if it did not contribute at
last to knowledge of what is worth doing. . . . The ultimate value of
sociology as pure science will be its use as an index and a test and a
measure of what is worth doing."[39] Sociology would provide a scientific
basis for an ethical perspective in life by studying the concrete context
of human associations within which values are realized; in demonstrat-
ing the limited and parochial nature of all existing value judgments,
sociology would press toward an evolutionary, universal ethic.[40]

For Small, as for many of his contemporaries, the absence of cultural
and moral unity was the overriding tragedy of modern life and the
major ethical problem to be solved.[41] The university, he thought, had
a special role to play in re-establishing cultural unity.[42] This, however,
was a task it could not fulfill until it put its own house in order, for the
moral confusion of modern culture was reflected in and exacerbated by
the intellectual and ethical chaos of the university itself. If the university were to be true to its proper task, it would have to center itself
around an ethical and unifying science of man—in short, around
sociology as Small conceived it.

Despite his and others' rhetoric to the contrary, however, Small's
vision of a synthetic, holistic social science was a misfit in the university
of his day.[43] To those social scientists who were busy delimiting their
own fields, the claims of a synthetic science sounded imperalistic and

39 Small, "The Significance of Sociology for Ethics," p. 119.

40 For my capsule account, I have relied especially on two studies of Small: Dibble,
The Legacy of Albion Small; and Ernest Becker, "The Tragic Paradox of Albion Small and
American Social Science" in *The Lost Science of Man* (New York: George Braziller, 1971),
pp. 3-70.

41 The deep concern among intellectuals of the period about the loss of common social
values is dealt with in R. Jackson Wilson, *In Quest of Community* (Oxford: Oxford University Press, 1968); and Jean B. Quandt, *From the Small Town to the Great Community:
The Social Thought of Progressive Intellectuals* (New Brunswick: Rutgers University
Press, 1970).

42 See Albion W. Small, "The Annual Phi Beta Kappa Address: The Social Value of
the Academic Career" (1906), reprinted in Dibble, *The Legacy of Albion Small*, pp. 185-
200. The address begins with the provocation: "If the world were governed by its wisdom
instead of its selfishness, would universities be promoted?"

43 Even though sociology had begun to find a focus in study of the social group, which
was not far removed from Small's own emphasis on the interrelatedness of human associations, and even though many others voiced similar concerns about over-specialization and
the need for integrating the special sciences, the pressures and rewards of scholarship ran
in a different direction. On the emerging focus of sociology on the social group, see Furner,
Advocacy and Objectivity, pp. 305-306. On the widespread expression of discontent with
specialization and of sentiment for a larger synthesizing vision among social scientists, see
Quandt, *From the Small Town to the Great Community*, pp. 102-25.

manifestly unscientific. The concept of an ethical science appeared, furthermore, to conflict with the canons of objective, value-free research. Small was fully aware of the problem. He knew that neither the university system itself nor the prevailing academic temper of mind provided much support for his view, and he sometimes criticized them on just that score.[44]

Yet Small was not always consistent. In his desire to see sociology acquire a disciplinary and professional base in the university, he was willing to trim his large claims for sociology, to keep a prudent silence about them, even to back down.[45] Owing much to Small's own indefatigable organizing labors, sociology was indeed established within the university, but at the price of having to abandon holistic, synthesizing pretensions and of having to assume the much more humble position of one discipline among many, a discipline with its own focus, its own language, its own carefully delineated problems.[46]

To the end, Small still clung to the hope that sociology would take up its true task. The conception of sociology that triumphed, however, the only one that in his day could have, was set forth very clearly by William F. Ogburn in his presidential address to the American Sociological Society three years after Small's death in 1929. "Sociology as a science," said Ogburn, "is not interested in making the world a better place in which to live, in encouraging beliefs, in spreading information, in dispensing news, in setting forth impressions of life, in leading the multitudes, or in guiding the ship of state. Science is interested directly in one thing only, to wit, discovering new knowledge."[47] Sociology had at last come of age as a bona fide discipline.

44 The decisive question in the university has usually been, he once wrote, "not what aspects of reality most urgently demand investigation, but with what sort of material one could most certainly establish oneself as a teacher. . . ." Quoted in Becker, "The Tragic Paradox of Albion Small," p. 23.

45 When, for example, Robert E. Park and Ernest W. Burgess, Small's associates at Chicago, published their *Introduction to the Science of Sociology* in 1921 setting forth their commitment to eschew system and to provide a sociology based on "modest searching in the spirit of an inductive science," they had Small's blessing. See Robert E.L. Faris, *Chicago Sociology, 1920-1932* (Chicago: University of Chicago Press, 1967), p. 128.

46 Becker argues that the tragedy of Small was that he never fully integrated in his own vision the concept of sociology as both synthesis and professional focus and in the end opted for the latter so that "one gained a new equality with other social sciences, but one lost social science." Becker, "The Tragic Paradox of Albion Small," p. 20. Dibble, on the other hand, argues, convincingly I think, that Small was internally consistent, but that his view was anachronistic in the university of his time and place. Both agree on the end result for sociology. Dibble, *The Legacy of Albion Small*, pp. 149-53.

47 Quoted in Becker, "The Tragic Paradox of Albion Small," p. 28.

The inward turn of the social sciences ensured the tightening of disciplinary boundaries, the development of increasingly esoteric bodies of knowledge accessible only to experts in each field, and a lack of concern, sometimes even of respect, for the general public and for the student. At the same time, it brought the social scientists organizational security and authority, a base for widening involvement with government and business, and the conditions for scholarly achievement and recognition. It also meant that the social sciences could no longer be looked to as a primary source and stimulus for the teaching of ethics in the college and university curriculum. The hope of many at the turn of the century that the social sciences would embrace the ethical tasks of their moral philosophy heritage, but fulfill them in ways appropriate to the modern world as the old course never could, had been abandoned.

ETHICS IN DEPARTMENTS OF PHILOSOPHY: THE EARLY DECADES

Philosophy was always the first legatee of the teaching of ethics, particularly the branch of ethics concerned with the intellectual theory of moral thought and action. Once it was clear that the social sciences would not continue their moral philosophy tradition, the teaching of ethics as a formal subject was left for the most part—though not entirely as we shall see—to departments of philosophy. What place ethics would occupy within departments of philosophy, what would be the dominant concern of ethics, how ethics would be related to other subjects, whether ethics would, for example, somehow step in to fill the vacuum left by the social sciences in their attempt to be value free, whether ethics would seek to continue the full panoply of the earlier moral philosophy concerns not only for the theory of ethics but also for the actual formation of character and conduct—these remained open questions even into the 1920s, although by then certain definite trends in the teaching of ethics were becoming evident.

For a time, there appeared in the undefined territory between philosophy and sociology courses in social ethics—taught sometimes in philosophy departments, sometimes in sociology, sometimes as a course in religion, and, on occasion, within departments of social ethics. In the late nineteenth century, the American Social Science Association (ASSA) had attempted to encourage colleges to introduce social science courses and topics oriented toward the study of current American social issues of the times. In response to the growing social problems facing the nation after the Civil War, the ASSA had been founded in 1865 by influential persons drawn from business, the older professions, literary circles, and academia, persons who were concerned to encourage social reform and to develop better methods of studying and understanding social problems. The ASSA represented a practical extension and application of moral philosophy to actual social conditions, and, as part of its effort to improve the social consciousness of American leaders, it encouraged during the 1870s and 80s the introduction into American colleges of courses in social science. In a survey conducted by the ASSA in 1885 over 100 colleges reported that they gave instruction in one or more topics in social science. Although one college, Wooster in Ohio, reported having just established a chair in Morals and Sociology, a close reading of the report suggests that most schools responding to the survey simply reported as social science topics those they were already giving in moral philosophy and political economy.[48] Little new came of these efforts, and it was not until the nineties and early twentieth century that social ethics began to appear in higher education from other sources.[49]

One of the first major experiments in the teaching of social ethics was the development of Harvard's Social Ethics Department under Francis Greenwood Peabody. The difficulty of establishing a subject area that lacked a clearly defined focus was well-exemplified by the Harvard Department. Peabody first began teaching ethics at Harvard in 1881 after some years as a lecturer on ethics at the Divinity School and as a minister in Cambridge.[50] Throughout the 1890s he conducted one of the college's most popular courses among undergraduates under the title, "The Ethics of the Social Question." Sociology was also being taught within the Economics Department but was still so closely tied to the methods and perspectives of that department that for many years there was little overlap or conflict.[51] And Peabody's own aim was not to develop sociology as such but was essentially to revive moral philosophy in a form he thought adequate to the problems of the day.

48 "Social Science Instruction in Colleges, 1886," *Journal of Social Sciences* (1886): xxxv-xix.

49 The attempt of the ASSA to establish closer relationships with the university and its rebuff by professionally minded academic sociologists, and its subsequent demise, are dealt with as part of the larger professionalization of the social sciences by Furner, *Advocacy and Objectivitiy*, and Haskell, *The Emergence of Professional Social Science.*

50 For my discussion here of Peabody and the Harvard Social Ethics Department I draw mainly on David B. Potts, "Social Ethics at Harvard, 1881-1931: A Study in Academic Activism," in Buck, *Social Sciences at Harvard, 1860-1920,* pp. 91-128. Also see, Jurgen Herbst, "Francis Greenwood Peabody: Harvard's Theologian of the Social Gospel," *Harvard Theological Review* 54 (January 1961): 46-52.

51 See Church, "The Economists Study Society."

Peabody emphasized ethics and social science as a unity, combining his own social gospel idealism with an attempt at empirical study and an emphasis on social action. David Potts has reported that by the end of the century over 400 Harvard students, products of "Peabo's drainage, drunkenness, and divorce," as they affectionately referred to his ethics course, were involved in various voluntary social work projects.[52] In 1906 Peabody organized the Social Ethics Department at Harvard with courses offered in "Ethics of the Social Question," "Criminality and Penology," and "Practical Social Ethics."[53] The eclecticism of Peabody's approach and his inability to be precise about the relation between ethics and social science, other than repeatedly to affirm it, resulted finally in social ethics' becoming neither sociology nor moral philosophy. When Peabody retired in 1913, although the courses in the Department were all listed as "social ethics," in their actual content the concern for ethics and value had almost totally disappeared and had been replaced instead by an emphasis on practical, technical, bureaucraticized social work.[54] Peabody had been attempting to revivify moral philosophy in the form of practical sociology and to build an entire department around this notion. Because of its vagueness and lack of focus, social ethics, as Peabody conceived it, failed to become a profession itself and at the same time was unable to resist the pressures and encroachments from another aggressive professionalizing group, the social workers.

Although few other schools to my knowledge attempted to follow Harvard's example under Peabody of trying to establish whole Departments of Social Ethics as a form of revitalized moral philosophy, social ethics courses were introduced in many philosophy departments to add a practical or applied orientation to the regular but more theoretic basic ethics course. Social ethics, in fact, would reappear again throughout the century as a fairly staple offering in philosophy departments. Typical, for example, were the two elective ethics courses taught in the Department of Philosophy of the University of Wisconsin in 1905: the first, a general introduction to ethics, and, the second, a course in "Social and Political Ethics," which examined "the rights of personal liberty, freedom of contract, property, national independence, and suffrage." In 1915 a third course in "Business Ethics" was added and re-

52 Potts, "Social Ethics at Harvard," pp. 95-96.
53 Harvard College, *Catalogue*, 1905-06.
54 Harvard College, *Catalogue*, 1915-16, p. 460. The Social Ethics Department continued in existence until 1931, when it was absorbed into the newly founded Department of Sociology, where any last vestige of ethics offerings disappeared.

mained a regular course with the other two well into the 1930s.[55] The Amherst College Department of Philosophy introduced a similar course in the early 1920s entitled "Social and Political Ideals."[56] Social ethics, however, was a kind of floating topic that could surface in sociology and religion as well as in philosophy departments. The Religious Education Department at Macalester College, for example, provided a course in "The Social Teachings of the Bible," essentially a course in Christian social ethics that sought to apply "the social message of the Bible . . . and its social principles to the solutions of current social problems" and was based on readings in the works of such leading social gospel figures as Josiah Strong, Walter Rauschenbusch, Shailer Mathews, and Francis Greenwood Peabody himself.[57]

In 1910 the University of Utah offered an "Orientation through Social Ethics" as an elective survey for freshmen.[58] In the early 1920s professors of sociology at Dartmouth College and at the University of Illinois's sociology department wrote textbooks and taught courses in social ethics still based on a conception they shared with Albion Small of sociology as a unifying science and a "scientific ethic."[59] What many schools did do, in addition to offering individual social ethics courses in various departments, was to begin to introduce, as part of their increasing vocational orientation, courses in social work along the narrow, practical lines that Harvard's Social Ethics Department later took. Even small traditional liberal arts colleges often began to provide prevocational social work training. These, however, offered no ethics and probably as little science.

During the first decades of the century the role assigned to ethics in the curriculum depended on the extent to which individual institutions had acceded to university influences and the elective principle. In most of the universities ethics was taught as one possible elective among hundreds of others. Institutions that attempted to preserve a liberal arts orientation and curriculum sometimes made ethics a required course within a prescribed core curriculum. Macalester College, for example,

55 University of Wisconson, *Catalogue,* 1904/05, p. 102; 1915/16, pp. 183-84; and 1935/36.

56 Amherst College, *Catalogue,* 1925/26.

57 Macalester College, *Catalogue,* 1915, p. 70.

58 Russell Thomas, *The Search for a Common Learning: General Education, 1800-1960* (New York: McGraw-Hill, 1962) , p. 76.

59 John M. Mecklin, *An Introduction to Social Ethics, The Social Conscience in a Democracy* (New York: Harcourt, Brace and Company, 1920) ; and Edward Cary Hayes, *Sociology and Ethics; The Facts of Social Life as the Source of Solutions for the Theoretical and Practical Problems of Life* (New York: D. Appleton and Company, 1921) .

215   *The Teaching of Ethics*

split its moral philosophy course into three—logic and scientific method, psychology, and ethics—all required.[60] Other liberal arts colleges simply made ethics the major requirement for upper-class students in an attempt to make ethics play a truncated version of the old moral philosophy.[61] Still others, among them some like Amherst that were outspoken critics of the university, abandoned ethics as a required course altogether.[62] By 1925 the pattern becoming prominent among universities and colleges alike was for ethics as such to be offered as an elective within departments of philosophy.

Reading material available to students for the study of ethics was by 1900 diverse and increasingly rich, sometimes confusingly so. The classic texts by America's nineteenth-century moral philosophers had all been almost totally abandoned. Their place had been taken by leading British ethicists whose works were available to American classes for at least selected reading assignments in the major ethical positions that set the context for turn-of-the-century theoretical discussion and debate: for instance, idealism in Thomas Hill Green's *Prolegomena to Ethics* (1883), intuitionism in James Martineau's *Types of Ethical Theory* (1885), and intuitionism and utilitarianism in Henry Sidgwick's *Methods of Ethics* (1874).[63] Moreover, a number of textbooks had appeared that presented a broad introduction to ethical thought, ancient and modern—texts such as Friedrich Paulsen's *System of Ethics*, translated in 1899 by Cornell's Frank Thilly, who the following year brought out a popular text of his own, *Introduction to Ethics*, Warner Fite's *An Introductory Study of Ethics* (1903), James Hyslop's *Elements of Ethics* (1895), S.E. Mezes' *Ethics: Descriptive and Explanatory* (1901), N.K. Davis' *Elements of Ethics* (1900), and others.[64] Some of these textbook writers—Mezes and Davis, for example—attempted to pull together and to present in condensed, simplified form some of the more

60 Macalester College, *Catalogue*, 1900/01, p. 42; 1909/10, pp. 30-31.
61 For example, Haverford College, *Catalogue*, 1905.
62 Amherst College, *Catalogue*, 1915.
63 All these books were on the reading list for the ethics course at Macalester College in 1900. Macalester College, *Catalogue*, 1900/01, p. 42. Thomas Hill Green, *Prolegomena to Ethics* (Oxford: Clarendon Press, 1883); James Martineau, *Types of Ethical Theory* (Oxford: Clarendon Press, 1898); and Henry Sidgwick, *Methods of Ethics* (London: Macmillan and Co., 1874).
64 Friedrich Paulsen, *System of Ethics* (New York: C. Scribner's Sons, 1899); Frank Thilly, *Introduction to Ethics* (New York: C. Scribner's Sons, 1900); Warner Fite, *An Introductory Study of Ethics* (New York: Longmans, Green and Co., 1903); James H. Hyslop, *Elements of Ethics* (New York: C. Scribner's Sons, 1895); S.E. Mezes, *Ethics: Descriptive and Explanatory* (New York: The Macmillan Co., 1901); and Noah K. Davis, *Elements of Ethics* (Boston: Silver, Burdett and Co., 1900).

daunting theoretical works. In addition the teacher of social ethics had by 1910 at least three bibliographies of literature in that field to draw upon.[65] A collection of readings in ethics from Socrates to Martineau—the first instance in ethics I have found of a type of classroom aide that would later become extremely popular—was compiled and published the same year by Harvard's librarian, Benjamin Rand.[66]

The publication of *Ethics* by John Dewey and James H. Tufts in 1908 was a major event for the teaching of ethics. Both a text covering the whole field of ethics and Dewey's first full length statement of his own position in ethics, the book was extremely popular. Adopted by thirty colleges within six months of its publication, *Ethics* went through twenty-five printings before Dewey and Tufts revised it in 1932.[67] The main appeal of *Ethics* for teachers was the clarity of its discussion and its three-part organization of the subject. Part one covered the history of ethics, part two the theory of ethics, and part three, "The World of Action," discussed the application of ethics to concrete social problems. This was a model of organization that was to remain standard until the 1950s and 60s when the topics covered in Dewey's and Tufts' part three would begin to disappear from the ethics textbooks. The book received immediate favorable notice, and many reviewers recommended it for the layman and general readers as well as for the student and "professional moralist."[68]

A random sampling of some of the texts used in the teaching of ethics during the first quarter of the century reveals the emergence of problems that to the present-day reader will appear familiar. One problem was that of overcoming the gap between theory and practice, between abstruse theoretical discussion and the actual needs and problems of students. "With the world calling for moral power and efficiency, and with the adolescent of college years in the nascent period of moral adjustment," wrote one early student of the teaching of ethics, "how insufficient, foreign, barbarian, do the arid ethical logomachies of most

---

65 These included the Harvard bibliography in social ethics, *Teachers in Harvard University: A Guide to Reading in Social Ethics and Allied Subjects* (Cambridge, Mass.: Harvard University 1910); a bibliography in business ethics, R.H. Edwards, "Business Morals," *Studies in American Social Conditions*, no. 7, Madison, Wisc., 1910; and a bibliography from the Fabian Society, *What to Read on Social and Economic Subjects* (London: King and Son, 1910).

66 Benjamin Rand, *The Classical Moralists* (New York: Houghton, 1909).

67 This book has just been republished with a newly edited text by the Southern Illinois University Center for Dewey Studies: John Dewey and James H. Tufts, *Ethics*, edited by Jo Ann Boydston (Carbondale and Edwardsville, Ill.: Southern Illinois University Press, 1978). My references are to this edition.

68 "Textual Commentary," Ibid., pp. 551-52.

textbooks appear?" Despite this, the same writer conceded that although the theoretical terms of ethical instruction, "stand for bewildering mazes of controversy" they, nevertheless, "conceal very real problems."[69] The question was how to give life to theory in such a way that it became more to the student than mere speculation. It was just this problem, and his own conviction that ethics should be free of abstract theory, that prompted Francis Peabody at Harvard to begin his teaching of ethics "inductively" as a study of specific social problems. It was a question also that continued to trouble textbook writers who felt that theoretical issues were important.

Almost all textbook writers not only indicated their awareness of the problem but stated as one of their main purposes an attempt to strike a balance between the theoretical and practical and to speak meaningfully, as one put it, to "concrete contemporary problems." "The purpose of a study of ethics," said this writer, "is, primarily, to get light for the guidance of life."[70] Another writer affirmed his hope that his book would make clear to every reader that "morality is nothing more or less than the business of living."[71] And the opening sentence of Dewey's and Tufts' text in ethics was a statement that the true significance of their work lay "in its effort to awaken a vital conviction of the genuine reality of moral problems and the value of reflective thought in dealing with them."[72] One way text writers could try to cope with the problem was, like Davis, an earlier writer, to urge for all an introductory course in the fundamentals of ethics and to postpone treatment of theoretical controversies until later, and then only for those who were interested. This, however, was easier said than done, if the elementary course were to provide students with much more than obvious moral truisms.[73] The better textbooks followed Dewey's and Tufts' example by giving attention to both theoretical and practical topics. Whether they actually divided their work into separate sections as did Dewey and Tufts, most authors tried to make explicit the concrete problems, personal and social, to which they felt their ethical reflections applied.[74]

69 Edward S. Conklin, "The Pedagogy of College Ethics," *Pedagogical Seminary* 18 (December 1911) : 427-28.

70 Durant Drake, *Problems of Conduct, An Introductory Survey of Ethics* (Boston: Houghton Mifflin, 1914) , p. vi.

71 Walter Goodnow Everett, *Moral Values: A Study of the Principles of Conduct* (New York: Henry Holt and Company, 1926) , p. vii.

72 Dewey and Tufts, *Ethics*, p. 3.

73 Davis, *Elements of Ethics*.

74 See, Drake, *Problems of Conduct;* Everett, *Moral Values;* Warner Fite, *Moral Philosophy, The Critical View of Life* (New York: Lincoln MacVeagh, 1925) ; and Mary Whiton Calkins, *The Good Man and the Good: An Introduction to Ethics* (New York: The Macmillan Company, 1918) .

A second problem, closely related to the first and in many respects only a variation of it, had to do with the formation of the conduct and character of the individual student. In this the teachers of ethics still tried to fulfill what had been considered a main purpose of the nineteenth-century college and its moral philosophy course. Nineteenth-century moral philosophers had themselves achieved a questionable degree of success in the effort, and with the greater freedom accorded students in the twentieth century the task for the teacher of ethics appeared more formidable than ever. Nevertheless, if the textbooks can be taken as a true indication, it was an undertaking that teachers of ethics still saw as one of their most important jobs. G. Stanley Hall had early criticized the gap between the teaching of ethics and the actual moral ideas and conduct of students. He argued that ethics should be taught not in a general course on the subject but in courses that touched directly on the students' own personal interests and emotions. Hall's choice was personal hygiene. "I have begun a course of ethics for lower college classes," he wrote late in the century, "and for two or three months have given nothing but hygiene; and I believe the pedagogic possibilities of this mode of introduction into this great domain are at present unsuspected and that, instead of the arid, speculative casuistic way, not only college but high school boys could be infected with real love of virtue and a deep aversion to every sin against the body."[75] Although hygiene was a much discussed topic of the early twentieth century—often in connection with eugenics—few, if any, followed Hall's lead in making it the pedagogical focus for the teaching of ethics (it did provide a major topic of study in social ethics courses).

The problem of conduct and character, however, remained of concern to ethics teachers and writers. It is a problem that runs throughout Dewey's and Tufts' *Ethics*—ethics, they defined, as "the science that deals with conduct, in so far as this is considered as right or wrong, good or bad"—and it was their reason for presenting the history of ethics before the theory.[76] To begin with the history of moral evolution, the development of actual moral principles and conduct, Dewey and Tufts felt, provided the student with a vivid sense of the reality and personal social setting of moral problems which could only then be dealt with analytically and theoretically in a meaningful way.[77] Other authors made personal conduct or the ethics of the individual the focus of their

75 G. Stanley Hall, *Educational Problems*, vol. I (New York: Appleton, 1911), Chapter 5.
76 Dewey and Tufts, *Ethics*, p. 6.
77 Ibid., pp. 8-10.

entire textbooks as a way of relating ethical theory, psychology, and sociology to the personal interests and concerns of the student.[78] Ironically, just as ethics teachers were making a last effort to keep alive an interest in the relation between theory and personal conduct, the triumph of the elective principle meant that in actuality the teaching of ethics was reaching only a relatively small percentage of students.

The growing isolation within the college and the curriculum and the practical ineffectuality of the undergraduate ethics course were symbolized by the blossoming of interest after 1910 in professional ethics. The ethics of the medical profession, of the law, of journalism, and of business were suddenly being discussed as never before.[79] On the one hand, this was a responsible and needed attempt to grapple with the problems posed by the new professional organization of American life. On the other hand, it represented something of a concession to a deepening sense that undergraduate instruction in ethics made little discernible difference in meeting the concrete problems of later life. If undergraduate instruction in ethics was lacking or failing, perhaps the moral dikes could be repaired later on by arousing a professional ethical sensitivity. This made sense, but the temptation it carried simply to concentrate on professional ethics also meant a retreat, for a professional ethic was by definition a limited ethic, a stopping short of the universality that most thinkers had always maintained the highest ethical standards should seek to achieve.

During the 1930s and 40s the challenge to ethics of the dominant scientific conceptions about how we know, and about what we can and cannot know, began to produce a radical shift in the study and teaching of ethics. Although science had, indeed, posed problems for ethicists long before this, it would probably be inaccurate to speak of any kind of deep crisis of confidence about ethics before the late 1920s and early 30s—if for no other reasons than that before then the strength of evolutionary optimism and progressive idealism had helped to blur the seriousness of impending problems. Moreover, a certain skepticism had always been of the essence of a rigorous study of ethics; such questions as the reality of other selves, of universal standards versus the diversity of moral codes and practices, of intuitionism versus utilitarianism, of free will versus necessity, had all constituted the age-old, perennial

78 Drake, *Problems of Conduct;* Fite, *Moral Philosophy;* and Calkins, *The Good Man.*
79 See, Theodore Day Martin, "Instruction in Professional Ethics in Professional Schools for Teachers" (Ph.D. diss., Columbia University, 1931) ; and Jesse Hickman Bond, "The Teaching of Professional Ethics in the Schools of Law, Medicine, Journalism and Commerce in the United States (Ph.D. diss., University of Wisconsin, 1915) .

issues of ethical discussion and debate. The growing force of scientific naturalism, however, began to appear to upset the balance in these venerable controversies and to bias the outcome irresistibly more in one direction than the other, more toward subjectivism, toward ethical relativism, toward functionalism, toward moral determinism. Within this larger intellectual context, and in reaction and response to it, the study and teaching of ethics took shape and acquired its own distinct problems and concerns. It is to this development and its consequences for the teaching of ethics from the 1930s through the 1960s that we now turn.

THE TWENTIETH-CENTURY CRISIS IN THE TEACHING OF ETHICS

During the thirties it became painfully apparent to ethical thinkers that the sciences, social and physical, rested on epistemological and methodological assumptions that threatened the very possibility of rational ethical discourse and action. Increasingly, scientific method was being regarded as the only valid mode of knowing and the objects of science the only things about which genuine knowledge could be had. The outlook of science, with its exclusive focus on quantities, particulars, chance and probability, when transferred to other fields left qualities, wholes, purposes, and ideals, the subject matter of ethics, with no ground to stand on. From the point of view of the physical sciences, value qualities, the very thing ethical statements were presumably about, simply did not exist. It would be a gross oversimplification to say that this view was taken over wholesale and uncritically by the social sciences and that there was no resistance to it. The general trend of thought, nevertheless, moved overwhelmingly in this direction.

The growing prestige of behaviorism has already been noted. By explaining all human behavior as either expressions of genetic endowment or responses to environmental influences, behaviorism left no room for the autonomy, self-deliberation, and volitional activity on which the conception of man as a moral agent depends.[80] The notion of a deliberating, deciding, and freely acting subject was often regarded as an unscientific myth, or at least as an imprecise designation for phenomena that could only be truly understood by breaking them down to their environmental and physiological components. In anthropology and soci-

80 In attempting to make sense of the very complex developments dealt with summarily in this and the following paragraphs, I have found two discussions especially helpful for both interpretational and bibliographical leadings: Purcell, *The Crisis of Democratic Theory;* and Frederick A. Olafson, *Ethics and Twentieth Century Thought* (Englewood Cliffs, N.J.: Prentice-Hall, 1973).

ology the tendency to view all beliefs, religions, and values as expressions
of more fundamental biological and economic needs of social groups
was pronounced. In an important article in 1926 Bronislaw Malinowski
gave to this approach of the social sciences the name "functionalism."
Although the notion has been much criticized, refined, and made more
precise since, it signified for Malinowski, as for most of his contemporary social scientists, the general view that any social practice, custom,
or belief was to be understood not by any intrinsic meaning, rational or
moral, it might have in itself, but only with reference to its consequences for the larger social group.[81]

Sociologists, perhaps more than others, tended to preserve the tension
between the older reformist, value-oriented role of social science and
the newer objectivist, empirical, and strictly disciplinary orientation;
and during the 30s and 40s there remained sociologists who continued
the attempt to counteract the dominant objectivistic, value-free conception of sociology.[82] As Edward A. Purcell has indicated, however, it is
significant that even those social scientists who endeavored to keep
questions of value and meaning alive in their discipline were severely
handicapped because they also shared with their opponents one all-
important assumption, namely, that while ethical values could be asserted and affirmed, genuine knowledge and rational justification were
possible only of the empirical data with which science dealt.[83] By the
late thirties the possibility of establishing and validating ethical norms
and values was one that few social scientists would have defended, had
they been interested.

Most social scientists not only held that social science is a totally
objective, value-free enterprise, but also that ethical values themselves
are expressions of subjective preferences. Ethical values were seen as
non-cognitive, non-rational, frequently as mere epiphenomena of underlying biological, economic, and social forces. Some objectivist scholars did acknowledge that researchers often could not avoid bringing
their own value judgments into their work, but since these represented
merely irrational biases and lapses, their primary task was to weed them
out as completely as possible.

81 Bronislaw Malinowski, "Anthropology," *Encyclopaedia Britannica*, 13th ed., supplement I (Chicago, 1926).
82 Sociology has continued to produce at least a minority of important scholars who
have continued to raise ethical, normative questions from within and about sociology
itself. One thinks of a line running through Albion Small, Robert Lynd, Robert McIver,
Pitirim Sorokin, Gunnar Myrdal, C. Wright Mills, Alvin Gouldner, Peter Berger, and
Robert Bellah.
83 Purcell, *The Crisis of Democratic Theory*, pp. 44-45.

This is not to say that social scientists were uninterested in leading an ethical life as individuals or in contributing to the creation of a more humane society. At least three positions were taken by objectivist social scientists in relation to ethical ideals and values. By far the most common response among them was simply to accept the conventional values of society uncritically and without question. Many were committed as individuals to humane and democratic ideals derived from religious and cultural sources they were no longer able or willing to recognize, ideals for which they would have found it difficult to provide a rational evaluation and defense had they been asked. The alleged neutrality of social science research did not raise for these social scientists any disturbing questions about the traditional ideals of American life that they took on faith. Another position that usually went hand in hand with the first was to continue to view science itself as by nature progressive and as leading irresistibly toward a more harmonious and humane social order. As with the first position, however, scientists would have been hard-pressed to give a justification for this faith that would have satisfied their canons of objective, scientific knowledge. Nor was there any contradiction between these attitudes and the determination of many social scientists to concentrate, in what was thought to be the manner and the key to the success of the physical sciences, on developing the methodology of their discipline and to ignore any substantive and normative questions about its meaning and application.

Appealing directly to the physical sciences as his model the social scientist George A. Lundberg said in 1929:

It is not the business of a chemist who invents a high explosive to be influenced in his task by considerations as to whether his product will be used to blow up cathedrals or to build tunnels through the mountains. Nor is it the business of the social scientist in arriving at laws of group behavior to permit himself to be influenced by considerations of how his conclusions will coincide with existing notions, or what the effect of his findings on the social order will be.[84]

The putative value-neutrality of the social sciences allowed the scholar to hold to his own value preferences uncritically, and, at the same time, absolved him of any responsibility for the uses others might make of his research results.

84 G.A. Lundberg, R. Bain, and S. Anderson, eds., *Trends in American Sociology* (1929), quoted in Robert K. Merton, *Social Theory and Social Structure* (Glencoe, Ill.: The Free Press, 1963), p. 543.

It was within this larger intellectual context that, beginning in the late twenties and becoming fully manifest in the thirties, major shifts in the field of ethics occurred. Ethics, however, took much longer than did the social sciences to reflect the pervasive influence of scientific ways of knowing. One reason for this was the lingering strength in American philosophy of late nineteenth- and early twentieth-century idealism, not only within philosophy departments but among the informed public as well.[85] Common to almost all forms of idealism, both popular and professional, was a three-fold conviction that mind is the fundamental reality, that ideas, therefore, are in some ways as real or more real than the objective world, and that a community of thought joins the individual, society, and nature. While idealism appeared to provide a solid epistemological ground for ethical evaluations and judgments, it was unable to withstand the new intellectual pressures.

In the first place, idealism tended all too often in practice to become a form of subjective idealism in which ideas and ideals served not so much to change reality as to justify and sanction it. This made idealism especially vulnerable to those functionalist interpretations of the social sciences that viewed ideas and values as mere rationales for subjective preferences and group interests. In the second place, idealism had real difficulty in finding an adequate place within its outlook for the biological and psychological elements of human behavior that science was uncovering. In the third place, idealism stressed community of thought and culture precisely at a moment when the culture of learning was fragmenting and scholars, including, ironically, idealistic philosophers themselves, were enjoying the protective boundaries of disciplinary compartmentalization. Finally, idealism was linked with the values and purposes of the humanities at a time when the prestige of the humanities was in decline. Throughout the twenties and into the thirties idealism still exerted a strong influence on the teaching of ethics, but this situation was rapidly to change.

For a time, so-called philosophic naturalism, represented preeminently by John Dewey, offered another possible direction for ethics to take. Throughout his long life, whether he was dealing with political and social philosophy, education, aesthetics, logic, or with ethics itself, Dewey returned again and again to questions of morality and value. Dewey insisted that there exists an integral, inseparable relationship

---

85 On the many schools of idealistic philosophy that flourished in America during the early twentieth century, see Herbert W. Schneider, *A History of American Philosophy* (New York: Columbia University Press, 1946), pp. 454-96.

between knowledge and action, research and its consequences, science and ethics, the natural world and human values. Dewey preserved the moral idealism, reform orientation, and synoptic vision of the earlier social science, but attempted to bring these, shorn of their metaphysical overtones, into conjunction with modern science and the problems of the modern world. "Moral science," Dewey said, "is not something with a separate province. It is physical, biological, and historic knowledge placed in a human context where it will illuminate and guide the activities of men."[86]

Because Dewey himself has frequently been portrayed as an uncritical champion of modern science, a brief closer look at Dewey's understanding of the relationship between science and ethics is in order. It is true that Dewey usually spoke of science as synonymous with organized intelligence, and throughout his life urged this conception of science as the model for all thinking. But there was another side to his thought that was critical of modern science. Because Dewey himself never fully developed this aspect of his thought, it has been frequently overlooked, and Dewey cannot be held blameless for often being regarded as an unquestioning defender of modern science. A look at this other, somewhat furtive strain in Dewey's thinking may help to throw light not only on why Dewey's naturalistic ethics did not find wider acceptance but also on why ethical theory and teaching took the turn they did. If it seems that inordinate attention is given to Dewey here, it is because Dewey's work, perhaps more than that of any other, helps bring into sharp focus some of the central problems that have been involved in the study and teaching of ethics in the modern world.

Central to Dewey's writing was his concern to overcome the widening gap between scientific knowledge and morality. "Certainly," he wrote, "one of the most genuine problems of modern life is the reconciliation of the scientific view of the universe with the claims of the moral life."[87] The split had arisen, Dewey was convinced, because, on the one hand, ethics had failed to keep pace with the advances of physical science and its technological applications, and, on the other hand, because science often was improperly conceived and practiced. Dewey devoted much of his writing to showing the correct view of science that he thought was demanded by an understanding of the relational character of experience. Dewey's understanding of the interconnectedness of all experience—

86 John Dewey, *Quest for Certainty* (1929), quoted in Mary Warnock, *Ethics Since 1900* (London: Oxford University Press, 1960), p. 77.

87 John Dewey, *Philosophy and Civilization* (New York: Capricorn Books, 1963; originally published 1931), p. 43.

reflected in those key phrases, "interaction," "transaction," and "community," that are hallmarks of his work—ran counter to many assumptions held by scientists and social scientists. In the first place, it denied the subject-object dichotomy that positivistic science took for granted. From Dewey's standpoint there was no place for the notion of a detached onlooker coolly observing the world and serving up the facts about it with neither he nor they being affected in the process. Furthermore, it challenged the assumption that an adequate understanding of complex phenomena is to be attained by reducing them analytically to their parts rather than seeing that they could only be understood with reference to the whole. Finally, a relational view of the world brought to light the importance of the initially non-cognitive as an essential element in experience and a potential source of genuine knowledge. Here Dewey was attacking the fundamental problem posed to ethics by an atomistic, positivistic science. He was attempting to establish that qualities and ideals could be given a status in knowledge fully as solid as that enjoyed by the numbers, measurements, and energies of physical science. Failure to recognize that the initially non-cognitive can in itself be a source of genuine knowledge was a primary reason, Dewey felt, why every form of knowledge except scientific knowledge is constantly on the defensive. In his writings in the 1930s he began to make this position explicit. "It tends to be assumed," he wrote, "that because qualities that figure in poetical discourse and those that are central in friendship do not figure in scientific enquiry they have no reality, at least not the kind of unquestionable reality attributed to the mathematical, mechanical, or magneto-electric properties that constitute matter." And, again: "That esthetic and moral experience reveal traits of real things as truly as does intellectual experience, that poetry may have a metaphysical import as well as science, is rarely affirmed."[88] In this view ideals need not, indeed, must not, be regarded as mere epiphenomena of material processes.

It is not often pointed out how disturbed Dewey seemed to be at times about the way science was actually conceived and practiced. For there to be a unity of science and ethics, science could not, in Dewey's view, be too far removed from everyday, common experience. And yet science seemed in actual fact to be moving farther and farther away. As a consequence Dewey criticized what he considered to be misinterpretations of scientific concepts and even began in the 1930s to argue on

---

88 John Dewey, *Experience and Nature* (London: George Allen & Unwin, Ltd., 1929),
p. 19.

occasion for a fundamental reconception and reorientation of science itself.

While Dewey had great appreciation for the abstractive power of science, he warned against what he called "the fallacy of selective emphasis," his version of Whitehead's "fallacy of misplaced concreteness." The "fallacy of selective emphasis" is committed whenever scientific concepts, which, for Dewey, are properly only instruments of control, are identified with reality itself.[89] Mistaking the concepts of science for something actually in nature or, worse, making them into a general world picture, Dewey argued, had disastrous consequences. "Since all value traits are lacking in objects as science presents them," he explained, "it is assumed that *Reality* has not such characteristics."[90] In place of a living, multi-leveled, complex world, there is substituted for it one which, by definition, has no place for enjoyment, purpose, creativity, meaning, or moral striving. By introducing the kind of simplification that has proven so effective for science into social and moral subjects, Dewey warned, "We eliminate the distinctively human factors —reduction to the physical ensues."[91] Dewey was very clear: Science has its own proper but limited domain, within which its power is second to none; extended beyond, unintentionally or by design, it lays waste.

Strictures against "the fallacy of selective emphasis," however, were not enough. Dewey began to sense that not all conceptions of science were compatible with his own point of view. When he contemplated the highly abstract and arcane character of most actual natural science, he became uncomfortable. He recognized the procedural necessity for abstraction, but he was suspicious of its remoteness from common experience. Dewey considered the distinction between pure science and applied science to be artificial and pernicious in its consequences. It fostered an esoteric knowledge inaccessible to the public and controlled by an elite few, who because of the actual connection between science and technology threatened to become not merely an intellectual elite, but a power elite also.[92] Furthermore, the undemocratic tendencies of abstract science were not its only danger. It threatened also to alienate man from his own true nature. Science divorced from the common experience, from "the primacy and ultimacy of the material of ordinary

---

89 Dewey, *Experience and Nature*, pp. 25-28.
90 Dewey, *Quest for Certainty*, p. 137.
91 Ibid., p. 216.
92 John Dewey, *The Public and Its Problems* (Chicago: The Swallow Press, Inc., 1927), pp. 173-78, 208.

experience," creates "a world of things indifferent to human interests."[93] To avoid the alienating tendencies of modern abstract science, Dewey began to edge toward a reconception of science that would keep it connected with human interests and the qualities of everyday experience.

When Dewey began to think in this way he took as his model for the scientist, not the mathematician and logician, but the old craftsman, the artisan, and "the intelligent mechanic."[94] The scientist as craftsman, as artisan, deals with problems that arise out of everyday experience. He produces knowledge that feeds back into the life of the community and is accessible to its control. His is a knowing by doing. This was all strictly in keeping with Dewey's pragmatic, instrumentalist conception of the relation between knowing and action, and it preserved the unity of knowledge, but it was not modern science. It is revealing that Dewey was emphasizing a practical, workshop notion of science at precisely a time when scientists were actually ascending to ever higher and more rarified levels of abstraction. It was in this latter direction, not Dewey's, that ethics would follow.

During the 1930s, just as Dewey was broadening his explorations of the relationships between empirical knowledge and ethics, the movement of thought known as logical positivism began to exert a strong influence on American philosophy. Although on the surface the positivists appeared to have much in common with Dewey, they constituted in actuality an alternative and a direct challenge to Dewey and other naturalists like him. Their influence was to give a decisive new direction to ethical theory, and, with it, to the teaching of ethics. Whereas Dewey had begun to search for a redefinition of science in order to find support in it for his conception of ethics, the logical positivists accepted fully the outlook and canons of modern science and undertook instead to redefine ethics.

Logical positivism increasingly became a force in American intellectual life through the work of a number of European thinkers who, originally concentrated in Vienna, began during the 1930s to assume university positions in the United States. Taking its leads directly from science, logical positivism accepted both the scientific emphasis on empirical data that naturalists like Dewey also prized, but at the same time emphasized the abstract logic of science that Dewey was beginning

93   Ibid.; and Dewey, *Experience and Nature.*
94   Dewey, *Experience and Nature;* and John Dewey, *Art as Experience* (New York: Capricorn Books, 1958, originally published 1934), pp. 5-6.

to find objectionable. Furthermore, they categorically rejected any form of ethical naturalism, such as Dewey's, that posited an inseparable connection between descriptions of the natural world and ethical values.

Two philosophers, G. E. Moore and Ludwig Wittgenstein, whose work the logical positivists drew upon for support, were to assume ever greater importance in twentieth-century ethical thought and, hence, deserve here at least passing note. In his *Tractatus Logico-Philosophicus,* published in 1922, Wittgenstein, seeking to purify and cleanse language by showing what it can and cannot do, insisted at the time that the chief function of language is to describe the structure of the empirical world and that any non-empirical, non-verifiable language is also non-sense. This the positivists interpreted as bolstering both their own concern with the use of language and also their view that only the empirically observable and verifiable is real. Likewise, the earlier work of G. E. Moore was selectively hauled into service to provide backing for the positivists' cause. As with Wittgenstein the positivists found in Moore an emphasis on clarifying ethical concepts that fit well with their own preoccupation with the analysis of logic and language. At first glance, however, the substance of Moore's thought might seem to have made him an unlikely source of support for the positivists and those who followed them. In his *Principia Ethica* (1903) Moore had labeled as "the naturalistic fallacy" any attempt to define, describe, or analyze ethical qualities in terms of the properties or characteristics of things in the natural observable world. His purpose in repudiating naturalism was to secure the autonomy of ethics against all efforts to reduce goodness, the chief ethical quality with which he was concerned, to something other than the indefinable, immediately intuited reality he considered the good to be. Moore's own primary intentions, therefore, were quite different from those of the positivists. The latter, however, had only to reject Moore's intuitionism to find in his notion of "the naturalistic fallacy" arguments for their own view not merely that, as Hume had put it, "is" does not imply "ought," but that, more radically, all talk about those non-empirical entities with which the oughts of ethics had traditionally been thought to deal simply had no warrant.[95]

95 It may be worth observing that those who drew most on Wittgenstein and Moore, the positivists and the analysts who succeeded them, seem to have been able to do so only by bypassing or mis-interpreting central elements in both. Wittgenstein appears not only to have changed his mind about the primary function of language as set forth in the *Tractatus,* but also, from the very beginning, to have repudiated both logical positivism and linguistic philosophy. Only temerity would lead one to pronounce unhesitatingly on the true interpretation of Wittgenstein, around whose work an enormous literature of

There are, the positivists argued, only two kinds of true or meaning-ful statements. One kind, exemplified in mathematics and logic, is true by definition and logical deduction but has no necessary connection with the empirical world. The other kind of meaningful statement is that which can be tested by experiment and verified by sense experi-ence. From the point of view of their radical empiricism all metaphy-sical, religious, poetic, and ethical concepts that are incapable of scientific verification were clearly meaningless. In the phrase of A. J. Ayer, whose 1935 book, *Language, Truth, and Logic,* was perhaps more influential than any other in setting forth most starkly the implications of logical positivism for ethics, ethical statements were "peudo-con-cepts"; they had no cognitive significance. Ethical statements served at most to express or arouse emotions of approval or disapproval.[96]

Presented at first iconoclastically and in mere outline by such spokes-men as Ayer, this emotive theory of ethics, as it came to be called, came under immediate attack from critics. Nevertheless, its influence grew. Probably the most important representative of the emotive theory in American philosophy has been Charles L. Stevenson. In articles pub-lished in the late thirties and then in 1945 in a book, *Ethics and Lan-guage,* which has been dubbed "the bible of emotive theory," Stevenson made refinements and distinctions that produced a much more complex and sophisticated version of the emotive theory than had hitherto ex-isted.[97] Perhaps Stevenson's main difference, among several, from earlier emotivists was his insistence that the central function of ethics was not so much to express emotions as to influence other people. At bottom, however, ethical judgments rested as much for Stevenson as for other positivists on subjective feelings and attitudes. In the final analysis ethical statements were subjectivistic, relativistic, and ultimately arbi-trary because they could not be rationally validated or justified, only asserted.

96   A.J. Ayer, *Language, Truth, and Logic* (London: Victor Gollanez, 1936) .

97   See, Charles L. Stevenson, *Ethics and Lanuguage* (New Haven: Yale University Press, 1944) ; and Warnock, *Ethics Since 1900,* p. 75.

comment has grown. The bibliography of K.T. Fann's book on him, for example, is sixty-five pages long. "I must confess," Professor G.E.M. Anscombe, one of his students has written, "that I feel deeply suspicious of anyone's claim to have understood Wittgenstein. That is perhaps because, although I had a strong and deep affection for him, and, I sup-pose, knew him very well, I am very sure that I did not understand him." K.T. Fann, *Wittgenstein's Conception of Philosophy* (Cambridge: Blackwell, 1969) ; Paul Englemann, *Letters from Wittgenstein with a Memoir* (Cambridge: Blackwell, 1967) . On the highly selective use of Moore by the analysts who have claimed him as one of their own, see Warnock, *Ethics Since 1900.*

Although the emotive theory as formulated by Stevenson was quickly subjected to criticism, its influence helped to give a decisive new direction to ethical theory and eventually to the teaching of ethics. With the positivists and the emotivists there came a shift toward an increasing emphasis on the analysis of ethical terms and their meanings and a diminishing attention to normative questions and practical problems. For the emotivist the main task of the ethicist was to analyze the terms and "pseudo-concepts" of ethics to show that they had no connection with science and to uncover the real psychological and sociological meanings hidden within them. Although by the mid-fifties there seem to have been few proponents of a pure emotive theory, linguistic analysis had become a dominant concern in ethics. Increasingly the term metaethics, as contrasted with normative ethics, came to be used to describe the central task of ethics as one of analyzing the meanings of ethical terms and judgments and their justification.[98]

By baldly denying the rationality of ethical statements the positivists and emotivists had laid down a challenge and set the agenda of subsequent ethical inquiry. If the emotivists were not correct, how and in what way could ethical judgments in fact be said to have a rationality and integrity in their own right? This substantive problem, as much as the awareness that, as the emotivists had indeed demonstrated, many terms in ethics are often employed indiscriminately and with careless disregard of their precise meaning, helps account for the increasing emphasis among all those who followed them on analysis and metaethics. If only the language of ethical discourse could be clarified, so the hope seemed to be, the true subject matter and rational standing of ethics woud finally emerge.

What was the impact of all this on the actual teaching of ethics? Evidence, such as class notes, course syllabi, and reading lists, that might shed light on what was in fact taking place in classrooms is hard to come by. Again, however, textbooks may at least provide some clues. A glance at textbooks indicates that throughout the 1940s and 1950s the actual teaching was probably much broader and more eclectic than a history of main currents of ethical theory might suggest.[99] No one system or outlook dominated the scene. The emotive theory was discussed,

98 For a comprehensive definition of metaethics, see Robert N. Hancock, *Twentieth Century Ethics* (New York: Columbia University Press, 1974), p. 2.

99 My comments on the teaching of ethics from roughly World War II through the mid-1960s are based on a survey of topics dealt with in a random sampling of popular texts and readers. These include: 1940-1959: Charles A. Baylis, *Ethics and the Principles of Wise Choice* (New York: Henry Holt and Company, 1958); Richard Brandt, *Ethical Theory* (Englewood Cliffs, N.J.: Prentice-Hall, 1959); A.C. Ewing, *The Definition of*

evaluated, and criticized as one highly influential outlook among others. Much attention, however, was also being given to existentialism in its various forms, and the writings especially of Sartre, Heidegger, and Kierkegaard, among others, stirred new excitement. At the same time the more traditional theories and positions of an older generation of American philosophers—the intuitionism of a Wilbur Marshall Urban, the idealism of a William Ernest Hocking, the naturalism of a John Dewey—were still represented along with linguistic analysis and the newer religious and existentialist ethics. Moreover, the perennial problems of ethics, for examples, the controversy concerning free will and determinism, the issue of ethical relativism, particularly as this had been raised by anthropologists and social psychologists, and the problems of social ethics, all continued to receive attention.

Good (New York: Macmillan Company, 1947); Stuart Hampshire, *Thought and Action* (London: Chatto & Windus, 1959); R.M. Hare, *The Language of Morals* (Oxford: Clarendon Press, 1952); Oliver Johnson, ed., *Ethics* (New York: Dryden Press, 1958); C.I. Lewis, *Knowledge and Valuation* (La Salle, Ill.: Open Court, 1946); Wayne A.R. Leys, *Ethics and Social Policy* (New York: Prentice-Hall, 1941); A.I. Melden, ed., *Ethical Theories: A Book of Readings* (New York: Prentice-Hall, 1950); A.I. Melden, ed., *Essays in Moral Philosophy* (Seattle: University of Washington Press, 1958); Edwin T. Mitchell, *A System of Ethics* (New York: Charles Scribner's Sons, 1950); Alan Montefiore, ed., *A Modern Introduction to Moral Philosophy* (London: Routledge & Kegan Paul, 1958); P.H. Nowell-Smith, *Ethics* (Penguin Books, 1954); Charles H. Patterson, *Moral Standards: An Introduction to Ethics* (New York: Ronald Press, 1952); William Henry Roberts, *The Problem of Choice: An Introduction to Ethics* (Boston: Ginn and Company, 1941); Wilfred Sellars and John Hospers, *Readings in Ethical Theory* (New York: Appleton-Century-Crofts, 1952); Charles L. Stevenson, *Ethics and Language;* Harold H. Titus, *Ethics for Today* (New York: American Book Company, 1947, 2nd ed.; first edition 1936); Stephen E. Toulmin, *An Examination of the Place of Reason in Ethics* (Cambridge: Cambridge University Press, 1950); and Philip Wheelwright, *A Critical Introduction to Ethics* (New York: The Odyssey Press, 1949, rev. ed.; first edition 1935). *1960-1969:* Raziel Abelson, *Ethics and Metaethics* (New York: St. Martin's Press, 1963); Robert E. Dewey et al., eds. *Problems of Ethics* (New York: The Macmillan Company, 1961); Joel Feinberg, ed., *Moral Concepts* (London: Oxford University Press, 1969); Phillipa Foot, ed., *Theories of Ethics* (London: Oxford University Press, 1962); Harry K. Girvetz, ed., *Contemporary Moral Issues* (Belmont, Calif.: Wadsworth, 1963); Thomas English Hill, *Contemporary Ethical Theories* (New York: The Macmillan Company, 1960; first edition, 1950); John Hospers, *Human Conduct: An Introduction to the Problems of Ethics* (New York: Harcourt, Brace and World, 1961); W.T. Jones, et al., eds., *Approaches to Ethics* (New York: McGraw-Hill, 1962); Joseph Katz, et al., eds., *Writers on Ethics* (Princeton, N.J.: D. Van Nostrand, 1962); Joseph Margolis, ed., *Contemporary Ethical Theory* (New York: Random House, 1966); Milton K. Munitz, *A Modern Introduction to Ethics* (Glencoe, Ill.: The Free Press, 1961, 2nd printing; 1958, first printing); Andrew Oldenquist, ed., *Readings in Moral Philosophy* (Boston: Houghton Mifflin, 1965); Evelyn Shirk, *The Ethical Dimension* (New York: Appleton-Century-Crofts, 1965); Paul Taylor, ed., *The Moral Judgment* (Englewood Cliffs, N.J.: Prentice-Hall, 1963); Judith J. Thompson and Gerald Dworkin, eds., *Ethics* (New York: Harper & Row, 1968); and W.H. Werkmeister, *Theories of Ethics: A Study of Moral Obligation* (Lincoln, Neb.: Johnson Publishing Company, 1961).

Striking in the texts is the prominence given throughout the forties and fifties to normative ethics and practical problems. Along with the attention devoted to theoretical ethics the texts dealt with such topics as "the nature of capitalism and business ethics," "the ethics of physical and mental health," "professional ethics," "ethics and the media of communication," "morality and race relations," "marriage and the home," "religion and ethics," "education and ethics," and others. Most of the textbooks were still marked by a concern, as one author said, "to deal with the actual problems which men and women face in the world today," and by a conviction that the study of ethics will be of value to students in their later lives, to enable them, as another author put it, "to live at their best in a society of free men and women."[100] Some authors continued to express the hope that they were writing not for a small professional group, nor even for college students, but also for the general educated public.[101] The eclectic nature of the texts and the range of topics they covered should caution against making simple generalizations about the dominance of one viewpoint or approach in the teaching of ethics during the decades of the forties and fifties. Nevertheless, despite the hopes and pieties of textbook authors, the trend toward an ever more exclusive emphasis on analysis, metaethics, and curriculum isolation was continuing and would become fully apparent during the turbulent decades of the 1960s.

By 1965 three tendencies in ethics, each directly affecting the teaching of ethics, were clearly apparent. First, the central theoretical task of ethics remained that of discovering some rational grounding for morality. Or, to use an older formulation with which the newer theorists, to be sure, would not have felt fully comfortable, the task still remained that of trying to establish and secure "the place of value in a world of fact." In this effort the work of British ethicists—such persons as R. M. Hare, Stephen Toulmin, P. H. Nowell-Smith, Philippa Foot, Stuart Hampshire—had become highly influential.[102] The positivist and emo-

100 Titus, *Ethics for Today*, p. v; and Patterson, *Moral Standards*, p. v.

101 Patterson, *Moral Standards*, p. vii; and Hill, *Contemporary Ethical Theories*, p. vii.

102 The development of ethical theory during the past quarter century has been extremely complex, and the distinctions separating one ethicist from another are often drawn exceedingly fine. To help me wend my way through this very intricate thicket, I have relied heavily on Warnock, *Ethics Since 1900;* Olafson, *Ethics and Twentieth Century Thought;* Hancock, *Twentieth Century Ethics;* Razial Abelson and Kai Nielson, "History of Ethics," and Kai Nielson, "Problems of Ethics," in *The Encyclopedia of Philosophy* (New York: Collier Macmillan, 1967) ; William J. Frankena, "Ethical Theory," in *Philosophy*, ed. Roderick M. Chisholm, et al. (Englewood Cliffs, N.J.: Prentice-Hall, 1964) , pp. 345-464; and G.J. Warnock, *Contemporary Moral Philosophy* (London: St. Martin's Press, 1967) .

tivist positions, if they had not been entirely discredited, no longer threatened to hold the field. Analysis remained the main preoccupation of the philosophers, nevertheless, and the names of Moore and Wittgenstein, because of what was taken to be their pioneering work in the analysis of language, were prominent as seldom before.[103] The emphasis of the new analysts, however, had shifted increasingly from the analysis of the meaning of ethical terms and more to the analysis of the logic and structure of moral reasoning as a whole. Ethics, it was being argued, constitutes a language and meaning structure in its own right, which cannot be determined by or reduced to something else as the positivists and emotivists had wanted to do. Ethical discourse, they pointed out, is for the purpose of guiding conduct, and close attention to the nature of ethical reasoning, they insisted, disclosed definite rules of procedure that make possible and give direction to moral discussion and activity.

The possibility of showing the existence of such rules of conduct, and of spelling out the criteria by which they were to be properly applied in regulating and justifying moral activity, offered the hope of establishing the autonomy of ethics on a firm foundation all its own. Some of the newer ethicists were also beginning to argue, however, that this could be done without Moore's repudiation of naturalism and were returning to one key notion of Dewey and other naturalists—that facts and values are related.[104] One of the ways we establish the morality of any action, some maintained, is by giving "good reasons" for it, reasons that in part describe the results, the factual outcomes, of that action. The emphasis on rules of procedure and on the need to justify moral statements and actions with persuasive reasons also underscored the social and public character of ethics in a way that had been lost to the positivists and emotivists.

And yet, there were those unconvinced that the new analysis had really achieved what it purported to have done, namely, to have rescued ethics from positivism. Deriving rules of moral conduct from the internal logic of language systems peculiar to some existing community of discourse seemed to some critics to suggest that the analysts had at best succeeded in grounding ethics only in social and institutional conven-

103 The posthumous publication of Wittgenstein's *Philosophical Investigations* in 1953 had given a boost to this interest. For some of the newer analysts Moore's notion of "the naturalistic fallacy," as well as his interest in the analysis of philosophical terms, lent impetus to the growing concentration on metaethics and to the neglect of normative ethics.

104 For criticisms of anti-naturalism from within the analytic perspective, see, for example, Philippa Foot, "Moral Beliefs," *Proceedings of the Aristotelian Society* 59 (1958-59) : 83-104, reprinted in Philippa Foot, *Theories of Ethics* (New York: Oxford University Press, 1967) , pp. 83-100; and Warnock, *Contemporary Moral Philosophy*, pp. 62-72.

tion. And why in the end an appeal to the mores and rules of conduct of a particular moral community should be any less arbitrary and subjective than the cruder formulations of the emotivists was not entirely clear. Moreover, the inability or reluctance of ethicists even to talk about the ultimate reality or non-reality of moral qualities or value properties—much in the manner that natural science extruded such qualities from its purview—suggested to some that the ethicists had after all still not overcome the separation between fact and value. Scientific naturalism continued, as it had throughout the century, to cast a shadow over the ethical enterprise. Despite the sophistication and refinements made in ethical theory, deep uncertainty about the actual status of ethics prevailed.[105]

Second, consequently ethics had become dominated by a concern with metaethics to such an extent that both normative questions about what is right and good as well as concrete problems were almost totally ignored. Textbooks and anthologies, while giving customary coverage to the traditional schools of thought, the great thinkers, and the perennial problems, approached even these more and more from the perspective of analysis and theory. Ethics was increasingly presented as a self-contained field of study with but a tangential connection to other disciplines and practical issues. Social thought and the concrete social problems of the earlier textbooks, when they did not disappear altogether, were treated primarily as material for metaethical analysis.[106] In 1964 William Frankena wrote that, "American philosophers have been relatively unpreoccupied in their official capacities with the practical and cultural problems of the day, a fact that has often disturbed their readers, as well as some of their own number. . . . They have usually contented themselves with offering general principles for the solution of such problems, and a very influential school of thinkers has disowned even the responsibility of doing this."[107]

---

105 Types of criticism of the ethical theory of the 1950s and 1960s may be found in Olafson, *Ethics and Twentieth Century Thought, passim,* esp. pp. 23-24; more specifically from within the analytic tradition in Warnock, *Contemporary Moral Philosophy;* from a naturalist point of view in Hancock, *Twentieth Century Ethics,* pp. 87-163; and from a metaphysical position in Henry B. Veatch, *For an Ontology of Morals* (Evanston, Ill.: Northwestern University Press, 1971), pp. 19-56.

106 For a more detailed discussion of recent ethics textbooks and pedagogical trends, which also notes the exceptional texts of the period, see, Jim Giarelli, "Primers in Ethics: Reflections on a Changing Field" (Paper presented at Southeastern Philosophy of Education Society meeting in Atlanta, February 1977). Unfortunately, Professor Giarelli's paper came to my attention after my study was complete, but I have drawn on it to the extent that this has been possible. I think that I am correct in finding substantial agreement in our conclusions regarding the texts of the sixties.

107 Frankena, "Ethical Theory," pp. 437-38.

For some this was a regrettable but unavoidable state of affairs. Only a few years after Frankena's observations, Kai Nielson noted that, "It is felt by many philosophers that the logical status of moral utterances and the nature of moral reasoning are so unclear that we cannot profitably do normative ethics until we have a far more adequate metaethics than we have at present. Because of such convictions, a central and pervasive question in metaethics is whether a normative ethics is possible."[108] Others were quite willing to make a virtue of the situation by affirming that the sole task of philosophy is analysis and that this is quite enough. As one philosopher said, for example, in introducing his own textbook of readings in ethics for college students, one of the few that did, in fact, attempt to relate metaethics to normative and practical issues, "Philosophy is not practical wisdom. . . . At its best, it can improve the clarity of our thought and the consistency of our reasoning—and this is a great deal."[109]

Third, ethics had become more isolated than ever within the college curriculum. This was not a new situation, but one that was exacerbated by the two characteristics of ethics that have just been examined. It is probably worth pointing out that the emphasis on analysis and meta-ethics fit well with a certain conception of professionalization that would make disciplinary boundaries watertight by focusing primarily on methodological problems and concerns.[110] Be this as it may, ethics had become increasingly a subject that would appeal mainly to philosophy majors and the occasional stray student from other fields seeking to fulfill a humanities requirement. Small liberal arts colleges, which usually had resources for only one general ethics course and, perhaps, a seminar for majors, were, ironically, probably worse off in this regard than the larger universities, which could offer a richer spread of courses. Among the several courses a large university was capable of providing were some that would deal with social problems and social theory in ways that would certainly raise broad ethical questions, although they were not offered specifically as ethics courses. Amherst, for example, in the mid-sixties offered one ethics course in its philosophy department

108 Nielson, "Problems of Ethics," p. 119.
109 Abelson, *Ethics and Metaethics*, p. vii.
110 The propensity of philosophers during this period to speak mainly to one another and to worry little about the wider consequences and applications of their work has frequently been explained as the result of a heightened guild mentality within academia. Whatever truth there may or may not be to this charge, it should be remembered that in the case of ethics, as with the social sciences as we have seen earlier, what may appear as professionalization is inseparable from the conception and focus of the discipline itself. The substance of philosophy and the structure of the profession have gone hand in hand, and an enquiry into the one must entail a looking into the other as well.

as an elective for sophomores.[111] The Philosophy Department of the University of Wisconsin, on the other hand, provided, in addition to three ethics courses as such, "Introduction to Social Philosophy," "Man, Religion, and Society," "Social Philosophy of John Dewey," and a course that had been a regular offering of the Department for a decade on the "Social Problems of Contemporary Art," which examined such ethical issues as censorship, freedom, and the social uses of art.[112] Nevertheless, regardless of how broadly the ethics course might be defined, within the overall college curriculum the study of ethics was for the few.

A 1964 article presenting a sampling of one hundred college and university catalogs—representing institutions of all types, large and small, public and private, religious and secular—found that only twenty seven institutions "required any philosophy at all for graduation with the bachelor of arts degree." And ethics was only one among several fields within philosophy itself. The author of that study noted that in his own institution of twelve thousand students the enrollment in ethics averaged eleven students per year.[113] His was probably fairly representative of other institutions. By the mid-sixties the teaching of ethics was in deep trouble.

Generalizations about a period as recent to our own as the last two or three decades must be offered tentatively and in the awareness that we may still be too close to judge in proper perspective. A couple of final observations about the period just examined are, therefore, in order. In the first place, it could be argued that in devoting themselves to metaethics, the philosophers were in a real sense dealing with the most practical problem of all—the intellectual difficulties that had made the theoretical foundations of all ethics so uncertain in the twentieth century. The question was whether metaethics as it was conceived was helping to reduce or to make worse that uncertainty. At the same time developments in ethical theory, and their implications for teaching, were not static. We have depicted the fifties and sixties with broad strokes of the brush highlighting major trends characteristic of the period but by necessity ignoring hints of possible new departures, including some within the analytic school itself.[114] We will return to some

111 Amherst College, *Catalogue*, 1965-66. Amherst also offered one ethics course at this time in the religion department.

112 University of Wisconsin, *Catalogue*, 1964/65, pp. 260-65. This course was still being offered ten years later. *Catalogue*, 1972/74.

113 George Henry Moulds, "The Decline and Fall of Philosophy," *Liberal Education* 50 (1964): 360-61.

114 To a historian writing in the year 2000 it may be precisely these, to us, still more hidden aspects of the sixties that will emerge as the most important marks of the period.

of these that appear to have surfaced in the seventies in the concluding pages.

THE TEACHING OF ETHICS IN THE LARGER CURRICULUM

Professional ethicists have not been the only persons in twentieth-century American higher education concerned with the teaching of ethics, nor has this teaching been the sole province of departments of philosophy. A full study of the teaching of ethics in the undergraduate curriculum, for example, would have to examine the continuing efforts to raise ethical issues in traditional humanities courses and in the social sciences. How often have students, for instance, enrolled in psychology —or literature or history or political science and government—courses in hopes, of which they have been perhaps only half-conscious, of finding there some enlightenment or guidance for pressing personal and social problems? To what extent have these disciplines addressed, by-passed, or suppressed these needs? Another area requiring further inquiry has to do with the ways in which ethics instruction has figured in undergraduate professional and vocational curricula. Have the "foundations" courses in undergraduate education programs, for example, or the "business and society" courses for undergraduate business majors, served in reality as forms of required moral philosophy courses? To deal with these intriguing areas and questions adequately would require a more extensive study than, unfortunately, is possible here, but to point to them may at least help to indicate the presence of the ethical dimension, even when ignored, throughout the undergraduate curriculum.

There have been other areas, however, that have been consciously and directly concerned with the teaching of ethics. Spokesmen for the variety of curricular reform described under the heading of general education have almost all viewed moral education as one of the prime purposes of undergraduate instruction. And some of the most lively teaching of ethics, at least since World War II, has taken place within departments of religions. Both, therefore, warrant a brief look.

THE GENERAL EDUCATION MOVEMENT

General education has represented in part a reassertion of the older liberal arts tradition that the teaching of ethics should properly be the responsibility not merely of a single course or department but of the entire institution of higher education and its curriculum. General education, however, has always been something of a rear-guard action to keep alive the liberal arts within hostile or indifferent circumstances and has had by necessity to exist as a compromise—and often compromised—movement. Consequently, it has been made to serve many purposes, not all of them compatible with one another. At its strongest and most vital, general education has presupposed that ethical concerns lie at the heart of the educational task and that the moral uses of knowledge and the integration of knowledge are intimately connected. In its weaker times general education has sunk to being little more than an administrative and rhetorical device for putting some order into a curriculum that has gotten entirely out of hand. Not surprisingly, general education has frequently found itself under fire from two sides: on the one, from reformers who feel that it makes too many concessions to traditional academic departments; on the other, from specialists who disdain it for being superficial. Yet despite its weaknesses, general education has been a source of some of the most interesting critiques and reform proposals in modern American higher education.

Early in the century a variety of attempts began to be made to stem the splintering of the curriculum that the elective principle and intensive specialization had produced. By the late 1930s virtually every type of curricular reform that has been attempted in the twentieth century had in one form or another made its appearance. There were first the introduction and adoption by most colleges and universities of the concentration and distribution system and the spread of the popular but frequently criticized survey and orientation courses. Then, during the twenties and thirties, there began those experiments that made up what has been known as "the general education movement" itself: the founding of new experimental colleges—Bennington, Sarah Lawrence, the new program at St. John's at Annapolis, the major curricular reorganizations of Columbia, The University of Chicago, and Reed College, and the organization of entirely new units within existing institutions as with the General College of the University of Minnesota, the General College of Boston University, and the Experimental College at the University of Wisconsin, among others.[115]

The foundation on which general education was based varied considerably among the different institutions: the two-year Contemporary Civilization and Humanities sequence at Columbia, the lower-college prescribed courses in the humanities and the natural, physical, and

115 Excellent accounts of the broad history of general education may be found in Russell Thomas, *The Search for a Common Learning: General Education, 1800-1960* (New York: McGraw-Hill, 1962); Daniel Bell, *The Reforming of General Education: The Columbia College Experience in Its National Setting* (New York: Columbia University Press, 1966); and Earl J. McGrath, *General Education and the Plight of Modern Man* (Indianapolis, Ind.: The Lilly Endowment, Inc. n.d.).

social sciences at the University of Chicago under President Robert Hutchins, the arts curriculum at Bennington, the ill-fated but imaginative two-year reading and group discussion program led by Alexander Meicklejohn at the Experimental College of the University of Wisconsin, based on an intensive study of Greek culture in the freshman year and contemporary culture in the sophomore year, and the so-called "Great Books Program" at St. John's College in Annapolis. Despite such differences, however, the major advocates of these experiments all indicated that their central concern was moral education, the turning out of persons with the breadth of knowledge, intellectual discipline, and ethical sensitivity needed to grapple with the personal and social problems of the modern world. Looking back many years later, Harry Carman described the motives that had led him and a group of young faculty members at Columbia University in 1917 to convert the course, "Issues of the War," begun to acquaint students with the causes and purposes of the war, to a "peace issues" course, which as "Contemporary Civilization" laid the basis for the development of Columbia's full-scale general education program over the next three decades. "The college, we agreed," wrote Carman, "should be concerned with education for effective citizenship in a democratic society: citizens with broad perspective and a critical and constructive approach to life, who are concerned about values in terms of integrity of character, motives, attitudes, and excellence of behavior; citizens who have the ability to think, to communicate, to make intelligent and wise judgments, to evaluate moral situations, and to work effectively to good ends with others."[116] This was the theme that in various formulations was common to all the pioneer experiments in general education.

Lacking, however, was consensus on what should be the integrating principle of the curriculum. In 1922 President Alexander Meiklejohn of Amherst published an article analyzing the tasks and difficulties facing those who would seek a unified curriculum. Meiklejohn, since his inauguration at Amherst in 1912, was a major voice in criticizing the elective principle and in calling for common purposes in the liberal college; he argued that there could be no genuine unity in the curriculum without an underlying unity of knowledge itself, the very thing that, as yet, no one had been able to supply. He argued that the fragmentation of learning was the result of the overweening influence of

116 Quoted in McGrath, Ibid., p. 29. Also see, James Gutman, "The Pioneers of Columbia's General Education Curriculum," *Columbia College Today* (Jan./Feb., 1979) : 11-13.

natural science. "First," he said, "it is chiefly Natural Science which is responsible for the opinion that knowledge has no unity. Second, it is chiefly that view which has brought our college teaching into incoherence and confusion."[117] The problem, then, was nothing less than to discover and defend a philosophical foundation for the curriculum that would by definition challenge the very conception of knowledge and knowing dominant in the university. This was general education's most formidable obstacle, and one its proponents have as yet never successively overcome.

By the mid-thirties at least four different positions on the problem had emerged. One was based on course content and sought to find the unity of the curriculum in the humanities and the humanistically-oriented social sciences. This was the solution represented, for example, by the general education program at Columbia University. The strength of this position was that as long as the humanities commanded respect they could bring to bear on the curriculum the weighty ethical and value heritage of Western civilization. Because the validity of these values, however, was in the main simply accepted without question, when they were seriously challenged the general education based on them had little defense to fall back upon. Moreover, this conception of general education was to suffer deep erosion as the models for knowing and professionalization within the humanities themselves were increasingly drawn from natural science.

A second position was to locate the integrating principle of the curriculum not in subject matter or content but, rather, in the method to be employed in dealing with significant cultural problems. This was Meiklejohn's own position, and he argued that this method was not the same as the techniques of scholarly research, but rather "a common unspecialized form of study" that cuts across all specialized interests and inquiries and that combines analysis and synthesis, the past and the contemporary, the humanities and science, interpretation and empiricism. Meiklejohn called this form of study "intelligence." The prescribed course at the Experimental College devoted to the study and discussion of significant cultural problems sought to show that "intelligence" in this sense was a reality and that it provided both the goal and the means of a liberal college education. Meiklejohn's hostility to graduate research, his rejection of the disciplinary classification of knowledge, and his holistic conception of intelligence did not favor

---

117 Alexander Meiklejohn, "The Unity of the Curriculum," *New Republic* 32 (October 25, 1922): pt. 2, pp. 2-3, quoted in Thomas, *The Search for a Common Learning*, p. 71.

widespread acceptance of his position. Nevertheless, Meiklejohn anticipated many reform proposals that were to be made later.[118]

A third position was that taken by Dewey and his followers, which
attempted to find the unity of the curriculum in the solution of concrete life problems through the method of science. This bore resemblances to Meiklejohn's outlook but unlike his was, on the one hand,
hostile to prescribed courses, and, on the other, more narrowly pro-
grammatic in its insistence that the method of intelligence was the
method of the natural sciences. If general education be identified not
with a prescribed course of study, but more accurately with the attempt
to establish a unifying principle and ethical orientation in the curriculum, Dewey clearly was part of the "search for a common learning." As
Laurence Veysey has observed, Dewey's approach could be interpreted
in two opposite ways, either as favoring a planned program based on
"life situations" or as fostering total individual elective freedom—the
one leaning toward more prescription than Dewey favored, the other
threatening the very fragmentation Dewey, like the others, wanted to
overcome.[119] The deeper problems of Dewey's approach we have examined in detail.

The fourth position made metaphysics the basis for an integrated
curriculum. In 1936 Robert Hutchins published an essay, *The Higher
Learning in America,* in which he effectively marshalled most of the
current criticisms of American higher education, calling it to task for
its commercialism, its vocationalism, its curricular confusion, its anti-
intellectualism, and its ethical relativism. The fundamental problem
for Hutchins, however, was the scepticism of scientific naturalism,
which made all talk about truth and value impossible. There was little
that was radically new in this criticism although Hutchins had advanced
it with much verve and provocation. Where Hutchins did deviate dra-
matically from others was in saying that only a thoroughgoing metaphysics—and Hutchins embraced the Aristotelian-Thomistic natural law
tradition—could bring order to knowledge and provide a solid foundation and justification for ethical values.[120]

118 Alexander Meiklejohn, *The Liberal College* (Boston: Marshall Jones, 1920) and
Alexander Meiklejohn, *The Experimental College* (New York: Harper & Brothers, 1932).
There is an excellent brief discussion of Meiklejohn's experimental curriculum in Laurence
Veysey, "Stability and Experiment in the American Undergraduate Curriculum," in *Con-
tent and Context: Essays on College Education,* ed. Carl Kaysen (New York: McGraw-Hill,
1973), pp. 54-57.

119 Veysey, Ibid., p. 54.

120 Robert Hutchins, *The Higher Learning in America* (New Haven: Yale University
Press, 1936).

Hutchins' essay touched off a rarity in the history of American higher education, an intense public dialogue on the purposes and philosophy of education. Hutchins' position was immediately subjected to a many-sided criticism of its own, both from major spokesmen for the university, as well as from John Dewey, who actually shared much of Hutchins' diagnosis of the university's ills, but abhorred his recommendation for a remedy. Hutchins' appeal to tradition was condemned as antiquarian and irrelevant to the solution of contemporary problems. His assertion of the existence of a higher non-empirical level of reality was judged inconceivable by modern canons of knowledge. And, finally, his claim that the problems of the modern university and world could be put right only by a recognition of absolute metaphysical principles was deemed, especially by Dewey and his followers, as authoritarian and reactionary.[121] Whatever the merits or weaknesses of his own solution, Hutchins had forced attention to the central question: How necessary was an integrating principle within the curriculum and on what grounds could it be established? The outbreak of the war brought the debate to an end as the nation and the universities turned from trying to justify the values of democracy to the more immediate task of defending them. It would be some time before the debate would be resumed.

Just as in World War I college "war aims" courses had given an impetus to the beginnings of general education, so also World War II helped touch off a renewed surge of interest in the movement. This time Harvard University took the lead. In 1943 President James Conant of Harvard appointed a committee to study "the objectives for general education in a free society." Two years later the committee issued its report under the title *General Education in a Free Society*.[122] Reflecting war-time anxiety about the stability of democratic society in the face of fascism and the rising threat of communism, as well as concern about possible post-war social disorientation at home, the report stressed the role of education in the creation of common social values. Foreseeing continual growth and diversification of higher education after the war,

121 In fact, in an increasingly rancorous debate each side succeeded in associating the other with fascism: the scientific naturalists were charged with abetting Hitler because of their ethical relativism; the metaphysicians because of their alleged authoritarianism. See, for example, John Dewey, "President Hutchins' Proposals to Remake Higher Education," *The Social Frontier* 3 (January 1937): 103-104; and Mortimer J. Adler, "God and the Professors," in his *Science, Philosophy, and Religion, A Symposium* (New York: n.p., 1941), pp. 120-37.

122 *General Education in a Free Society: Report of the Harvard Committee* (Cambridge, Mass.: Harvard University Press, 1945).

the report sought to avoid any further fragmentation of the curriculum and of American cultural values this might entail.

The aim of general education was viewed primarily as one of training up intelligent and capable citizens committed to the values necessary for a full and responsible participation in democratic society. The integration of the curriculum would center in a combination of the religious and humane values of the Western cultural heritage with the methods of the physical and social sciences taught as the means of implementing those values. Through a program of general and specific courses distributed among the three areas of the natural sciences, the social sciences, and the humanities, general education would prepare students "to think effectively, to communicate thought, to make relevant judgments, to discriminate among values." This was traditional enough, but somewhat unique to the report was the notion that general education must be a continuing ethical education. "Unless," wrote Conant in his preface to the report, "the educational process includes *at each level of maturity* [his italics] some continuing contact with those fields in which value judgments are of prime importance, it must fall far short of the ideal." In other words, general education as the formation of ethical discernment and capacity for action must extend throughout all education and all of life.[123]

For all of its several virtues, *General Education in a Free Society* lacked in important respects the precision and sharp analysis of the problems of moral education that had begun to be evident in the general education programs and debates of the 1930s. The report accepted without question the humane values of Western culture as the center of the curriculum as though their validity were self-evident and beyond challenge. It assumed equally without question that these given values were fully compatible with the critical methods of modern science and philosophy and only awaited transmission to the students. "The impulse to rear students to a received idea of the good," read the report, "is in fact necessary to education. It is impossible to escape the realization that our society, like any society, rests on common beliefs and that a major task of education is to perpetuate them." The report sought to avoid any suggestion of implied indoctrination in such a manner of speaking by invoking the spirit of John Dewey, pragmatism, and scientific experimentation.[124] The report sought an easy and eclectic amalgamation of the traditional and the modern, the humanities and

123 Ibid., pp. vii-ix.
124 Ibid., pp. 46-47.

science, the "spiritual" and the "material," the given and the experimental, in the faith that by presenting both together an integral balance between them would of itself be achieved and maintained. This unexamined faith, however, simply meant staving off the hard questions that sooner or later would have to be faced once the values embodied in the report and the justification for them had been challenged or, just as fatal to the program, ignored.

The immediate response, however, was a renewed enthusiasm for general education throughout the country. As they spread, general education programs varied considerably from campus to campus. Many were little more than a reshuffling and expansion of previous distribution requirements; some like the senior seminar and symposia at New College in Florida, Bowdoin College, Macalester, and other institutions appeared very much like full-fledged modern versions of the old moral philosophy course; others like those at Columbia, Harvard, and other institutions attempted to be more thoroughgoing reconstructions of the curriculum.[125] In the *Journal of General Education,* founded in 1946, the movement had its own voice and forum for the exchange of ideas. By 1955, Earl McGrath has observed, probably half the colleges of the nation were experimenting with some form of general education.[126]

The decline of post-war general education, however, was even more rapid than its rise. The erosion of general education began in the late fifties and within little more than a decade the movement was nearing total collapse.[127] The response to the launching of Sputnik in 1957 brought enormous prestige and funding to scientific and technological research, at the expense of the humanities, and encouraged colleges and universities to return to the specialized orientation of the old distribution system. That same year a widely discussed, if controversial, study of the influence of college teaching raised serious questions about the very ability of higher education to affect student values in any substantial way whatsoever.

In a broad survey of student attitudes and assumptions entitled, *Changing Values in College: An Exploratory Study of the Impact of College Teaching* the author, Philip E. Jacob, concluded that colleges had little, if any, effect on student values.[128] In ordinary times the data

125 Macalester College, *Catalogue,* 1953/55; and Rudolph, *Curriculum,* pp. 248-49.
126 McGrath, *General Education,* p. 23.
127 Earl McGrath documents in detail the erosion of the general education programs at Harvard, Columbia, and Chicago during this period. Ibid., pp. 20-49.
128 Philip E. Jacob, *Changing Values in College: An Exploratory Study of the Impact of College Teaching* (New York: Harper & Brothers, 1957).

and conclusions presented by Jacob might well have supplied arguments for the champions of general education. Coming as it did, however, at the height of the post-war general education experimentation, it may—we can only speculate here—very well have taken the heart out of efforts to defend the importance of teaching and to resist the resurgence of research specialization and concentration.[129]

The decline of general education, however, would not have been so rapid had not even deeper problems already begun to manifest themselves—problems that cast grave doubt on general education as any kind of effective source for the teaching of ethics and values. First, the essential question of establishing a genuine integrating principle for the curriculum had never been answered and since World War II had scarcely been addressed. As a result, many of the general education schemes were little better than administrative efforts to balance a variety of competing faculty interests. Second, the lack of such an integrating principle left general education vulnerable to serving simply the distribution needs of the traditional subject matter disciplines. When this happened, prescribed general education courses were accorded low priority, relegated to graduate teaching assistants, and became merely an ordeal to be endured by students on their way to fulfillment of non-major requirements. This was exactly one charge brought against such courses by dissident students and critical faculty during the 1960s.[130] Finally, the deeper philosophical problems that had begun to be raised during the thirties regarding the very possibility and justification of moral education in the university had not been rigorously dealt with within the post-war general education movement. Indeed it seemed that at times they had been deliberately ignored. As a consequence, although it could still function as a means of softening and mitigating the worst excesses of extreme early specialization, general education had been nearly deprived of its own ultimate justification. In retrospect, it is hardly surprising that the sixties and early seventies witnessed a veritable rush to dismantle prescribed courses and programs of every kind.

Experiments with the undergraduate curriculum continued throughout most of the 1960s, but these were mainly administrative rearrange-

---

129 For a contemporaneous discussion of Jacob's study, see John E. Smith *Value Convictions and Higher Education* (New Haven: The Edward W. Hazen Foundations, 1958). For discussions on the problems of values in higher education still reflecting the influence of the Jacob study a few years later, see Jack F. Cully, ed., *Contemporary Values and the Responsibility of the College* (Iowa City: State University of Iowa, 1962).

130 Harold Taylor, *Students Without Teachers: The Crisis in the University* (New York: McGraw-Hill, 1969), pp. 131-63.

ments of no real consequence.[131] Although he presented a fascinating analysis of higher education, Daniel Bell's 1964 effort at Columbia to restate the case for general education aroused no interest even at his own university. By making methods of disciplinary inquiry the basis for integrating the curriculum—a much different, and narrower conception of method than that proposed by Meiklejohn and others thirty years earlier—Bell's proposal may have seemed to the traditional advocates of general education like handing them over to their enemies and to the specialized research interests, who were in the ascendant anyway, a bit like carrying coals to Newcastle.[132] "By 1976," Frederick Rudolph has written, "concentration was in charge of curriculum."[133]

Already the pendulum has swung, and today, once again, there is a resurgence of interest in general education. One expression of this interest appears in the larger context of the kind of concern that motivated Jacob's study mentioned earlier regarding the influence of the total college experience on student values. The nineteenth-century conception of "the college as a community" has never entirely disappeared. And recent years have witnessed a mounting number of efforts to take yet another look at the impact of "college life" on students.[134] Some investigators, such as Theodore Newcomb and Kenneth Feldman, have concluded, like Jacobs before them, that, all told, the college has

131 Paul L. Dressel and Frances H. DeLisle, *Undergraduate Curriculum Trends* (Washington, D.C.: American Council on Education, 1969).

132 Bell, *The Reforming of General Education.*

133 Rudolph, *Curriculum*, p. 248.

134 Among the most important works of a voluminous and growing literature are. Arthur W. Chickering, *Education and Identity* (San Francisco: Jossey-Bass Publishers, 1972); Kenneth Feldman and Theodore M. Newcomb, *The Impact of College on Students,* 2 vols. (San Francisco: Jossey-Bass Publishers, 1976); Douglas H. Heath, *Growing Up in College* (San Francisco: Jossey-Bass Publishers, 1968); Joseph Katz, et al., *No Time for Youth* (San Francisco: Jossey-Bass Publishers, 1969); William G. Perry, *Forms of Intellectual and Ethical Development in the College Years* (New York: Holt, Rinehart, & Winston, 1968); and Harold Webster, et al., "Personality Changes in College Students," in Nevitt Sanford, ed., *The American College* (New York: John Wiley & Sons, 1962). Also see, Martin Trow, "Higher Education and Moral Development," *AAUP Bulletin* (Spring 1976): 20-27.

These represent latter-day manifestations of what in actuality has been a rather long-standing interest among values-interested social scientists. For some early examples of the genre, see Harry William Foot, "A Psychological Approach to the Problem of Character-Training in Institutions of Higher Education". (M.A. thesis, Columbia University, 1932); G.J. Dudycha, "The Moral Beliefs of College Students," *International Journal of Ethics* 43 (1933): 194-204; A. Snyder and K. Dunlap, "A Study of Moral Evaluations by Male and Female College Students," *Journal of Comparative Psychology* 4 (1924): 289-324; and W.H. Crowley and W. Walker, "A Study of Student Life," *Journal of Higher Education* 6 (1935): 132-42.

relatively little effect in altering student values; others, such as William Perry, have presented evidence suggesting that the actual and potential impact of the college experience may be very important indeed.[135] As yet interest in studies of this sort continues strong.

General education has also experienced a resurgence among those involved in reconceiving a "liberal core" in the undergraduate curriculum as a means of countering excessive specialization and curricular fragmentation.[136] As we have seen, this is a problem endemic to the modern university, and reform efforts intended to deal with it wax and wane with cyclic regularity. Curriculum reforms of this sort, however, as has also been observed, concentrate not so much on keeping ethical concerns and value questions alive in higher education, but more on providing students with cross-disciplinary understanding and methodological breadth. It remains to be seen whether the most recent attempts in this regard will preserve at their center any notion of "the educated person," including "the ethical person," or whether they will devolve, at best, into a streamlined refurbishing of the old system of distribution, or, at worst, into the politics of departmental representation.

A final, and still different, call for general education has come from those who seek an issue-oriented curriculum as distinct from either the content- or method-oriented approaches of other general education attempts. There are antecedents of this issue-orientation, but the main impetus for the present proposal has come from issues raised by student protestors in the sixties, and, now more recently, from those who see the possibility of addressing those issues directly within higher education. "The point of departure," Earl J. McGrath, one of the main spokesmen for the issue-orientation, has written, "must be the problems with which this and succeeding generations must deal—ecology, energy, crime, hunger, war, and the rest."[137] The hope of making issues the focus of a reformed curriculum is to unite once again relevance, moral commitment, and knowledge, and to avoid having the movement captured by the subject-matter interests of the faculty and the existing divisions of the curriculum.

The main problem that has continued to plague both the teaching of

135 See note above. Mine is a gross summary of some very intricate studies.
136 See, for example, Malcolm G. Scully, "Tightening the Curriculum: Enthusiasm, Dissent, and 'So What Else Is New?'" *The Chronicle of Higher Education* 18 (May 8, 1978) : 1, 12; and Gerald Grant and David Riesman, *The Perpetual Dream: Reform and Experiment in the American College* (Chicago: The University of Chicago Press, 1978), pp. 355-82.
137 Earl J. McGrath, *Values, Liberal Education, and National Destiny* (Published by the Lilly Endowment, Inc., n.p., 1975), p. 36.

ethics and general education has been the modern tendency to regard only scientific knowledge as genuine and to look upon other concerns as somewhat out of place in the university. It will have achieved little to make issues the central focus, if in the end the scientific and technological solutions to them are the only ones that enjoy philosophic and social standing. Unless this problem is addressed, one would expect continuing problems for the present movement. In the meantime, the vision of a meaningful general education will continue to appeal to many who would insist on raising questions concerning the moral uses of knowledge and who seek a concrete arena within which personal and social ethics can be taught in relation to the whole curriculum.

RELIGION AND ETHICS

Throughout the twentieth century the teaching of ethics in American higher education has maintained vestiges of the special relationship with religion that it enjoyed in earlier periods. This relationship finds expression, for example, in the familiar phrase "religion and ethics," still sometimes used to describe, not always with approval, the domain of moral concerns within higher education. One difficulty, in fact, in identifying the sources of the teaching of ethics in higher education is that religious programs and courses, even when they lack a specific emphasis on ethics as such, have almost invariably been taught with ethical aims in view. Thus, courses in biblical studies, in the philosophy and psychology of religion, and in comparative religion have often been justified not only as being culturally important, but also as providing a necessary framework within which to understand the most important problems of personal and social life.

During the first half of the twentieth century most of the teaching of religion in higher education was concentrated within private colleges sponsored by religious bodies, mainly Protestant and Roman Catholic but including a few explicitly Jewish institutions. Private nonsectarian colleges, many of which had originated as denominational schools, often bent over backwards in excluding religious courses from their curriculum programs in their desire to establish their autonomy and status as independent institutions. State universities, however, which had a much longer and closer connection with the teaching of religion than is often supposed—many of them in their earlier years were nearly indistinguishable from other nineteenth-century church-related colleges in being suffused with pan-Protestant values and religious concerns—were actually more flexible than many nonsectarian private schools. Concern about church-state conflicts inhibited the inclusion of religion courses and departments within the regular curriculum of public institutions during the late nineteenth and early twentieth centuries, but gradually more and more schools of this sort began to make provision for the study of religion in a variety of different programs.[138] A major study of the teaching of religion in American colleges and universities conducted in 1936 concluded that in Roman Catholic colleges all students received religious instruction, that in Protestant colleges one out of two students did so, and that in private nondenominational colleges and in state universities and colleges the respective figures were one out of eight and one out of twenty. In all these programs courses in ethics were among the major offerings, although a still smaller number of the students enrolled in religious studies would have taken courses specifically in ethics.[139]

The two decades following World War II witnessed a dramatic growth of religion departments within private, nonsectarian schools and within state universities. By 1950, Clarence Shedd reported, nearly sixty percent of state universities and land grant colleges were offering instruction in religion on an academic credit basis, and their number continued to increase.[140] The proliferation of religious programs was

138 See, John F. Wilson, "Introduction: The Background and Present Context of the Study of Religion in Colleges and Universities," in *The Study of Religion in Colleges and Universities,* ed. Paul Ramsey and John F. Wilson (Princeton: Princeton University Press, 1970), pp. 3-22.

139 The study reported that in public institutions three groups of courses competed closely for first place in being most frequently offered in religious programs: Biblical studies, ethics, and philosophy of religion. Among Protestant schools, explicit ethics courses were prominent, but ranked along with Biblical studies, the life and teachings of Jesus, and religious education, though, again, within these last, it would be undoubtedly difficult to draw a hard and fast line between the ethical and nonethical dimensions of what was taught. Only two subjects stood out prominently within Roman Catholic colleges: doctrine and ethics. Gould Wickey and Ruth A. Eckhart, *A National Survey of Courses in Bible and Religion in American Universities and Colleges* (Printed for The Indiana Council on Religion in Higher Education, 1936). With the exception of Roman Catholic colleges and universities, much more data than is now available is needed to assess the exact nature of these religiously-based ethics courses. A more complete study would have to look in much greater detail than has been possible in this paper at the tradition of the teaching of ethics in Roman Catholic institutions.

140 Clarence Prouty Shedd, "Religion in the American State Universities: Its History and Present Problems," in *Religion in the State University: An Initial Exploration,* ed. Henry E. Allen (Minneapolis: Burger Publishing Co., 1950), p. 25. A copious literature soon developed to deal with the issues raised by the rapid growth of religious studies. Among some of the more useful examples are Ramsey and Wilson, *The Study of Religion,* which contains an extensive bibliography; Clyde A. Holbrook, *Religion, A Humanities Field* (Englewood Cliffs, N.J.: Prentice-Hall, 1963): and Robert Michaelson, *The Study of Religion in American Universities* (New Haven, Conn.: The Society for Religion in Higher Education, 1965).

just as rapid among private nonsectarian institutions. This surge in the intellectual study of religion reflected in part a growing awareness of the religious dimensions of many other fields of study such as sociology, psychology, anthropology, literature, and so forth. It was also due in part to the availability of highly-trained graduates from interdenominational seminaries—Yale, Harvard, Duke, Union-Columbia, Chicago—to staff the new programs. These graduates were imbued with the intellectual and religious excitement stemming from the theological renewal of the 1930s, 40s, and 50s—often associated in Protestantism with so-called neo-orthodoxy, but actually limited neither to Protestantism nor neo-orthodoxy—in which these seminaries had played a leading part. One hallmark of the newer theological outlook was an intense appreciation of the central intellectual and ethical importance of the Judeo-Christian tradition in the development of Western culture.

The result for the teaching of ethics was threefold. First, the treatment of ethical and moral questions in their broadest political, social, and philosophic dimensions was accorded a central position in the study of religion. Both religious ethics—stimulated by the theological works of such persons, among others, as Paul Tillich, Karl Barth, Reinhold and Richard Niebuhr, Jacques Maritain, Nicholai Berdyaev, and Martin Buber—and nonreligious ethical viewpoints—such as that of Jean Paul Sartre—were dealt with as bearing directly on the ultimate concerns of man. Second, a main characteristic of this theological renewal was its concern with the large problems of political and social ethics, rather than with a narrow, individualistic interpretation of religious morality. As a consequence, normative ethical issues and major social issues probably received much more attention during the fifties and sixties within the teaching of ethics in religion departments than within departments of philosophy.[141] Third, an existentialist outlook and attitude was, likewise, probably much more prevalent within religion departments than in departments of philosophy, both because of the importance of existentialism in much twentieth-century religious thought and because it combined intellectual analysis with a call for commitment in dealing with crucial ethical issues of the day. Although existentialism made personal decision the sole basis for authentic moral

141 It is probably no accident, for example, that one of the exceptional texts of the early sixties that focused entirely on concrete ethical problems opened with readings from the theological-ethical perspectives of Karl Barth and George F. Kennan and contained substantial sections on "Church and State" and "The Church and Social Reform," with readings from the Niebuhr brothers, John Courtney Murray, and others. Girvetz, *Contemporary Moral Issues.*

action and was, therefore, for the most part unabashedly subjective, perhaps its being taught within the framework of a religious perspective may have seemed to provide existentialism with a foundation it lacked in the more analytic and positivistic climate of departments of philosophy. At any rate, it would probably be safe to conclude that during most of the 1950s and 60s some of the most vital teaching of ethics in American higher education took place within departments and programs of religion.[142]

At the present the situation seems to have changed. The theological renewal of the mid-century was unable to stem the fundamental modern skepticism about religious knowledge, and, consequently, a religiously-based teaching of ethics also appears to have lost the promise it held out for a time of being able to command the attention and respect of a wide audience. Compounding the problem is that in their desire to establish the full academic status and respectability of their fields, members of departments of religion were, perhaps, even more zealous than others to adopt the standards of graduate school oriented professionalism with all of the unresolved, perhaps unavoidable, problems of curriculum isolation and compartmentalization that this has historically entailed. In order, however, to assess the degree to which the combination of these two factors has actually affected the teaching of ethics in departments of religion would require a much more extensive analysis of present programs than is possible here.

RETROSPECT AND NEW DEPARTURES

Two things happened during the nineteenth and twentieth centuries that were to have momentous consequences for higher education and modern society in general, as well as for the teaching of ethics in particular. Both were centuries-long developments that reached a kind of culmination in the 1890s, although it was not for several decades thereafter that their full impact and implications began to become clearly manifest. One development was the splintering of the culture of learning into many different, self-contained disciplines of knowledge. We have considered some of the main aspects of this development, and the so-called professionalization process that accompanied it, as these affected the decline of moral philosophy and a widening separation of the social sciences from the teaching of ethics. The other development—essentially much more important than the first—was that one of these

---

142 A comprehensive discussion of the content and issues of Christian ethics is the bibliographic essay by James Gustafson, "Christian Ethics," in *Religion,* ed. Paul Ramsey (Englewood Cliffs, N.J.: Prentice-Hall, 1964), pp. 285-354.

branches of knowledge, namely natural science, began to be regarded as the one and only valid mode of knowledge.

As this conception of knowledge became increasingly dominant, it began to make extremely difficult any consideration of values other than those already embedded in natural science and its technological application. The eventual impact of this attitude on the teaching of ethics—in fact, on all attempts to determine the very place of ethics in higher education—was profound. Subjects that traditionally had most to do with values and meaning—art, religion, literature, and philosophy—were increasingly called into question as sources of genuine knowledge. The growing conviction that science alone dealt with an objective world of knowledge meant that these nonscientific subjects were more and more regarded not as modes of knowing or sources of new knowledge, but as, at best, merely expressions of subjective feelings and preferences, or as repositories of folk customs and social habits, or as ideological manifestations of group interests. They even began to have difficulty finding a place within the university except insofar as they sought to model themselves after the natural sciences. Doing this, however, meant the sacrifice of their own integrity and identity as independent sources of value and ethical judgment.

From the beginning there have been surges of awareness that other values besides the scientific and technological are essential to a humane society. Periodically, throughout the twentieth century, there have been attempts to redress the balance by introducing consideration of values into the university curriculum. In effect, the loss of the role played by the old moral philosophy course has been keenly felt, and attempts have been made repeatedly to find some meaningful substitute for it—usually to little avail. Programs for general education, for the study of professional ethics, for renewing the arts and humanities, have come and gone again and again during the past seventy-five years.

Today we are experiencing a rebirth of concern for moral philosophy and the teaching of ethics of an extent and magnitude perhaps unprecedented in modern American education. The reasons for this renewal are many and complex. The multiplicity and enormity of problems demanding moral decision and action confronting humankind today have become simply unavoidable. Student demands of the last decade for "relevant" courses, whatever else their effects, challenged faculties to re-examine the connection between knowledge and values, between the discovery of knowledge and its ethical applications. And mounting concerns, and doubts, regarding the ethical sensitivity and commitment of public leaders have spurred professional groups and educators as seldom before to grapple with the tasks of moral education.

This renewed attention to the teaching of ethics is manifest at nearly every point in the curriculum. Professional philosophers and ethicists themselves have begun on a wide front to deal with pressing normative and practical problems. Leading philosophers, many of them directly within the analytic tradition itself, have frequently been at the forefront in reflecting on such issues as social justice, equality, personal and social freedom, war, and the ethical problems of science.[143] Perhaps the persistent involvement of the analytic school with language has itself helped foster within its once narrow and technical domain the re-establishment of connections with the great classical traditions of humanistic political and social theory.[144] The founding of new publications has signaled the desires of philosophers to deal with a variety of specific problems only recently out of fashion; ethics textbooks and anthologies of readings for undergraduates have begun increasingly to make normative and practical issues a central focus of instruction.[145] Moreover, not only within philosophy, but also within the other humanities and the sciences as well have appeared a growing awareness of the ethical dimension and devotion to the pedagogical problems of moral education.[146]

Perhaps most important, across a broadening spectrum are to be glimpsed indications that some of the most fundamental theoretical

143   For example, see, Richard M. Hare, *Applications of Moral Philosophy* (Berkeley: University of California Press, 1972) ; Thomas Nagel, *The Possibility of Altruism* (Oxford: Clarendon Press, 1970) ; Robert Nozick, *Anarchy, State, & Utopia* (New York: Basic Books, 1974) ; John Rawls, *Theory of Justice* (Cambridge: Harvard University Press, 1971) ; and Kersten J. Struhl and Paula R. Struhl, eds., *Ethics in Perspective* (New York: Random House, 1975) .

144   See for example, John Rawls, *Justice*.

145   Among recently founded journals especially noteworthy in this context are *Philosophy and Public Affairs* and *Journal of Medicine and Philosophy*. For examples of new approaches and emphases among texts and anthologies, see, Raziel Abelson and Marie-Louise Friqueqson, eds., *Ethics for Modern Life* (New York: Random House, 1975) ; A.K. Bierman and James A. Gould, eds., *Philosophy for a New Generation* (New York: Macmillan Company, 1970) ; Thomas A. Meppes and Jane S. Zembaty, eds., *Social Ethics: Morality and Social Policy* (New York: McGraw-Hill, 1977) ; Carl Wellman, *Morals and Ethics* (Glenview, Ill.: Scott, Foresman and Company, 1975) . Also see, for example, Thomas Nagel, et al., eds., *War and Moral Responsibility* (Princeton: Princeton University Press, 1974) ; Thomas Nagel, et al., eds., *The Rights and Wrongs of Abortion* (Princeton: Princeton University Press, 1974) ; Thomas Nagel, et al., eds., *Equality and Preferential Treatment* (Princeton: Princeton University Press, 1977) ; and Thomas Nagel, *Philosophy, Morality, and International Affairs* (New York: Oxford University Press, 1974) . Also see Giarelli, "Primers in Ethics."

146   The Hastings Center study of the teaching of ethics is eloquent testimony to this growing interest. See Daniel Callahan and Sissela Bok, eds., *The Teaching of Ethics* (New York: Plenum, 1980) .

problems underlying the teaching of ethics are once again being addressed.[147] Within psychology, for example, the work of such persons as Piaget, Lawrence Kohlberg, and William Perry suggests to some that moral issues are part and parcel of the basic process of education. A revived concern with general education has again called attention to the inseparable connection between the moral uses and unity of knowledge. And especially promising are the voices within science who are calling, like Dewey at one point, though not along his lines, for a reconception of science that would recognize the all important role of creative insight and the values of the knower in all knowing. From this last perspective comes the suggestion that a fundamental unity joins scientific insight, artistic insight, and moral insight and that the vision of an ethical, intellectual, and integral curriculum may yet be a genuine possibility.[148]

147 Some aspects of these developments are discussed in Carl Wellman, "Ethics Since 1950," *Journal of Value Inquiry* 6 (1972): 83-90; and Donald S. Klinefelter, "The Place of Value in a World of Fact," *Soundings* 58 (1975): 363-79.

148 Klinefelter, Ibid. See Michael Polanyi, *Personal Knowledge* (Chicago: University of Chicago Press, 1958); see especially the articles by the theoretical physicist David Bohm, "Imagination, Fancy, Insight, and Reason in the Process of Thought," in *Evolution and Consciousness: Studies in Polarity*, ed. Shirley Sugarman (Middletown, Conn.: Wesleyan University Press, 1976), pp. 51-68; and David Bohm, "On Insight and Its Significance, for Science, Education, and Values," *Teachers College Record* 80 (February 1979): 403-18. Also provocative and relevant in this context is Huston Smith, "Excluded Knowledge: A Critique of the Modern Western Mind Set," *Teachers College Record* 80 (February 1979): 419-45.

William James as an Educator:
Individualism and Democracy

PAUL F. BOLLER, JR.
Texas Christian University, Forth Worth

William James was a confirmed individualist. He did of course have strong social loyalties — to family, friends, local community, university, state, region, nation, and international community of scholars — and he was the most cosmopolitan of men; but he was an unreconstructed individualist for all that and his philosophy of education as well as his metaphysics, epistemology, and ethics were highly individualistic. Though he took for granted later in life the gradual movement of modern industrial nations like the United States toward increasing socialization of economic arrangements, he remained devoted to individual values to the end.[1] He was not, to be sure, a "rugged" individualist in the self-centered, socially irresponsible economic sense; but he was an individualist all the same. History, he insisted, was the result of "the accumulated influences of individuals, of their examples, their initiatives, and their decisions."[2] Education, he thought, should be directed toward the development of superior individuals. "There is very little difference between one man and another," he said, "but what little there is, *is very important.*"[3] There were both aristocratic and democratic elements in James's outlook. He was elitist enough on occasion to please the most devout Ivy Leaguer; but

---

1 William James to Henry James, Cambridge, Mass., December 19, 1908, *The Letters of William James,* ed. Henry James, 2 vols. (Boston: Little, Brown, 1926), vol. 2, pp. 317-18. See also Paul Woodring, Introduction to William James, *Talks to Teachers; and to Students on Some of Life's Ideals* (New York: The Norton Library, W.W. Norton, 1958).

2 William James, *The Will to Believe and Other Essays in Popular Philosophy* (New York: Dover Publications, 1956), p. 218.

3 Ibid., p. 256.

there was also a profound democratic note in his individualistic philosophy that enabled him in the end to transcend the aristocratic social and academic milieu in which he lived and worked in ways that were inconceivable to most of his colleagues.

James's own education, it has often been noted, was informal and haphazard. It involved tutors and governesses, four private schools in the United States, and a variety of schools in Germany, France, and Switzerland. It also included the powerful influence of his father, Henry James, Sr., a talented thinker and writer who followed his son's intellectual development with eager concern. James's education may have been highly irregular; but it was a first-rate education nevertheless and few Americans in James's day were privileged to receive anything nearly as good. Before entering Harvard University in 1861 at the age of nineteen, James had ready widely and thoughtfully in literature and philosophy, studied painting, mastered French and German, and learned enough science to pick chemistry as his specialty at college. Partly under the influence of the celebrated naturalist Louis Agassiz he switched from chemistry to biology and physiology at Harvard and then went on to take his medical degree in 1869. "M.D., if I choose," he exclaimed proudly after passing his Harvard Medical School orals and receiving his first and only academic degree. But he did not so choose. He considered the practice of medicine a drudgery and he became a teacher instead of a physician.[4]

James's Harvard studies were interrupted frequently by illnesses, trips to Europe, and by a field trip to South America with Louis Agassiz to collect zoological specimens. Still, James was coming gradually to know himself during his student years and to develop his major interests and concerns. Severe emotional problems as a young man led him to psychology; and psychology itself, for James, involved basic philosophical issues (like freedom and determinism) that were to engage his lifelong interest. James soon discovered that the life of the mind was most congenial to his own individual make-up, and his experience on the Agassiz expedition in 1865–1866 convinced him that he was better fitted for a speculative than an active life. When President Charles W. Eliot offered him a position as instructor in physiology at Harvard in 1872, he decided, after some hesitation (he would have preferred philosophy), to accept. He quickly discovered that he liked teaching and he was soon flourishing both personally and professionally in the academic world. At Harvard, James soon moved into psychology: He developed a course in physiological psychology, established the first psychological laboratory in the United States, and

4 Gay Wilson Allen, *William James, A Biography* (New York: Viking, 1967), p. 158.

wrote his famous textbook *Principles of Psychology* (1890), which was widely adopted by colleges throughout the country. James's first love, however, was philosophy, and he gradually shifted from psychology into philosophy during his years at Harvard. By the 1890s he was offering courses in Kant, Cosmology, and Metaphysics.[5]

James was by all accounts a superb teacher. Dynamic, vibrant, energetic, and witty in the classroom, he was "always throwing off sparks" as he talked.[6] "To see him," said one student, "was never to forget what it means to be alive."[7] Courses were adventures of ideas for James; he expected to learn along with his students from the inquiries launched at the beginning of the year. His lectures were exploratory, not pontifical; they were sprinkled with "ifs" and "maybes." James was interested in "making conventionalities fluid again."[8] At the same time his ability to *"feel* ideas," according to one observer, "lent a kind of emotional or aesthetic color which deepened the interest."[9] James not only welcomed questions in class (unusual for his day); he also talked to students after class and engaged them in highly animated discussions if he happened to meet them outside of the classroom. He was, moreover, probably the first college teacher in the United States (if not the world) to ask students for criticisms of his courses at the end of the year. "He changed topics, textbooks and methods frequently," according to President Eliot, "thus utilizing his own wide range of reading and interest and his own progress in philosophy, and experimenting from year to year on the mutual contacts and relations with his students."[10] Dickinson Miller, a James student who went on to teach philosophy at Bryn Mawr, Harvard, and Columbia, was struck by James's "absolutely unfettered and untrammeled mind, ready to do sympathetic justice to the most unaccredited, audacious, or despised hypotheses, yet always keeping his own sense of proportion and the balance of evidence . . . ." Yet for all his classroom brilliance, James, according to Miller, "never quite outgrew a perceptible shyness or diffidence in the lecture-room, which showed sometimes in a heightened color. Going to lecture in one of the last courses he ever gave at Harvard, he

5   *Letters of William James,* vol. 2, p. 3.

6   Allen, *William James,* p. 301.

7   Ibid.

8   William James, "The Teaching of Philosophy in Our Colleges" (1876), in his *Essays in Philosophy* (Cambridge: Harvard University Press, 1978), p. 4.

9   Dickinson S. Miller, "Beloved Psychologist," in *Great Teachers,* ed. Houston Peterson (New Brunswick: Rutgers University Press, 1946), p. 224.

10   *Letters of William James,* p. 4n.

said to a colleague whom he met on the way, 'I have lectured so and so
many years, and yet here am I on the way to my class in trepidation!' "[11]

Like most serious people, James could on occasion become quite exas-
perated with his chosen profession. "*Dang* all schools and colleges, say I,"
he once exclaimed. "What an awful trade that of professor is—paid to
talk, talk, talk! . . . It would be an awful universe if *everything* could be
converted into words, words, words."[12] James found "our damned academic technics and Ph.D.-machinery and university organization" personally distasteful and he expressed great irritation with "the gray-plaster
temperament of our bald-headed young Ph.D.'s, boring each other at
seminaries, writing those direful reports of literature in the 'Philosophical
Review' and elsewhere, fed on 'books of reference,' and never confound-
ing 'Aesthetik' and 'Erkentnisstheorie.' "[13] Too many graduate students
seemed like "young fogies" to James; they were "bald-hearted" as well as
bald-headed and they bored one another (and James) with "the pedantry
and technicality, formless, uncircumcised, unabashed and unrebuked, of
their 'papers' and 'reports' . . . ." Worst of all, perhaps, was the uncouth
English they wrote.[14] In his last years at Harvard James began complain-
ing about the "treadmill of teaching,"[15] and he was undoubtedly being
quite candid when he told his brother Henry after meeting his last class at
Harvard in January 1907: "You can't tell how happy I am at having
thrown off the nightmare of my 'professorship.' As a 'professor' I always
felt myself a sham, with its chief duties of being a walking encyclopedia of
erudition. I am now at liberty to be a *reality*, and the comfort is
unspeakable—literally unspeakable, to be my own man, after 35 years of
being owned by others. I can now live for truth pure and simple, instead
of for truth accommodated to the most unheard-of requirements set by
others."[16] Responding a few weeks later to Théodore Flournoy's congratu-
lations on his retirement, James assured his Swiss friend of his deep
satisfaction at having retired and he then added: "A professor has two
functions: (1) to be learned and distribute bibliographical information;
(2) to communicate truth. The *1st* function is the essential one, officially

11   Ibid., pp. 15-16.
12   Allen, *William James*, p. 434; and William James to Grace Norton, Florence, December 28,
1892, *Letters of William James*, vol. 1, pp. 337-38.
13   William James to George Santayana, Orvieto, May 2, 1905, *Letters of William James*, vol. 2,
pp. 228-29.
14   William James, "A Great French Philosopher at Harvard" (1910), in James, *Essays in
Philosophy*, p. 167; and "G. Papini and the Pragmatist Movement in Italy" (1910), ibid., p. 145.
15   William James to John Jay Chapman, Cambridge, Mass., May 18, 1906, *Letters of William
James*, vol. 2, p. 256.
16   William James to Henry James, Salisbury, Conn., May 4, 1907, ibid., vol. 2, pp. 279-80.

considered. The *2nd* is the only one I care for. Hitherto I have always felt like a humbug as a professor, for I am weak in the first requirement. Now I can live for the second with a free conscience."[17]

James had of course always emphasized the search for more knowledge and understanding in his teaching. But he was by no means deficient in bibliography. Dickinson Miller reported that James would tell his graduate students, "I am no man for editions and references, no exact bibliographer" and then fill the blackboard with lists of books in English, French, German, and Italian. His reading, Miller pointed out, was "immense and systematic," despite his modesty about it; but, he added, when James was deeply engaged in an issue of great concern to him, he talked "the language of perception, insight, sensibility, [and] vision of possibilities."[18] But though James spoke to Flournoy of "communicating truth" as the professor's chief function, he never himself actually attempted any such thing in the classroom. He was the most unauthoritarian of personalities; and he expressed his own deepest convictions without a trace of dogmatism. He did not communicate truth; he energetically sought for it and he encouraged others to join the search. Students "felt his mind at work" during the class period, according to Dickinson Miller, and the result was that he conveyed to his classes (and his readers) the excitement and sense of adventure and high importance to humane living of the quest for insight into reality in which he was engaged.[19] Inspiring students to embark on the quest for truth—or, rather, truths, for James was a pluralist—was, James thought, a professor's chief function, though he never quite put it that way.

What fundamental truths did James put forward as possible ways of viewing reality in his teaching and writing? Four in the main: pluralism, radical empiricism, indeterminism, and pragmatism. All four provided a basic foundation for the kind of individual autonomy and creativity that he cherished so highly and regarded as the ultimate aim of the educational process. Early in his teaching career he wrote: "If the best use of our colleges is to give young men a wider openness of mind and a more flexible way of thinking than special technical training can generate, then philosophy is the most important of all college studies."[20]

James was, first of all, a pluralist; he rejected monism as a compelling approach to the universe that we know from experience. He insisted that

17 William James to Théodore Flournoy, Cambridge, Mass., March 26, 1907, ibid., vol. 2, p. 268.
18 Ibid., vol. 2, pp. 14, 12.
19 Allen, *William James*, p. 300.
20 *Letters of William James*, vol. 1, p. 190.

we live in an "open universe," that is, in an evolutionary world that is continually changing, growing, and developing, and whose future is to a large extent undetermined and unpredictable. He had a temperamental dislike for closed systems of thought that purported to explain everything in the universe, once for all, according to a few basic principles or according to one big principle. "The reader," he warned in the preface to *Principles of Psychology*, "will in vain seek for any closed system in the book."[21] James vigorously discarded what he called "block universes," that is, systems of thought portraying the universe as a consolidated unit and taking universal determinism for granted. According to block-universe theories (whether in religion, philosophy, or science), the world is a tightly knit system in which everything is related to everything else and in which whatever takes place does so because of immutable laws fixed for all eternity. James called this a "through-and-through universe" and he thought that the "through-and-through philosophy" was "too buttoned-up and white-chokered and clean-shaven a thing to speak for the vast slow-breathing unconscious Kosmos with its dread abysses and its unknown tides." In a striking metaphor that delighted Bertrand Russell, James said that the necessities of the block universe made him feel "as if I had to live in a large seaside boarding-house with no private bed-room in which I might take refuge from the security of the place."[22] James believed that some things were related to other things in his incompletely integrated universe, but he denied that the universe was totally unified. For James, nature was loose-jointed and strung-along; it was a "turbid, muddled, gothic sort of affair," in which "each part of the world is in some ways connected, in some other ways not connected with its other parts. . . ."[23] James's "multiverse," as he sometimes called it, was "superabounding, growing, ever-varying, and novelty-producing."[24]

James was also a radical empiricist. He held that we must take reality for what it appears to be in our experience, with all its multifariousness and waywardness; we must assume that things and the relations between things are just what they are experienced as and we must not permit our abstract categories (colossally useful though these may be for some purposes) to mislead us into thinking that there is more order in the universe than there actually is. James did not regard experience as chaotic; he

21 William James, *The Principles of Psychology*, 2 vols. (New York: Dover, 1950), p. vii.

22 William James, *Essays in Radical Empiricism* (Cambridge: Harvard University Press, 1976), p. 142.

23 William James, *A Pluralistic Universe* (Cambridge: Harvard University Press, 1977), pp. 26, 41.

24 James, *Essays in Philosophy*, p. 169.

thought that "the relations between things, conjunctive as well as disjunctive, are just as much matters of direct particular experience, neither more so nor less so, than things themselves."[25] Relations of time, space, difference, likeness, change, rate, and cause were for James not Kantian categories imposed on experience by the human mind; they were "just as integral members of the sensational flux as terms are . . . ."[26] Experience and reality were thus identical for James; they involved a "field of consciousness including its objects [and their relations] thought or felt, plus an attitude in regard to these objects, plus a sense of self to which this attitude belongs."[27] There was enough connection between things in our immediately felt experience, in short, to make it possible for human beings to formulate useful generalizations about reality; but there was also enough looseness among things to leave room for individual freedom.

James was, in the third place, an indeterminist. Universal determinism, so widespread among scientific scholars in James's day, was James's special bête noire. He did not of course deny the presence of uniformities in the world of experience; there were enough regularities, he thought, to enable human beings to devise satisfactory explanations (and make useful predictions) about natural events and thus gain some measure of control over their lives and surroundings. Yet he also insisted that human experience revealed irregularities as well as regularities and that there was enough loose-jointedness and elbow-room in the world to make room for human freedom. By freedom James did not mean the mere absence of external restraint or constraint that determinists like Thomas Hobbes asserted. Nor did he mean the kind of freedom that rational determinists like Benedictus de Spinoza affirmed: the emancipation from ignorance and prejudice and narrow impulse that rational and moral understanding brings about. James did not regard proponents of circumstantial (Hobbes) and rational (Spinoza) freedom as real libertarians; he called them "soft determinists." He insisted on a measure of real indeterminism and unpredictability in the world; he was anxious to keep a place open for freedom of the will in his philosophy. Free will is of course an individualistic concept; it pertains to the inner life of the individual person and, according to its proponents, it transcends both the biological conditions and social pressures shaping individual volitions. For James, free will appeared in the special effort of attention that an individual gives to one concern rather than to another (when confronted with alternatives) and

25   William James, *The Meaning of Truth* (Cambridge: Harvard University Press, 1975), p. 7.
26   James, *Pluralistic Universe*, p. 126.
27   Théodore Flournoy, *The Philosophy of William James*, trans. Edwin B. Holt and William James, Jr. (New York: Henry Holt, 1917), p. 94.

that eventuates in an unpredictable and individually shaped choice. More broadly, it involved what James called "the experience of activity," that is, the inward striving an individual exerts in order to articulate something elusive, solve a problem, formulate an idea, and, in general, to bring to the surface of his consciousness something new and unexpected in his experience. In this respect free will was for James identical with the act of creation by which an individual generates unforeseen novelties in himself, objectifies them, and thus helps to produce intellectual and social change in the world.[28] In a series of popular lectures to school-teachers in Cambridge, Massachusetts, and elsewhere, James urged his audiences to think of the student as "a little sensitive, impulsive, associative, and reactive organism, partly fated and partly free . . . ."[29]

James's fourth doctrine, pragmatism, was a new way of looking at the ideas human beings formulate for dealing with their experience and it, too, had an individualistic emphasis in James's thinking. Ideas were not discoveries for James; they were not mere copies of external reality. They were, rather, human creations devised by people to understand the flux of experience more adequately and thus to get around the world more satisfactorily than mere sensory experience by itself made possible. Ideas were tools or instruments or guides for thinking and acting; they helped individuals comprehend and thus gain some control over their environment. But pragmatism was a method as well as a theory of ideas for James; it was a method of testing ideas. One tests an idea, James declared, by inquiring into its concrete results when put into practice; if the idea puts one into a satisfactory relation with reality, then that idea may be judged as true, and if it does not, the idea is false. We test ideas, in short, by getting down to concrete cases; we ask ourselves what practical difference the ideas will make in our experience. The origin of an idea, its basic premises, its internal consistency or coherence, its logicality or reasonableness, and its elegance or simplicity are all of secondary importance; the main thing about an idea is its practical consequences (in terms of the sensations it will produce and the behavior it will evoke) when put to work in the stream of experience. "Grant an idea or belief to be true," exclaimed James, "what concrete difference will its being true make in any one's actual life; How will the truth be realized? What expe-

---

28 For James's analysis of "personal activity-situations," see his *Essays in Radical Empiricism*, chap. 6, "The Experience of Activity" and his *Some Problems of Philosophy* (New York: Longmans, Green, 1911), pp. 210-18. For a detailed study of James's view of freedom, see Paul F. Boller, Jr., *Freedom and Fate in American Thought: From Edwards to Dewey* (Dallas: SMU Press, 1978), chap. 7, "William James on Freedom as Creative Effort."

29 James, *Talks to Teachers*, p. 131.

riences will be different from those which should obtain if the belief were false? What, in short is the truth's cash-value in experiential terms?" And his answer was: *"True ideas are those that we can assimilate, validate, corroborate, and verify. False ideas are those that we cannot."*[30] James's pragmatism was far more individualistic than was the pragmatism of Charles S. Peirce (from whom James freely acknowledged he had learned so much). Peirce stressed the logical consequences of ideas and their general or habitual effects; he was also more interested in the consequences of ideas for the community than for the single individual. James did not deny the importance of the social test for ideas; but here as elsewhere his emphasis was individualistic and he put great stress on the importance of ideas of special interest to the individual person all by himself. In the realm of religion and philosophy, in particular, he argued that an individual had a "right to believe," that is, the right to adopt any idea or belief that had fruitful consequences for his own personal life so long as it did not clash with other vital pragmatic beliefs or produce social harm.[31] James's powerful individualism, in short, pervaded his pragmatism as well as his pluralism, radical empiricism, and indeterminism. When he wrote a book about religion, he called it *The Varieties of Religious Experience.*[32] But all human experience, including the educational experience, possessed abundant varieties for the individualistic James. He regarded teaching as an art that could learn something from the science of psychology, but he also believed that "many diverse methods of teaching may equally well agree with psychological laws."[33]

Compared with John Dewey, James wrote very little directly about education, but whenever he did so the individualistic note was dominant. In the essay "The Ph.D. Octopus" for the *Harvard Monthly* of March 1903, he deplored the increasing emphasis in American colleges on the necessity of the doctoral degree for teaching and he warned against the development of the "Mandarin disease" in America. James made the obvious point that the Ph.D. degree was no guarantee of either good teaching or meaningful scholarship.[34] But he was chiefly concerned about the threat of the "Doctor-Monopoly" to individual initiative, independence, and creativity in

30   William James, *Pragmatism* (Cambridge: Harvard University Press, 1975), p. 97.
31   William James, "The Will to Believe," in James, *The Will to Believe and Other Essays in Popular Philosophy,* pp. 1-31.
32   William James, *The Varieties of Religious Experience, A Study in Human Nature* (New York: Longmans, Green, 1902).
33   James, *Talks to Teachers,* p. 24.
34   William James, "The Ph.D. Octopus" (1903), in his *Memories and Studies* (New York: Longmans, Green, 1911), p. 334.

the world of scholarship.[35] He insisted that the increasing demand in American graduate schools for meeting specified requirements for taking a doctorate tended to "interface with the free development of talent" among students, to "transfer accredited value from essential manhood to an outward badge," to "divert the attention of aspiring youth from direct dealings with truth to the passing of examinations," and, in general, to foster academic snobbery.[36] American universities

> should never cease to regard themselves as the jealous custodians of personal and spiritual authority. They are indeed its only organized and recognized custodians in America today. They ought to guard against contributing to the increase of officialism and snobbery and insincerity as against a pestilence; they ought to keep truth and disinterested labor always in the foreground, treat degrees as secondary incidents, and in season and out of season make it plain that what they live for is to help men's souls, and to decorate their persons with diplomas.[37]

James thought it was curious that the passion for titles was growing up in a nation in which "recognition of individuality and bare manhood have so long been supposed to be the very soul." Pointing out the "throttling influences upon individuals" of the emphasis on titles, ranks, and grades in Europe, James exclaimed:

> But are we Americans ourselves destined after all to hunger after similar vanities on an infinitely more contemptible scale? And is individuality with us also going to count for nothing unless stamped and licensed and authenticated by some title-giving machine? Let us pray that our ancient national genius may long preserve vitality enough to guard us from a future so unmanly and so unbeautiful![38]

James no doubt would have been appalled by the new "octopus" emerging in the late twentieth century: the proliferation of busywork in the groves of academe growing out of the development of the publish-or-perish rule for advancement and the multiplication of academic conferences and journals to accommodate that rule. And he probably would have sympathized to some extent at least with the students revolting in the 1960s against the growing bureaucratization and impersonalization of the American educational enterprise. In the essay "The True Harvard,"

35 Ibid., p. 338.
36 Ibid., p. 336.
37 Ibid., pp. 343-44.
38 Ibid., pp. 346-47.

written in 1903, he singled out his alma mater's "persistently atomistic constitution," her "tolerance of exceptionality and eccentricity," and her "devotion to the principle of individual vocation and choice" for special praise.[39] The best universities for James were nurseries for "independent and lonely" thinkers: "Our undisciplinables are our proudest product."[40] He would have been put off, though, by the anti-intellectualism of the 1960s and by the scorn, in some circles, for standards of excellence in our colleges. "*Thoughts*," he declared, "are the precious seeds of which our universities should be the botanical garden."[41] In an address at Stanford, where he served as a visiting professor for a semester in 1906, he urged the new university to assemble a faculty of first-rate thinkers ("real geniuses") to set the tone for the place and keep it in ferment.[42] "Education," he said,

> in the long run is an affair that works itself out between the individual student and his opportunities. Methods of which we talk so much, play but a minor part. Offer the opportunities, leave the student to his natural reaction of them, and he will work out his personal destiny, be it a high one or a low one. Above all things, offer the opportunity of higher personal contacts.[43]

The following year at Radcliffe College he announced that the main point of a college education was to "*help you to know a good man when you see him*" and he suggested emphasizing "biographical history" in the curriculum in order to familiarize students with "standards of the excellent and durable" in all fields and to develop young people's critical sensibilities.[44]

James's emphasis on individuality in education undoubtedly led him at times into elitism. In his Stanford address he urged special treatment for outstanding faculty members:

> They have to be treated tenderly. They don't need to live in superfluity; but they need freedom from harassing care; they need books and instruments; they are always overworking, so they need generous vacations; and above all things they need occasionally to travel far and wide in the interest of their soul's development.[45]

39   William James, "The True Harvard" (1903), in ibid., p. 353.
40   Ibid., p. 355.
41   Ibid., p. 354.
42   William James, "Stanford's Ideal Destiny" (1906), in ibid., p. 362.
43   Ibid.
44   William James, "The Social Value of the College-Bred" (1908), in ibid, pp. 309, 313.
45   Ibid., p. 366.

James may have had himself in mind when he made this point. He had suffered poor health through much of his life and he needed "freedom from harassing care" to lighten his burdens; he also had a restless temperament and quickly became bored with the academic routine and needed vacations and travel abroad to preserve his sanity. Like many other fine teachers who have spent many hours in instruction, moreover, James became weary of the demands of the classroom in his later years and anxious to devote full time to his philosophical inquiries. In his Stanford speech, therefore, he even suggested that the newly founded institution become "less a place for teaching youths and maidens than for training scholars; devoted to truth; radiating influence; setting standards; shedding abroad the fruits of learning . . . ."[46] But the aristocratic note in James's view of education was even more pronounced in his speech at Radcliffe College in 1907. At Radcliffe he frankly entrusted to college graduates the "mission of raising the tone of democracy." College-trained people, he said, in an amazingly naive view of the matter,

> more than others should be able to divine the worthier and better leaders. . . . In our democracy, where everything else is so shifting, we alumni and alumnae of the colleges are the only permanent presence that corresponds to the aristocracy in older countries. We have continuous traditions, as they have; our motto, too, is *noblesse oblige*; and, unlike them, we stand for ideal interests solely, for we have no corporate selfishness and wield no powers of corruption. . . . If we are to be the yeast-cake for democracy's dough, if we are to make it rise with culture's preferences, we must see to it that culture spreads broad sails. . . . It all reverts in the end to the action of innumerable imitative individuals upon each other and to the question of whose tone has the highest spreading power. . . . As a class, we college graduates should look to it that *ours* has spreading power. It ought to have the highest spreading power.[47]

But James's view of college people was not entirely dewy-eyed. In his essay on Harvard in 1903 he acknowledged that an elite education did not necessarily produce superior moral and intellectual insight when it came to public affairs. "We see college graduates on every side of every public question," he pointed out.

> Some of Tammany's stanchest supporters are Harvard men. Harvard men defend our treatment of our Filipino allies as a masterpiece of

46 Ibid.
47 Ibid., pp. 319-21.

policy and morals. Harvard men, as journalists, pride themselves on producing copy for any side that may enlist them. There is not a public abuse for which some Harvard advocate may not be found.

In the successful sense, then, in the worldly sense, to be a college man, even a Harvard man, affords no sure guarantee for anything but a more educated cleverness in the service of popular idols and vulgar ends.[48]

Even more important: In *Talks to Teachers* (1899), a little volume consisting of lectures to school teachers on psychology and pedagogy and talks to students on life's ideals, James made the important point that even the most highly educated people can be quite obtuse when it comes to matters that lie outside of their own personal experience. Two essays in *Talks to Teachers* are of particular interest: "On a Certain Blindness in Human Beings" and "What Makes a Life Significant." In these essays, James showed that his individualism (like his pluralism, radical empiricism, indeterminism, and pragmatism), far from being elitist in nature, was fundamentally democratic at heart. The "blindness" that James talked about in the first essay (and enlarged on in the second) referred to the insensitivity most people have to the innermost ideals, feelings, interests, and callings of other people, particularly those who belong to another social class or who live quite different lives from their own. James was thinking particularly of humble people — North Carolina mountaineers, Russian peasant women, urban laborers, miners, sailors, cowboys — whose lives, he suggested, might be replete with courage, patience, kindness, and quiet heroism of which educated people like himself might be quite unaware and whose active virtues college people like himself might totally lack. The moral of his analysis was humility about one's own particular way of life, sensitivity to other people's inner ideals and springs of action, and tolerance and imaginative sympathy in human relations.[49] (Once he told a psychology class that had just visited some insane asylums: "President Eliot might not like to admit that there is no sharp line between himself and the men we have just seen, but it is true.")[50] The tolerance and respect for diversity that James called for was of course firmly grounded in his pluralistic or individualistic philosophy:

Neither the whole of truth nor the whole of good is revealed to any single observer, although each observer gains a partial superiority of in-

48 Ibid., pp. 352.
49 James, *Talks to Teachers*, pp. 149-91.
50 James, *Letters of William James*, vol. 2, p. 15.

sight from the peculiar position in which he stands. Even prisons and sickrooms have their special revelations. It is enough to ask of each of us that he should be faithful to his own opportunities and make the most of his own blessings, without presuming to regulate the rest of the field.[51]

It is difficult not to believe that, given the basic fact of human diversity, there is not something of enduring value in James's way of looking at things.

Education for James centered in helping individuals to discover their own special "blessings" (to use his own word) and encouraging them to make the most of their own particular opportunities. "What doctrines students take from their teachers," wrote James, "are of little consequence provided they catch from them the living, philosophic attitude of mind, the independent, personal look at all the data of life, and the eagerness to harmonize them."[52] Like Ralph Waldo Emerson, James believed that each individual knows some part of the world of reality that others fail to see and has some "single specialized vocation of his own," which it is education's task to develop.[53] But education also involved the cultivation of sensitivity to the "depth of worth that lies around you, hid in alien lives" and the realization that in this vast and complex open universe of ours no one individual has a final truth or an unassailable insight and that only by sharing our individual experiences and pooling our knowledge was it possible to gain a better grasp of things, devise better ways of living together, and move toward a more democratic, tolerant, and humane world.[54]

The spirit that James thought should animate the educational enterprise was one of intense curiosity, adventure, tolerance, sensitivity, and compassion. And it was precisely this spirit that James himself brought to the classroom. Dozens of students of his have testified to this fact. But perhaps George Santayana has caught the flavor of James in the classroom better than anyone else. Santayana was himself just about as far, temperamentally and philosophically, from James as it is possible for one person to be from another. Still, by an act of imaginative insight about as Jamesian as it could be, Santayana was able to capture the spirit of James the teacher. His reminiscences of his class with James are worth quoting at length. James, he said, was "a sort of Irishman among the Brahmins"

51 James, *Talks to Teachers*, p. 169.
52 James, *Essays in Philosophy*, p. 5.
53 James, *Talks to Teachers*, p. 156.
54 Ibid., p. 188.

who "didn't talk like a book, and didn't write like a book, except one of his own."

Even his pupils, attached as they were invariably to his person, felt some doubts about the profundity of one who was so very natural, and who after some interruption during a lecture—and he said life was a series of interruptions—would slap his forehead and ask the man in the front row "What *was* I talking about?" Perhaps in the first years of his teaching he felt a little in the professor's chair as a military man might feel when obliged to read the prayers at a funeral. He probably conceived what he said more deeply than a more scholastic mind might have conceived it; yet he would have been more comfortable if some one else had said it for him. He liked to open the window, and look out for a moment. I think he was glad when the bell rang, and he could be himself again until the next day. But in the midst of this routine of the class-room the spirit would sometimes come upon him, and, leaning his head on his hand, he would let fall golden words, picturesque, fresh from the heart, full of knowledge of good and evil. Incidentally there would crop up some humorous characterization, some candid confession of doubt or of instinctive preference, some pungent scrap of learning; radicalisms plunging sometimes into the sub-soil of all human philosophies; and on occasion, thoughts of simple wisdom and wistful piety, the most unfeigned and manly that anybody ever had.[55]

55 George Santayana, *Character and Opinion in the United States* (New York: The Norton Library, W.W. Norton, 1967), pp. 94-96.

CONTRIBUTORS

PETER A. BERTOCCI is Borden Parker Bowne Professor Emeritus of Philosophy, 1953–1975, Boston University. He was a Fulbright Research Scholar in Italy, 1950, and held the same post in 1960 in India. He was also a Guggenheim Fellow, 1967–1968. He has published about 150 articles and contributions to various reference works. His books include *Empirical Argument for God in Late British Thought* (1938), *Introduction to Philosophy of Religion* (1951), *Religion as Creative Insecurity*, (1958), *Personality and the Good: Psychological and Ethical Perspective* with Richard M. Millard, Jr. (1963), *Sex, Love and the Person* (1967), and *The Person God Is* (1970).

DAVID BOHM has taught at Princeton University, Universidade de Sao Paulo (Brazil), and Technion, Haifa, Israel. Since 1961 he has been Professor of Theoretical Physics at Birkbeck College, University of London. His main interests have been in plasma theory, in the fundamentals of relativity and quantum theory, and, especially, in their significance for philosophy and, more broadly, for general notions current in life as a whole. He is also deeply interested in psychology, education, and related fields.

PAUL F. BOLLER, JR., who teaches American intellectual history at Texas Christian University in Fort Worth, has written about William James's pragmatism in *American Thought in Transition* (1967) and about his concept of freedom in *Freedom and Fate in American Thought* (1978). He is author of *American Transcendentalism, 1830–1860*, and other books.

HARRY S. BROUDY is Emeritus Professor of Philosophy of Education at the University of Illinois at Urbana. His recent writings have been concerned with the uses of schooling, a new rationale for general education, and the importance of the aesthetic components of the curriculum.

SEBASTIAN DE GRAZIA is Professor at the Eagleton Institute of Politics, Rutgers University, where he teaches political philosophy in the graduate school. Formerly on the faculty of the University of Chicago, he is author of the Twentieth Century Fund study *Of Time, Work and Leisure*. His present fields of study are the American theory of the state and the role of military technology in political change. His most recent book is *Masters of Chinese Political Thought* (1973).

HENRY FRIEDLANDER is Associate Professor of Judaic Studies at Brooklyn College, City University of New York. He received his Ph.D. in European history from the University of Pennsylvania; served with the German War Documents Project at Alexandria; and taught history at Louisiana State University, McMasters University, University of Missouri, and City College of New York. He is the author of *The German Revolution of 1918, On the Holocaust,* and editor of *Detente in Historical Perspective.* His most recent article was "The Language of Nazi Totalitarianism."

R.S. PETERS is Professor of Philosophy of Education at the University of London Institute of Education. He is a member of the American National Academy of Education. He is author of numerous articles and books, including *Ethics and Education.*

CATHERINE ROBERTS, a former microbiologist in Denmark, has now returned to Berkeley, California, where she is continuing her work on ethical and evolutionary problems within science and other fields of endeavor. She is author of *The Scientific Conscience,* and has written for *The American Scholar, Tract,* and numerous other journals.

ROGER L. SHINN is Professor of Social Ethics and Counselor to Graduate Students at Union Theological Seminary, and Adjunct Professor of Religion at Columbia University. He is author of a dozen books, most recently of *Wars and Rumors of Wars.*

DOUGLAS SLOAN is Associate Professor of History and Education at Teachers College. Columbia University, and editor of the *Teachers College Record.* He is the author of *The Scottish Enlightenment and the American College Ideal* and *The Great Awakening and American Education.*

HUSTON SMITH is Thomas J. Watson Professor of Religion and Adjunct Professor of Philosophy at Syracuse University. He is author of *The Purposes of Higher Education, The Religions of Man,* and the book that elicited the invitation to write the present article, *Forgotten Truth: The Primordial Tradition.*

JOHN E. SMITH is Clark Professor of Philosophy and Director of the National Humanities Institute, Yale University. Among his books are *Purpose and Thought, The Spirit of American Philosophy,* and *Experience and God.*

Index

Thilly, Cornell Frank, 215
Thomas, Dr. Lewis, 47
Thorndike, E. L., 207
Tillich, Paul, 88, 250
Tolstoy, Leo, 165
Toulmin, Stephen, 232
Toynbee, Arnold, 190
Tradition, 25, 33, 64, 65, 66, 113-114
Truth, 27, 29, 30, 31, 61, 79, 82, 99,
100, 101, 103, 172, 182; and democracy, 76-77; and subjectivity, 57,
169, 183
Truth Values, 100-101
Tufts, James H., 205, 206, 216,
217, 218

Ulrich, Robert, 23
Understanding, 76, 79-82
Universals, 58, 59
Universal Order, 8-9
University, The, 147, 148, 153; and
ethics, 200, 209, 238; funding of, 154,
155, 156; and government, 150, 154,
155, 156-159; and leisure, 148, 153,
154, 155-156, 159; the rise of, 201,
202; and the rise of experts, 202, 205-
211; and work, 150, 151, 153-158
University of Chicago, 208, 250
University of Wisconsin, 213, 236, 238,
239
Urban, Wilbur Marshall, 231

Values, 1, 2, 19, 93, 96, 97, 162, 167;
and acculturation, 111-113; aesthetic,
77-78, 107-110; and character, 101-
104; conflicts of, 114-116, 165; democratic, 72-85, 239, 242, 243; derivation of, 19; and education, 1-6, 60,
70, 71, 72; and ethics, 220-222, 241;
and experience, 97-99; exploration in,
113-114, 118, 120, 121; and insight,

19-22; intrinsic, 27; normative, 27,
162; religious, 116-118; and science,
9, 27, 30, 221-222, 226, 243, 252; and
truth, 13, 99, 100, 101-104; and
work, 104-106
Values Clarification, 1, 118
Value Judgments, 19-20, 64, 98, 209
Veysey, Laurence, 241

Wald, George, 186
Walzer, Michael, 199
Ward, Lester Frank, 208
Watson, James, 30
Watson, John, 207
Wayland, Francis, 195, 198
Weber, Max, 37, 44
Weil, Simone, 81
Weiss, Peter, 137
Weizenbaum, Joseph, 3
Welty, Eudora, 165
Whitehead, Alfred North, 85, 89, 108,
110, 226
Wirth, Louis, 114
Witherspoon, John, 196
Wittfogel, Karl, 139
Wittgenstein, Ludwig, 27, 28, 228, 233
Wolff, Kurt, 46
Work: and democracy, 83-85; and education, 83-85, 104-106, 150, 157, 161;
and leisure, 84, 150-153; and the
university, 150, 151, 153-158; and
values, 104-106
World War I, 206, 242
World War II, 242, 245, 249
Wyman, David, 141

Yahil, Leni, 141
Yale University, 192, 250
Yeats, William Butler, 43

Zamiatin, Eugene, 134

6 9 0 2